DEVELOPMENT AND UNDERDEVELOPMENT

Series editors: Ray Bromley and Gavin Kitching

Regions in Question

SPACE, DEVELOPMENT THEORY
AND REGIONAL POLICY

D1324637

In the same series

Already published:

Development and Underdevelopment in Historical Perspective:
Populism, nationalism and industrialization
Gavin Kitching

Development Projects as Policy Experiments:
An adaptive approach to development administration
Dennis A. Rondinelli

Development and the Environmental Crisis:
Red or green alternatives?
Michael Redclift

Forthcoming:

The Fragmented World:
Competing perspectives on trade, money and crisis
Chris Edwards

Multinational Corporations
Rhys Jenkins

Latin American Development Theories:
Structuralism, internal colonialism, marginality and dependency
Cristóbal Kay

Regions in Question

SPACE, DEVELOPMENT THEORY
AND REGIONAL POLICY

Charles Gore

Methuen
LONDON and NEW YORK

For Tom and Alice,
my parents

First published in 1984 by
Methuen & Co. Ltd
11 New Fetter Lane,
London EC4P 4EE

Published in the USA by
Methuen & Co.
in association with Methuen, Inc.
733 Third Avenue, New York,
NY 10017

© 1984 Charles Gore

Typeset by
Scarborough Typesetting Services
and printed in Great Britain by
Richard Clay
(The Chaucer Press) Ltd
Bungay, Suffolk

*British Library Cataloguing in
Publication Data*
Gore, Charles G.
Regions in question. – (Development
and underdevelopment)
1. Regional planning – Developing
countries
I. Title   II. Series
361.6'1'091724   HT391

ISBN 0–416–31410–4
ISBN 0–416–31420–1 Pbk

*Library of Congress Cataloging in
Publication Data*
Gore, Charles G.
Regions in question.
(Development and
underdevelopment)
Includes bibliographies and index.
1. Regional planning.
2. City planning.
3. Rural development.
4. Economic policy.
5. Social change.
I. Title.
HT391.G57   1984   338.9'009172'4
84–6589

ISBN 0–416–31410–4
ISBN 0–416–31420–1 (pbk.)

Contents

List of figures

List of tables

Series editors' preface

Development studies is a complex and diverse field of academic research and policy analysis. Concerned with the development process in all the comparatively poor nations of the world, it covers an enormous geographical area and a large part of the modern history of the world. Such a large subject area has generated a varied body of literature in a growing number of journals and other specialist publications, encompassing such diverse issues as the nature and feasibility of industrialization, the problem of small-scale agriculture and rural development in the Third World, the trade and other links between developed and developing countries and their effects on the development prospects of the poor, the nature and causes of poverty and inequality, and the record and future prospects of 'development planning' as a method of accelerating development. The nature of the subject matter has forced both scholars and practitioners to transcend the boundaries of their own disciplines whether these be social sciences, like economics, human geography or sociology, or applied sciences such as agronomy, plant biology or civil engineering. It is now a conventional wisdom of development studies that development problems are so multi-faceted and complex that *no* single discipline can hope to encompass them, let alone offer solutions.

This large and interdisciplinary area and the complex and rapidly changing literature pose particular problems for students, practitioners and specialists seeking a simple introduction to the field or some part of the field with which they are unfamiliar. The Development and Underdevelopment series attempts to rectify these problems by providing a number of brief, readable introductions to important issues in development studies written by an international range of specialists. All the texts are designed to be readily comprehensible to students meeting the issues for the first time, as well as to practitioners in developing countries, international agencies and voluntary bodies. We hope that, taken together, these books will bring to the reader a sense of the main preoccupations and problems in this rich and stimulating field of study and practice.

RAY BROMLEY
GAVIN KITCHING

Preface

This book has two immediate aims. The first is to provide an introduction to the theories of urban, regional and rural development which have been used to rationalize regional policy in developing countries. The second is to elaborate an argument which negates the validity of these theories.

These two aims may appear contradictory at first sight. The major theoretical contributions within the literature are summarized in a way which assumes no prior specialist knowledge of the reader, as the intention is to open up, for general readers, a field of knowledge which is at present marginal to major debates in development studies. Yet the argument about these theoretical contributions intends to show that they are, within their own terms, illogical – a conclusion which implies that ideas within the field may be safely ignored.

But the procedure of presentation and negation does have a rationale. That rationale stems from the observation that *space* is a neglected dimension within development studies (and social theory in general) and from a conviction that theories of social and economic change which treat societies and economies as if they were some spaceless aggregate are at best incomplete, and at worst misleading. The theories of urban, regional and rural development which have been constructed by geographers, regional scientists and regional policy analysts are important to address as they attempt to analyse spatial aspects of change. They take space seriously. But the argument of this book is that the way in which the relationship between space and society is conceptualized within these theories is mistaken. The literature is therefore important not only because it focuses upon the neglected spatial dimension of social life, but also because it shows how space should *not* be treated within social studies. By presenting ideas within the literature on spatial patterns of development, and then negating them in terms of the conceptualization of space, it is possible to emerge with a clearer view of how the significance of space in development may be understood.

Gaining such a view is the underlying purpose of this book, and it is in relation to that purpose that the two immediate aims make sense.

The book has been organized so that a reader who is new to the subject and who just seeks a concise guide to the regional development literature can do so without the complications of the general argument. The ideas of major theorists within the field are presented in certain sections of Part One and in Part Two of the book, and their analyses are summarized as faithfully as possible. But it is important to note that the underlying purpose of the book has determined both the *sequence* and *manner* of exposition. Throughout, the presentation seeks to uncover the assumptions about processes of development which have informed the work of regional theorists, and to show how these assumptions have been applied in a spatial context. But concepts which are introduced at one point in the argument are reappraised later from a different angle – and then reappraised yet again. At times, this approach may seem tedious. But the logical process of reworking the same material from different perspectives is a path by which one can get behind surface appearances and begin to see the deeper significance of ideas. Following that path is the method of this book.

The results of empirical studies of processes of urban, regional and rural development do not occupy a major part of the text. This, it must be emphasized, is not because I believe that such work is futile. Indeed, there is a pressing need for empirical studies which take account of spatial aspects of change in developing countries. The decision to lay more emphasis on logical argument than on empirical evaluation rather stems from a somewhat painful personal experience in my own empirical research, in which I found that the way in which questions are posed *predetermines* the types of answers which one derives. The ways in which empirical questions about urban, regional and rural development are posed are rooted in different conceptions of space, and those conceptions set strict limits to the conclusions that may be drawn. Identifying those limits is part of the task of this book. For then it is possible to see *how to pose questions* about social and economic change in a way which takes account of space.

But although the results of empirical research are not systematically presented in the text, one empirical fact is deliberately identified as the *context* of the argument. That is the fact that many developing countries have adopted some form of regional policy. This fact may not, in itself, appear to be surprising. But as the argument proceeds, it poses a puzzle. For as the theories which have been used to rationalize regional planning practice in developing countries are shown to be more and more illogical, the question which necessarily arises is: what is the rationality of regional policy? This question is the counter-point of the argument, and it runs as a latent theme throughout the main body of the text. The concluding chapter attempts to resolve the puzzle, and in doing so it seeks to show how the relationship between space and society may be reconceptualized in a way which allows deeper understanding of development issues.

The ideas contained within the book have crystallized over a long period of time, and I would like to thank a number of people who have influenced both my own way of thinking and the final form of the text.

First and foremost, thanks are due to my students at the Centre of Development Studies in the University College of Swansea. I have been teaching the subject-matter of the book as part of the Master's programme in Regional Development Planning at the Centre since 1978, and it was the students on the programme who initially forced me to write the book through their intelligent, probing questions. Their interest and enthusiasm sustained the protracted and seemingly endless task of writing, and our discussions in what were supposedly 'lectures' continually helped to clarify my thinking.

The Centre has been a maddening and wonderful place to work in, and it is in that environment, by a strange process of interdisciplinary alchemy (which, I believe, is the basic justification for 'development studies'), that my development education has taken place. Thanks are due to all the staff, but I would particularly like to acknowledge the influence and support of Michael Cowen, Gavin Kitching, David Marsden, Marcos Palacios and Angela Reidy.

Less directly, the thinking of a number of geographers and regional theorists has been important to me. Many of the arguments elaborated in *Regions in Question* are based on the insights of David Harvey, Doreen Massey, Gunnar Olsson, Robert Sack and Andrew Sayer. They may well disagree with my use of their ideas. But I have drawn much inspiration from their critical approach to regional studies, and I hope that my arguments will encourage readers to study their work further.

In the production of the final manuscript a number of people have helped. Thomas Gore read some early chapters and encouraged me throughout to seek clarity of expression. Ray Bromley and Gavin Kitching commented extensively on various versions of the text, and made many helpful suggestions. And Patsy Healey gave me useful general thoughts on what was, at that time, a 'final' version of the manuscript. The advice of these 'first readers' has helped me to improve my arguments, though in the end I am responsible for what I write.

Anthea Thomas typed and retyped the manuscript, and gave me some important reactions on the coherence of the argument. Tim Fernside drew the figures thoughtfully yet speedily. And Kay Edge copy-edited the text with great care.

★

The author and publishers would like to thank the following for permission to reproduce copyright material:

Edward Arnold (Publishers) Ltd and Halsted Press for Figure 1 from *Locational Analysis in Human Geography* by P. Haggett; Edward Arnold (Publishers) Ltd and the University of California Press for Figures 26 and 27 from *Territory and Function* by J. Friedmann and C. Weaver; The Free Press for Figure 18A from 'Hierarchical diffusion: the basis of developmental filtering and spread in a system of growth centres' by B. J. L. Berry in *Growth Centres in Regional Economic Development*, and for Table 4 from 'Development poles and related theories: a synoptic approach' by T. Hermansen in *Growth Centres in Regional Economic Development*; Johns Hopkins University Press for Figure 17 from *Regions, Resources and Economic Growth* by H. S. Perloff *et al.*; MIT Press for Table 1 from *Regional Development Policy* by J. Friedmann; Pergamon Press for Figure 16 from *Growth Centres in Spatial Planning* by M. J. Moseley, and for Figure 21 from 'Underdevelopment and spatial inequality: approaches to the problem of regional planning in the Third World' by D. Slater in *Progress in Planning*; Praeger Publishers for Table 7 from *Urbanization and Rural Development: A Spatial Policy for Equitable Growth* by D. Rondinelli and K. Ruddle; John Wiley & Sons, Inc. for an extract from 'Economic space: theory and applications' by F. Perroux in the *Quarterly Journal of Economics*; Sage Publications Ltd for an extract from *Urbanization, Planning and National Development* by J. Friedmann.

'Regions are simple generalizations
of the human mind.'

Walter Isard

'The region of the geographers is the
military region (from *regere*,
to command) . . .'

Michel Foucault

Introduction

Getting into space

'Regional planning has become a necessity in most countries. But nobody seems to know quite what it is, and no nation seems to know how to do it.'
(Ross and Cohen, 1974)

CONTEXT AND THESIS

Since 1960 most developing countries have adopted some form of regional planning. In some cases this has merely involved the locational programming of investments within a sector, for example in plans to promote industrial development away from the capital city, or plans to co-ordinate the location of roads, market centres and credit facilities within a region in order to accelerate agricultural growth. In others, it has entailed the creation of regional development agencies, such as SUDENE in north-east Brazil, charged with the task of accelerating development within a particular depressed region or the setting up of river basin authorities to manage water resources in a physically defined area. And in a few it has meant the adoption of growth centre strategies in which the development of different urban centres within a country is fully integrated into the national plan, or the pursuit of decentralization in which some of the powers and functions of government are transferred to a defined set of regions within a country. Utria's prediction of the early 1970s that 'like import substitution and industrialization in the fifties, and national planning and economic integration in the sixties, regional development appears destined to become one of the principal concerns of planners and strategists of Latin American development' (Utria, 1972, p. 61), may not have been realized to the extent envisaged in that continent, or elsewhere in the developing world. But certainly political rhetoric and plan documents are now much more concerned with the allocation of power and resources between *places* than they were twenty years ago. And if following Friedmann (1966) we catholically define regional planning as 'planning concerned with the where of development', then there has been a remarkable upsurge in the activity (see, for example, Kuklinski, 1975; El-Shakhs and Obudho, 1974; Mabogunje and Faniran, 1977; Lo and Salih, 1978; CEPAL, 1980; Stöhr and Taylor, 1981).

The technical basis for making decisions about where resources should be allocated and where projects located, where urban growth should occur and where particular types of agricultural land-use be encouraged, lies in a growing literature which may be designated as 'regional development theory'. This body of knowledge is both new, and now, in question.

The field is approximately twenty-five years old. The elaboration of regional development theory is generally said to have gathered momentum in 1958 following the independent publication of Gunnar Myrdal's study *Economic Theory and Underdeveloped Regions* and Albert Hirschman's discussion of the transmission of growth between regions in his book *The Strategy of Economic Development*. John Friedmann published a series of articles on locational aspects of economic development and regional planning in the late 1950s and early 1960s, and in 1964, with William Alonso, edited the first collection of readings on the subject, *Regional Development and Planning*. That work contained the first strong argument that, in planning development 'the arithmetic of macro-economics has need of and is made more powerful by the geometry of regional considerations' (p. 1). But at the same time Friedmann and Alonso noted that 'the conceptual structure for the intelligent making of policy is in its infancy' (p. 1).

The reader laid the basis for the budding new field of knowledge and helped to establish its conceptual structure. Yet despite the vast literature which now examines spatial and regional disparities within countries and proposes ways in which spatial and regional considerations may be integrated into development planning, regional development theory is currently in crisis. Many influential regional thinkers (for example, Friedmann, Stöhr and Hilhorst) have come to doubt the validity of their theories and the utility of their prescriptions. Some argue that regional planning is ineffective as an agent of social change (Blaikie, 1980). Others suggest that there is a need to reassess the central issues in regional development theory (Hilhorst, 1980; Dunham, 1982; Weaver, 1981). And a few are attempting to engineer a paradigm shift within the field (Friedmann and Weaver, 1979; Stöhr and Taylor, 1981).

The paradox of the moment, in which there is a proliferation of regional planning in poor countries while many theoreticians confess the poverty of regional theory, is the context of this book. The loss of confidence in the theories of course reflects a wider crisis in the social sciences.

The impulse to plan for, and in, regions similarly reflects broad trends towards an expansion of state intervention in developing countries. But this book argues that, within these general trends, the poverty of regional development theory may be traced back to the way in which theorists conceptualize the relationship between 'space' and 'development', and that the purposes behind the adoption of regional policies in so many developing countries can only be understood if this relationship is reassessed.

To make this argument the book focuses upon the Anglo-American theoretical tradition, which underpins regional planning in capitalist developing countries. It has been suggested that this is the dominant intellectual tradition in regional development theory (Friedmann and Weaver 1979), but it is important to emphasize that there is a lively French and Latin American literature on regional issues and that some of the most elaborate attempts at regional planning have been undertaken in socialist countries. For reasons of space, these ideas and practices will only be considered to the extent that they have been incorporated within the Anglo-American literature.

REGIONAL SCIENCE, REGIONAL ECONOMICS AND THEORETICAL GEOGRAPHY

Anglo-American regional development theory is rooted in three overlapping academic disciplines which first began to flourish in North America and Britain in the late 1950s – regional science, regional economics and theoretical geography. At the time, each of the three subjects was being promoted as new and important fields of study, and arguments were made to define their specific contribution to the social sciences. In each case, their distinctiveness was said to lie in their commitment to studying the spatial dimension of social affairs, their commitment to solving practical problems, and their commitment to the construction of scientific knowledge, often using statistical methods and mathematical models. To understand the conceptual structure of Anglo-American regional development theory, it is necessary to understand the characteristics of these three academic disciplines.

Regional science emerged as a new discipline in the United States in 1954. It was organized through the newly formed Regional Science Association and propagated through a new journal, the *Papers and Proceedings of the Regional Science Association*. Walter Isard, the founding father of the subject, shaped the field through a long series of articles published during the late 1940s and early 1950s, and in one of them provides a definition of the nature and scope of the field. In broad terms,

Isard (1956) considered the subject-matter of regional science to be the relationship between man and the physical environment. But he argued that 'it would be folly to define regional science so broadly as to embrace several other disciplines' (p. 15). Such a definition would mean that regional science 'would meet with stern opposition' from scientists in 'standard disciplines' such as geography, sociology, economics, political science and anthropology. He thus argued that regional science should exclude 'the study of problems whose spatial dimensions are only incidental to the resulting or projected interaction. It limits itself to problems for which a spatial or regional focus is central' (p. 14).

It is difficult to imagine exactly what such problems are, and indeed, as I shall argue later, it is a moot question whether 'spatial problems' may be identified at all. However, a clearer picture of the nature of regional science may be gathered through an examination of the first two texts which Isard wrote – *Location and Space Economy* (1956) and *Methods of Regional Analysis* (1960).

As the title of his first book suggests, his main initial concern was to add a spatial dimension to economic theory. The term 'space economy' was a literal translation of the German word *Raumwirtschaft* and Isard drew heavily on the work of German location theorists. Thus he wrote in 1960 that his earlier book was an attempt to reduce to common simple terms 'the basic elements in von Thünen, Weber, Predöhl, Ohlin, Palander, Hoover, Lösch, Dunn and others', and thereby 'to synthesize the separate location theories into one general doctrine, and, where possible to fuse the resulting doctrine with existing production, price and trade theory'.

The key to this massive undertaking is the concept of *transport inputs*, in abstract terms, the movement of a unit weight over a unit distance. Transport inputs, which may be measured, for example, by the costs of assembling raw materials and distributing finished products, are regarded as important as 'usual' factors of production in Isard's analysis, and just as labour can be substituted for capital or land in the spaceless economy, so in the space economy an entrepreneur making a decision where to locate can substitute the transport inputs needed for production at one location with those needed in another. Similarly, because there are differences in labour costs and agglomeration economies between locations, the entrepreneur can substitute expenditures on transport inputs for expenditures on production inputs. *Location and Space Economy* shows how this substitution approach may be used to synthesize classical Weberian theory of industrial location, Lösch's ideas on market areas and a hierarchy of central places, and von Thünen's agricultural land-use theory, and theories of interregional trade, and the book concludes by exploring, both mathematically and graphically, the conditions of equilibrium of a space economy on a hypothetical plain.

In assessing the limits of this work, Isard wrote that 'it is fully recognized that a general theory of location is of little direct use in treating the concrete problems of reality (Isard, 1960, p. vii). *Methods of Regional Analysis* was thus designed to complement the first text by providing the basic tool-kit through which the competent regional scientist could tackle the problems of the world. The key operational techniques are evident from the chapter headings of the book: population projection; regional income estimation and social accounting; interregional flow analysis and balance of payment statements; regional business cycle and multiplier analysis; industrial location analysis and related measures; interregional and regional input-output techniques; industrial complex analysis; interregional linear programming; and gravity, potential and interaction models. This battery of computational devices was designed to solve such problems as the efficient location of specific industries, individually or in interrelated groups; the improvement of the welfare of the population of a region; the reduction in the cyclical sensitivity of economic activity within a region; the planned industrial development of a region with rich resources; or the planned use of resources in a region with a poor natural endowment.

If it is accepted that in practical terms *Location and Space Economy* and *Methods of Regional Analysis* define the scope of regional science in its formative years, then the new discipline was, in its early period, almost synonymous with regional economics. Later there was more emphasis on an interdisciplinary perspective which incorporated the analysis of economic-ecological systems and of coalition formation and conflict resolution, and which abandoned the assumption that all the actors in regional systems only responded to economic forces (Isard *et al.*, 1969; Isard, 1975). But the focus on the study of 'social problems *with* spatial or regional dimensions' remained (Isard, 1975, p. 2).

The overlap between regional science and *regional economics* makes it unnecessary to consider the latter discipline in any detail. The latter has been defined as 'the study of man's economic behaviour in space' (Siebert, 1969, p. 1) and more pithily by Hoover (1975, p. 3) as the study of 'what [economic activity] is where, why — and so what?'. Meyer (1963), in the standard survey of the early development of the field, notes that the phrase 'regional analysis' only came into common professional usage after 1950, and argues that the interest in the subject was stimulated by a concern for urban and regional policy problems, particularly disparities in income and growth between regions, and urban transportation patterns. As he put it, 'regional analysis apparently has filled a void by developing tools applicable to economic planning problems at a time when economic planning has been increasing in favour in many circles and governments' (p. 51). The tools of regional analysis are exactly those listed by Isard, and indeed Meyer suggests that 'interregional multiplier analysis, interregional input-output models and mathematical programming along with location theory, constitute the "theoretical foundations" of modern regional analysis' (Meyer, 1963, pp. 29–30).

Theoretical geography evolved in the 1950s in the United States as a new orientation within an old subject. 'Evolution' is undoubtedly too weak a word to describe this process of academic change. The new orientation was an *anti*-thesis to established definitions of the nature of geography (Sack, 1974a) and, as one of its leading protagonists later explained, the process of change was more like a battle (Gould, 1979).

The new geographers distinguished themselves from the old guard first by promoting human geography as a science, and second by focusing on spatial variables and spatial systems (Johnston, 1979). The subject had traditionally examined questions of location. But the old school was primarily concerned to understand the areal differences on the earth's surface by studying specific regions, such as the American South, and emphasizing the unique synthesis of physical and human characteristics found within them. Theoretical geographers decried such 'exceptionalism', arguing that geography is 'the science concerned with the formulation of the laws governing the spatial distribution of certain features on the surface of the earth' (Schaefer, 1953).

To formulate such laws, a critical change of perspective was required. Instead of studying the distribution of phenomena in terms of their *absolute location* (for example, what industries are found in Sao Paulo? what agricultural activity is undertaken in the Midwest of the USA?), the geographers studied spatial distributions in terms of *relative location* – searching for recurrent empirical regularities in, for example, the distribution of agricultural land-uses with increasing distance from a large city, or the spacing of cities of different sizes in a region.

In attempting to explain these recurrent spatial patterns theoretical geographers identified the *friction of distance*, that is, the costs of moving commodities, people or information between places, as a key variable. An extreme example of this viewpoint is expressed by Bunge (1966) in his book *Theoretical Geography*. Asserting that geography is 'the science of spatial relations', he wrote that:

Every *explanation* we have of how geographic phenomena obtained their location involves the notion of movement. Whatever the type of movement it leaves its mark on the face of the earth. That is, it *produces* the geometry. In turn, the geometry *produces* the movement. Thus, geometry and movement are the inseparable duals of geographic theory. (p. 200)

Thus agricultural land-use patterns are 'produced' by farmers shipping their commodities to market, residential zones within cities are 'produced' by families seeking homes in relation to their workplace and service facilities, and even the morphology of the physical landscape is 'produced' by streams moving earth material to the sea. The costs of movement and the need for accessibility are such important explanatory variables in Bunge's scheme that movement is designated as *spatial process*, which is said to be the 'generator' of *spatial structure*, that is, the locational arrangement of phenomena on the earth's surface.

Not all theoretical geographers advocated that the subject should be as narrow a geometric science as that proposed by Bunge, but a cursory examination of the main textbooks which served as the educational vanguard of the new geography shows that some of Bunge's basic ideas were in common currency (Haggett, 1965; Morrill, 1970; Abler, Adams and Gould, 1971).

In North America, *spatial organization* was used as the key word which encapsulated the new approach. The term implies more than *spatial structure* or *spatial system*, which merely refer to the physical arrangement of phenomena on the earth's surface and the patterns of movement. Spatial *organization* suggests that phenomena are distributed to achieve some objective. As Morrill (1970) puts it in a succinct summary of the theoretical geographer's perspective:

1 Societies operate to achieve two spatial efficiency goals:
   (i) to use every piece of land to the greatest profit and utility; and
   (ii) to achieve the highest possible interaction at the least possible cost.
2 Pursuit of these goals involves four types of location decisions:
   (i) the substitution of land for transport costs when seeking accessibility;
   (ii) substituting production costs at sites for transport costs when seeking markets;
   (iii) substituting agglomeration benefits for transport costs; and
   (iv) substituting self-sufficiency (higher production costs) and trade (higher transport costs).
3 The spatial structures resulting from these decisions include:
   (i) spatial land-use gradients; and
   (ii) a spatial hierarchy of regions.

These are somewhat distorted by environmental variations to produce:
(iii) more irregular but predictable patterns of location.
Whereas over time distortion may result from:
(iv) non-optimal location decisions; and
 (v) change through processes of spatial diffusion.
                    (Morrill, pp. 175–6, as summarized in Johnston, 1979)

The similarity to Isard's 'transport inputs' is readily apparent in this
analytical framework and as with regional science, geographic theory
was often elaborated in an 'isotropic' environment, i.e. an imaginary
plain which had uniform environmental conditions, equal transport
costs in all directions and an equal distribution of population with equal
capacities and preferences. Through this method, the distance variable
could be isolated and mathematical models which explained the pure
geometry of spatial systems, 'undisturbed' by the 'distortions' of the
'real' world, could be constructed.

THE DISPLACEMENT OF THE REGION

One important characteristic of regional science, regional economics and
theoretical geography is that each discipline is more concerned with
space than with *regions*. This is readily apparent in Isard's initial attempt
to define the nature and scope of so-called 'regional' science (Isard,
1956b). There he says that a region is 'both a concept and a concrete
reality', but enigmatically goes on to assert that:

> in certain contexts the region, either as a concept or a concrete reality,
> disappears into thin air and leaves as a residue a continuous set of
> points in space. Identified with this context is an extreme degree of
> abstraction, which, nonetheless, furnishes one fruitful approach to the
> development of the concept of the region.   (p. 18)

He invokes the image of an astronaut peering down at the earth's surface
from a space-platform to explain this riddle:

> Imagine our observer in space pilots his platform to a position fairly
> close to the earth's surface, and yet not so close that he fails to see the
> forest for the trees. He attentively watches circulation patterns –
> people moving, goods in transit. If he were endowed with supra-
> human powers and curiosity, he would also observe communications
> phenomena whether via telephone, television, or financial clearing
> operations. He would gradually perceive that the variation of volume
> and intensity of flows with distance, whether value-added flows,

commodity flows, telephone messages and others, could be described by certain statistical distributions. Over time he would note certain stabilities in these flows – in the analytical forms that might be used to characterize their statistical distributions. In approaching the earth's surface, he might have already been forcefully struck by the spatial density configurations formed by the loci of population and by the physical structures and facilities constructed by man. Upon retreating into space, he might curiously regard these broad density configurations a second time, and perceive certain unchanging characteristics. He would speculate upon all these distributional stability characteristics, especially since he would have noted the constant state of flux of the individual units contained within any system. His speculations might be classified as pure spatial analysis.   (p. 18)

Such 'pure spatial analysis', with no reference to the region, describes some of the activities of regional scientists, but Isard argues that the spaceman/regional scientist needs the region in order to test his speculations and develop good theory. To make any empirical tests the regional scientist is compelled to collect data which refer to areal units and it is at that point, as a method of hypothesis testing, that the region re-enters analysis. As Isard puts it, 'even the most pure spatial theorist, if he is to be an effective theorist, must be a regional scientist' (pp. 18–19).

But the region, according to Isard, may also enter analysis as 'a concrete reality, sharply definable in terms of a particular problem at a point in time and in a position of dominance in the analysis of the particular problem' (p. 21). Such regions are said to be 'broad geographic areas significant for the human race' (p. 19), areas that 'would acquire a concrete form and character with respect to a pressing situation of reality' (p. 26). But what makes a region *significant* for humanity or what constitutes 'a pressing situation of reality' is left undiscussed. Isard considers the possibility that there is a single 'true' set of regions which are the most 'meaningful' in terms of 'the broad welfare objectives of society' (p. 19), but, as he later concluded, there are many different regions which are relevant to regional scientists. Any given region is not an arbitrarily demarcated area, however. Rather, it is 'an area which is meaningful because of one or more problems associated with it which we, as regional scientists, want to examine and solve' (Isard, 1975, p. 1).

Isard's clumsy discussion of the nature of regions is a telling comment on the place of the region in 'regional' science. Similar unease with the regional concept is found within regional economics and theoretical geography. In both these subjects much, of course, has been written on procedures for defining regions. The familiar division into three different types of region – the homogeneous region whose sub-areas have some characteristics, such as income level or cropping pattern, in common; the polarized (or nodal, or functional) region, whose sub-areas are all interrelated by flows of some kind; and programming regions, whose sub-areas all fall under the jurisdiction of a planning or administrating authority – is often repeated. But theoretical geography developed as a reaction against regional geography, and little attempt was made to reconcile the adherence of the old guard to studying the region as a *unique* integration of physical environment and human occupancy at a specific location on the earth's surface, with the commitment of the young Turks to searching for universal laws of spatial pattern (Sack, 1974a). One geographer in the new school who was very sensitive to older currents, Peter Haggett, did adopt the nodal region as the organizing concept for his classic text *Locational Analysis in Human Geography* (1965). But this was just a framework within which the various elements of spatial structure which together constitute the regional system could be analysed (Figure 1). For most theoretical geographers, regionalization was viewed as the act of classifying places, classification being a crucial first stage in scientific method (Grigg, 1967).

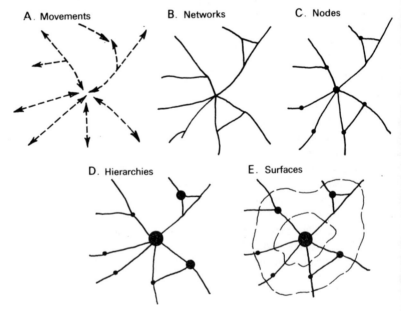

Figure 1 Elements of the spatial structure of a nodal region.

Source: Haggett, 1965, Figure 1.5.

Regional economics draws inspiration from location theory and inter-national trade theory. The former conforms to Isard's 'pure spatial theorizing', while the latter begins with pre-defined spatial units, that is, countries. In applying trade theory at a national level regional econom-ists have introduced the region by merely disaggregating the national economy into a set of homogeneous units which are spatially separate and then studying the nature of interregional relationships. This has been a common procedure in the elaboration of regional growth theory, but these 'regions' are in fact merely 'spaceless points separated by un-specified distances' (Richardson, 1973a).

When it comes to defining regions in practice, regional economists face major difficulties. Hoover, perhaps not entirely facetiously, says that one answer to the question 'what is a region?' is that 'a region means an area which a researcher gets a grant to study' (Hoover, 1975, p. 151). While Richardson (1978) asserts that 'defining regions precisely is such a nightmare that most regional economists prefer to shy away from the task and are relieved when they are forced to work with administrative regions on the grounds that policy considerations require it, or that data are not available for any other spatial units' (p. 1).

In much Anglo-American regional development theory, as in regional science, regional economics and theoretical geography, the region has been displaced from the centre of the stage. As Massey put it, the region is rarely 'constituted as an effect of analysis' (1978, p. 110). Rather, it serves as a methodological tool used in analysis, or a starting-point in which the problem under study – poverty or backwardness in a certain part of the country – is given definite boundaries.

The marginal position of the region within regional development theory has recently been noted and some of the efforts to engineer a paradigm shift within the field have been directed towards reasserting its importance (Friedmann and Weaver, 1979). This is also a major concern of this book. But it is argued here that recent efforts to reappraise the region have been misdirected. This is because its displacement is related to a much more deep-rooted tendency in the three mother disciplines – that is, the way in which the relationships between space and society are conceptualized – and until the nature of this tendency is identified, what regions actually are, how they are formed and why they are important in regional development theory cannot be fully analysed.

THE DOMINANCE OF THE SPATIAL SEPARATIST THEME

Regional science, regional economics and theoretical geography are all characterized by what Robert Sack has called 'the spatial separatist theme', that is, 'the notion that it is possible to identify, separate and evaluate the *spatial* as an independent phenomenon or a property of events examined through spatial analysis' (Sack, 1974b, p. 1). This is apparent in the foregoing description of the three disciplines, but exactly what it means may best be introduced through an example which applies spatial analysis to 'explain' a particular development problem.

The example of labour-supply reserves

Imagine a country, like Sierra Leone, which has a single large metropolis, its capital city. Almost all the urban demand for locally produced foodstuffs is concentrated in that city, where government offices and industries producing goods such as cloth and beer for local consumption are also located. Farmers cultivate cassava (manioc), maize or groundnuts. They spend part of their time producing for their own subsistence, but with taxation, school fees and a social norm which dictates that certain goods, such as kerosene, are necessities and have to be purchased, all producers are engaged in the monetary economy. In fact, their aim, once their subsistence is satisfied, is to maximize their cash income. The spatial analysts' problem is to determine what crops are grown where, and the areas over which *only* subsistence cultivation may be pursued and from which people earn cash by migrating to the city for work. These areas may be designated 'labour supply reserves'.

In order to isolate the effects of distance and location relative to the capital city on land-use it is common for the spatial analyst to begin by making certain simplifying assumptions about both the land surface and the population. Let us assume that the land surface is homogeneous in every respect, that is, it is an isotropic plain. There are no barriers to movement, physical resources are evenly distributed and soils are of equal fertility. The rural population living on this plain is equally distributed; has identical incomes, demands, tastes and productivity; has identical farm size and family size; and has perfect knowledge and acts to maximize cash income once subsistence needs are satisfied. There are no off-farm sources of income, so that maximizing cash income is equivalent to maximizing returns from the use of land. Also let us assume initially that all farms are of a size that farmers have enough land to meet their subsistence needs *and* produce a surplus for the market if it is profitable.

These conditions are highly unrealistic but a spatial analyst uses them to remove 'complicating factors'. They are, in effect, a spatial version of the economist's 'other-things-being-equal' assumption, and they may be relaxed later in the analysis if, for example, our imaginary country has local areas where farmers do not aim to maximize cash income, or where yields are less through lower soil fertility or more rudimentary techniques, or where farms are so small that producers can scarcely meet family subsistence needs. However, we may begin with our assumptions for they imply that production costs and yields are exactly the same all over the country. Thus the cash income which accrues to each farmer will vary according to his or her location *relative to* the capital city and the costs of shipping produce to that centre of consumption.

Let us assume further that producers do not directly engage in marketing but sell their goods 'at the farm gate' to traders who travel out from the capital city. In our imaginary country, too, let us suppose that marketing is competitive, and so the farm gate prices which the traders offer are equivalent to the market price in the capital city minus the costs which the traders have to bear in transporting produce from the farm gate to the city, and the market prices at which traders sell produce in the capital city are set by the prevailing conditions of supply and demand.

The cash income which the farmer obtains from selling a particular crop depends on his gross returns and production costs, and the net returns per unit of land may be expressed by the formula:

$$\text{Net returns per unit of land} = \underbrace{Y(p - td)}_{\substack{\text{gross} \\ \text{return}}} - \underbrace{Yc}_{\substack{\text{production} \\ \text{costs}}}$$

where Y is the yield per unit of land, c is the production cost per unit of produce, and the expression $(p - td)$ sets the producer price per unit of produce at any given location, with p equivalent to the market price in the capital city, t the transport rate per unit of produce per mile and d the distance in miles of any location from the capital city. As Y, t, p and c do not vary from place to place for any given crop, net returns per unit of land will diminish with increasing distance from the city until a point will be reached where it becomes unprofitable to grow a crop for sale.

Each crop has a different market price, different production costs and yields, and different transport rates, and using these figures it is possible to determine the net returns of different crops in different locations (e.g. Figure 2A). Figure 2A, based on purely notional data, shows that farmers aiming to maximize returns per hectare would grow cassava within twenty-five miles of the capital city, groundnuts in a belt between twenty-four and forty-eight miles, and maize up to a hundred miles from the city. *It would be unprofitable to grow any crops for market in all areas beyond this point.* In these outer areas, only subsistence cultivation could be pursued and cash would have to be earned by migrant labour (Figure 2B).

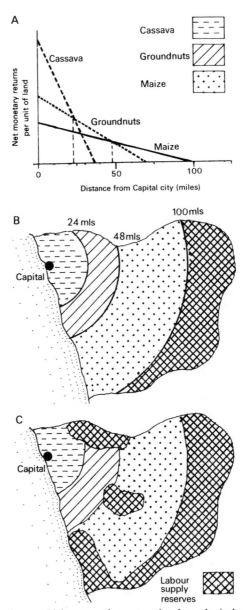

Figure 2 Land-use and labour supply reserves in a hypothetical country. A. Cash income from different land-uses at locations more and less accessible to the capital city. B. The spatial pattern of land-use, assuming farmers maximize cash income. C. Same, with localized 'distortions'.

This almost completes the analysis, but as a final step we may relax the assumptions about population and land-surface and 'distort' the regular concentric rings of land-use. Figure 2C includes three further pockets of subsistence production which are found: (i) in a small area in the centre of the country where soils are very infertile and so yields are low; (ii) along a coastal strip where there is a high population density and farms have become so small that producers have no surplus to sell once they have met their subsistence needs; (iii) an area along the northern frontier where yields are lower because farmers are unwilling to abandon some rudimentary outmoded cultivation practices.

This example demonstrates two important features of the spatial separatist theme. First, the object of study is to explain the location of social phenomena *in geographic space*, i.e. where things are located on the earth's surface. This may seem self-evident but it is necessary to stress it for there is a profusion of adjectives which distinguish different types of space – *social* space, *economic* space, *personal* space, *geographic* space, *topological* space, *physical* space, *perceptual* space, *absolute* space, *relational* space and *relative* space. Furthermore, one of the most influential figures in regional development theory, François Perroux, as long ago as 1950 argued that questions of location in geographic space were 'banal'. I shall argue in later chapters that the change in the conceptualization of space which he then advocated, to *economic space*, has been fatally, yet inevitably, misinterpreted. Regional development theorists may frequently use such epithets as economic space and are also willing to describe locations on the earth's surface in terms of cost-distance or time-distance, instead of physical (miles and metres) distance, and by doing so they may radically change maps of geographic spatial relationships (Figure 3). However, *their fundamental concern remains location in geographic space*, and regional development theory tries to explain *where* 'development' is located on the earth's surface and *where* it should be located.

The second important feature illustrated by the example is that location enters spatial analysis *twice*. The objective is not just to explain the locational properties of social phenomena, *but also to use spatial variables to explain these properties*. As Sack (1980) has clearly stated, in explaining any spatial distribution, the spatial separatist asks the question 'Why does this occur here?', rather than 'Why does this occur?', and produces answers which suggest that it is location *itself* which is important. The existence of labour-supply reserves is thus 'explained' by the costs of moving agricultural produce to the central city market and the effects of *accessibility* to market on the range of opportunities to earn cash from the land.

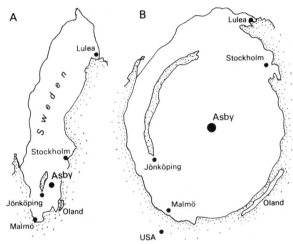

Figure 3 A migrant's perception of distance. A. Conventional map of Sweden. B. Same map, centred on Asby, with all distances transformed using a logarithmic scale. Represents the perception of distance by migrants from the village of Asby.

Source: adapted from Haggett, 1965, Figure 2.4.

The appeal of such pure spatial analysis lies in the fact that it satisfies an institutional need to define a distinctive and exclusive subject-matter for a separate social science in the academic community. This has been demonstrated by Sack for geography and is indeed explicit in Isard's initial definition of the nature and scope of regional science quoted above. But there may be a contradiction between the desire to carve out an independent academic territory and the analytical power and pre-scriptive utility of the discipline thus defined. Even in 1963, Meyer suggested that regional economics should turn away from the construc-tion of regional accounts and studying the effects of spatial separation for its own sake, and direct attention to analysing the way in which cities and regions grow. Such a research effort, he argued, would probably lead to the loss of distinctiveness of regional economics, but would yield more useful theory.

This book examines the spatial separatist theme at work within Anglo-American regional development theory and the logical weaknesses which arise from the way in which space is conceptualized within the field. It would be wrong to assume that explanations of regional develop-ment are as simple as the example outlined. Our example above does not consider temporal change, for instance, and regional development theor-ists have been attempting to examine distributions of human activity in geographic space *and* over time. But it is significant that Friedmann and Alonso (1964) in their pioneering reader, proposed that 'the problem of regional development may be reduced to one in spatial organization' (p. 20). A major aim of the book is to show just how extensive such a reduction in perspective is within the field and to deduce the logical weaknesses in regional development theory which follow from it.

SCIENTIFIC KNOWLEDGE AND THE RATIONALIZATION OF REGIONAL PLANNING

The displacement of the region and commitment to the spatial separatist theme are the major characteristics of regional science, regional economics and theoretical geography which are evident in Anglo-American regional development theory. But there is a third and final aspect of the three root-disciplines which must be considered in order to understand the way in which knowledge has been constructed within the field which is of interest to us. That aspect is the conception of 'useful knowledge' which has underpinned research work and theorizing in the root-disciplines.

Regional science, regional economics and theoretical geography were all promoted as social *sciences*. The conception of 'useful knowledge' which guided thinkers in each of the new disciplines was that such knowledge should be *scientific knowledge*. But their mental efforts were not based on *any* view of 'scientific' investigation. Their research work, at least until the mid 1970s, was founded upon a particular view of what it means 'to understand the social world scientifically'.

That view is positivist or instrumentalist. Within this frame of reference it is assumed that there is a categorical distinction between facts and values, between 'what is' and 'what ought to be'. Social scientists may construct normative arguments, which evaluate factual situations according to given value axioms – for example, whether or not the spatial distribution of health care facilities in a country is equitable in some defined sense. But the main thrust of scientific activity is to understand the social world as it is. And using scientific methods, which are modelled on the procedures of the natural sciences, it is assumed that it is possible to construct an *objective* account of how events are related. Such explanations of the facts of social life are not distorted by the scientists' values or wishes about the way the world ought to be. They are, rather, based on observations and rigorous reasoning processes which can be verified or falsified by others.

The assumption that it is possible to construct an objectively true account of the social world through systematic observation is fundamental to the positivist and instrumentalist conception of scientific activity. But on top of this, there is a particular view of what an *adequate* scientific account consists of. The details of this view will be discussed later in the book. For the present one aspect is important. It is that both the positivist and instrumentalist scientist seek an understanding of the world which can provide the basis for making conditional *predictions*. The positivist endeavours to construct general laws of a type which show that if an event X occurs in a set of conditions, C, then event Y will inevitably, or with known probability, also occur. And the instrumentalist attempts to calibrate the relationships between the variables in a mathematical model so that the model faithfully replicates the real world, and then manipulates those variables to show what would happen if similar changes were made in reality.

As the debates in the philosophy of science show, the positivist and instrumentalist view of 'scientific' knowledge is not the only view which has been put forward (see Keat and Urry, 1975 for a good introduction), and the recognition of alternative perspectives poses the question as to why this particular view was the basis for work in regional science, regional economics and theoretical geography. In part, it reflects the recent evolution of the social sciences, for it was not until the 1970s that alternatives to positivism were widely advocated (see Bernstein, 1976). But besides this, there is a basic rationale for constructing positivist and instrumentalist scientific knowledge. It is that this type of knowledge is 'useful' in the sense that it allows man to control the natural and social environment better. It offers a way of *rationalizing* planning intervention (Fay, 1975).

It supposedly does so by indicating the best means for the achievement of some set of goals. The scientist, it is argued, cannot decide the ends to which policy is directed. Normative arguments which evaluate factual situations can inform the choice of goals, but ultimately this choice rests on values. However, the knowledge which the positivist and instrumentalist construct is of a type which allows one to decide what must be done if one wishes to prevent the occurrence of an event which is not desired, or if one wishes to bring about an event which is desired. Because it provides the grounds for making conditional predictions, it offers a basis for what Popper (1957) has called 'piecemeal social engineering'. It intimates the steps open to us if we want to achieve certain results. And it does so in a way which excludes emotion and opinion. With such knowledge, one may formulate plans of action which are *technically rational*.

Both regional science and regional economics were not just promoted as bodies of 'objective' scientific knowledge, but also as bodies of knowledge which offered a technical basis for making planning decisions. And many of the theorists attempting to construct a new geography were similarly concerned to ensure that their analyses were both objective and 'relevant' to the practical issues of modern-day life. In each of the subjects there was an adherence to the spatial separatist theme *and* a commitment to constructing positivist and instrumentalist knowledge. The conception of scientific knowledge was the framework within which attempts to isolate 'the spatial' were made, and knowledge was constructed on the assumption that it could be used to rationalize planning activities.

As in the three root disciplines, adherence to the spatial separatist theme in Anglo-American regional development theory is linked with an endeavour to construct positivist and instrumentalist scientific knowledge. And like those disciplines, the field has evolved with a strong policy orientation. This book thus examines the spatial separatist theme at work within Anglo-American regional development theory. But it does so within a particular frame of reference. *It considers Anglo-American regional development theory as a body of scientific knowledge which offers a technical basis for the rationalization of regional planning activities.*

It must be emphasized here that there are strong arguments within the philosophy of science which suggest that it is impossible to construct objective, value-free knowledge of human action and social change. Moreover the assumption that plans based on positivist and instrumentalist knowledge are socially neutral has been powerfully contested (see especially Fay, 1975). If, then, one stands outside the narrow conception of 'useful knowledge' which permeates regional development theory and applies these general philosophical arguments to assess ideas within the field, the validity and utility of regional development theory may be immediately questioned. But this book will not make its case in this way. The purpose of the book is to lead the reader to a point where a change in perspective is *seen to be necessary*, and where such arguments *must* be addressed. And to achieve this Anglo-American regional development theory will be examined *in its own terms*. At the outset, therefore, I shall accept the view that positivist and instrumentalist scientific knowledge offers a neutral, technical basis for choosing the best means to achieve given ends, and consider, in the body of the argument, whether this view can be sustained for Anglo-American regional development theory, given the adherence to spatial separatism.

To do this, the discussion will focus upon both the logical structure of the field and the practical implications which follow when knowledge constructed within a positivist and instrumentalist frame of reference and with a spatial separatist's perspective is translated into practical action. Many logical weaknesses stemming from spatial separatism may be identified within the theory *itself*. But it is in the translation of theory into practice that the inadequacies of the spatial separatist theme are most fully exposed. And in the exposure of those inadequacies, the overall approach to understanding the world in regional development theory, and the assumptions about the uses of supposedly 'objective' scientific knowledge, will be called into question.

THE ORGANIZATION OF THE ARGUMENT

The book is organized in three major parts. Part One considers the goals of regional policy by examining three spatial patterns which are often designated as policy 'problems' in developing countries. Broadly defined, these three patterns are regional disparities in development, the size of the national metropoli, and rural–urban disparities. The view that these spatial *patterns* constitute *problems* which require planning intervention rests upon arguments which suggest that these *spatial* patterns have adverse *socio-economic* implications for national states and that without planning intervention the spatial patterns will persist. Chapters 1 and 2 consider these arguments.

Part One is mainly concerned with normative evaluations of spatial patterns. But some explanatory theory is introduced, as the arguments for state intervention to ameliorate these problems rest on analyses of the spatial outcome of the free play of market forces. Part Two extends the review of explanations of urban and regional development by examining the theoretical bases of rival regional planning strategies which have been suggested in the literature as means of promoting a supposedly more desirable spatial distribution of activity, income and population within developing countries. These alternative planning strategies are based on different explanations of how cities, regions and rural localities 'develop', which are, in turn, rooted in particular conceptions of what 'development' is and how it occurs. The aim of the second part of this book is to identify the developmental assumptions which underlie the rival regional planning strategies and show how they have been applied in a spatial context.

The discussion in Part Two is designed to introduce important contributions to regional development theory and thus attempts to summarize these contributions faithfully and not to criticize them. But the exposition indicates the extent to which the spatial separatist theme is at work within the field. Part Three offers a critique of the proposed strategies in terms of the way in which space enters the explanations on which the rival strategies rest, considering both the logical limitations and practical implications of the way in which knowledge has been constructed.

The argument is intended to lead the reader to the conclusion that the way that knowledge is constructed within Anglo-American regional development theory is, *within its own terms*, illogical. As a technical basis for regional planning it offers non-solutions to non-problems. The final chapter offers a way out of this impasse by changing the way in which the relationship between 'space' and 'development' is conceptualized, and by examining both the ends *and* the means of regional planning as *political choices*, that is, as choices which support or damage the interests of particular groups in society. In this reinterpretation, the region is brought back to the centre of analysis. But regional development theory, as a separate field of knowledge, ceases to exist. The task of understanding the spatiality of change in developing countries becomes a task for development theorists.

Part One

Common Regional Policy Objectives

1

Regional imbalance as a policy problem

There is a great range of regional planning strategies pursued in the developing countries of the world, but three common policy problems constantly recur: regional disparities in development, the excessive size of the national metropoli, and rural–urban inequality. The stated objective of regional policy in many developing countries is to alleviate one, or more, of these problems – that is, to reduce interregional and rural–urban disparities and to curb the growth of the national metropoli.

It is so often taken for granted that the achievement of these goals is desirable that it may seem naïve to question the judgement. But that is the aim of the first part of this book.

Closer scrutiny of the three 'problems' shows, first, that there is no single way in which any of them may be defined, and second, that each refers to a *spatial distribution* of some kind. Regional disparities in development and rural–urban inequality may be measured using various indicators, such as *per capita* income, employment opportunities, social facilities or infrastructure. But whatever indicators are chosen, they merely describe a spatial pattern. The number of people who are said to be inhabitants of a metropolis may similarly be calculated in different ways. But whatever metropolitan boundaries and criteria of habitation are used, the size of the national metropoli is merely an aspect of the spatial distribution of population within a country. In making these spatial distributions an object of policy, it is assumed that such spatial *patterns* are in fact social and economic *problems*. And it is often implied that the alleviation of these 'problems' will in some sense be beneficial for the 'nation' as a whole. The next two chapters examine the main normative arguments which have been elaborated in support of this contention.

The present chapter focuses on regional economic disparities and the argument that they constitute a policy problem because they represent a condition of disequilibrium. This argument is rarely stated explicitly, but it is evident in the common view that 'regional balance' should be a goal of public policy. Of course, the term 'balance' is widely used in political rhetoric for it is in effect meaningless until specified in detail, while at the same time it suggests harmony, stability and equality. However, *technically, balance means equilibrium*. And thus it is possible to interpret the argument that governments should intervene to reduce regional economic disparities because they constitute a condition of regional imbalance as saying that such disparities represent a condition of spatial disequilibrium and such a condition is undesirable. This interpretation of 'the problem of regional imbalance' is followed here. For although it is usually implicit, the use of equilibrium as a norm to judge spatial patterns and to characterize some patterns as problems is, I believe, deeply ingrained in regional development theory, and also, as I shall argue, highly misleading.

THE NATURE OF GENERAL SPATIAL EQUILIBRIUM

In order to sustain the argument that a spatial pattern is a problem because it represents a state of disequilibrium, it is necessary first to determine exactly what spatial disequilibrium looks like. This takes us into a complex, mathematical field which has occupied the minds of many regional scientists and regional economists. It is difficult to summarize the results of this intellectual endeavour succinctly, particularly as spatial equilibrium may be specified in many different ways. However, it is possible to illustrate the manner in which spatial equilibrium is determined by the simple models of two early theorists – Bertil Ohlin and August Lösch.

Both these highly creative economists worked on the problem of adding a spatial dimension to the formulation of general economic equilibrium which had been elaborated by Walras and Pareto among others. The idea of general equilibrium is that in any economy, with a given set of factors of production and commodities to be exchanged, there is a unique pattern of output and prices which will always be attained through individuals striving to achieve the 'best' position for themselves. Every economy moves towards its equilibrium as long as what are defined as exogenous variables – for example, technology, population and tastes – do not change. And the state of equilibrium has the added property that it is optimal in the sense that it provides the maximum aggregate satisfaction of wants given the limited resources, and no individual within the economy can improve his or her position without making another individual worse off.

General equilibrium theorists were not concerned with how the process of adjustment among producers and consumers would bring about equilibrium, but rather explored, through mathematical equations and argumentation, the conditions in which an equilibrium could be achieved. The mutual determination of outputs and prices in such analyses was instantaneous, and the drama of economic life took place, in effect, on the head of a pin. Ohlin and Lösch, in distinctly different ways, and with different results, tried to include the effects of space.

Bertil Ohlin and interregional income equalization

The main aims of Bertil Ohlin in writing his classic text *Interregional and International Trade* were to construct a theory of international trade which was 'in harmony with the mutual-interdependence theory of pricing', and to demonstrate that such a theory was part of a general location theory, 'wherein the space aspects of pricing are taken into full account' (1933, p. ix). Ohlin set about this task by extending 'the one-market analysis' of the general equilibrium theorists to include 'a number of more or less closely related markets' (p. 2).

Each of these markets is described as a 'region' which is distinguished from other 'regions' by its endowment of factors of production. A 'region', in these terms, may be a nation, and indeed much of his analysis examines problems of international trade. However, for Ohlin, 'international' trade is merely one type of interregional trade, and the analysis is intended to be equally relevant at any spatial scale whether the regions are whole countries or merely parts of countries.

Ohlin begins by assuming that factors of production are inter-regionally immobile and intra-regionally freely mobile, and that no transfer costs are incurred in trade. Furthermore, the production function, which relates level of output to levels of input used, is assumed to be identical in every region. In these simplified conditions, trade will only occur when it is possible for a region to buy and import commodities from another region more cheaply *in monetary terms* than they can be produced within the region. And this situation arises in Ohlin's frame of analysis when there are differences in factor endowments between regions. 'Each region has an advantage in the production of commodities into which enter considerable amounts of factors abundant and cheap in that region', he writes (p. 12), and economic benefits are maximized in a region if it can specialize in production of those commodities and trade.

Supposing that trade does occur between regions, what is its effect on the pattern of production and prices? Ohlin argues that the outcome is difficult to determine precisely for both commodity and factor prices in each region form part of a system of mutual interdependence. The total demand for a commodity in a region, for example, depends on income in that region, which depends further on both the volume of interregional trade and returns to factors of production (among other things). The total demand for each factor of production in a region depends on both the structure of production for domestic consumption, and the structure of production for export and thus is affected by demand in other regions. If the regions have separate currencies, then the way all prices are compared depends on the *foreign* (i.e. interregional) *exchange rate* which specifies the relative value of each region's currency and which depends on conditions of reciprocal demand for both commodities and factors of production in each region. Without a mathematical analysis, which Ohlin does not attempt, it is impossible to determine the equilibrium pattern of output and prices. But through a 'crab-like' analysis, in which certain variables are held constant, a result obtained, and then released one by one, he does identify major tendencies within the interregional system.

The general equilibrium which is achieved is characterized by a geographical division of labour in which different regions specialize in the production of different commodities according to their factor endowment. But there are also important elements of regional economic equality. In the absence of transport costs and tariffs, 'the effect of interregional trade is to equalize commodity prices' and 'there is also a tendency toward equalization of prices of factors of production' (p. 34).

It should be noted that the latter trend occurs even though there are no factor movements. And exactly why this is so may be simply illustrated. Imagine an economy in which the only two commodities are steel and textiles, the former highly capital-intensive, the latter labour-intensive; and there are only two regions, the north which has abundant cheap capital and scarce expensive labour, and the south which has abundant cheap labour and scarce expensive capital. Without interregional trade, each region must produce both commodities; but with trade, the north would specialize in steel production and the south in textiles. The change in the structure of production would force down labour prices in the north, because in the switch from textiles to steel, more labour would be shed than could be absorbed, and at the same time, less capital would be released than required, and so capital prices would be forced up. The switch from steel to textiles in the south would similarly increase labour prices, and reduce capital prices (see Armstrong and Taylor, 1978).

Transfer costs between regions provide an obstacle to interregional trade and mean that commodity prices are different in different regions. And for any particular commodity, if the costs of transfer are greater than the differences in the costs of production in the various regions, then no trade will occur. But in these circumstances, interregional factor

movements can have equalizing effects. There is a trend towards factor
price equalization whenever capital and labour can move freely and
moves to where it achieves the greatest return (Figure 4).

For this reason, Ohlin writes, 'Factor movements act as a substitute for
the movement of commodities. Interregional price equalization seems to
be furthered either by both movements or the one that meets with less
resistance' (p. 116). The process of factor movement clearly changes
factor endowments in different regions and it may be thought that interregional trade then becomes unnecessary. But 'psychological obstacles'
reduce the mobility of capital and labour, and natural resources are
immobile. In the long run, this immobility of natural resources is 'the
controlling element' on the whole system of prices and output (p. 124).

The tendencies towards regional economic equality which Ohlin
identifies are, as he readily acknowledges, conditional upon a number of
assumptions. The restrictive assumption of identical production functions has already been noted, but the analysis is also elaborated for a

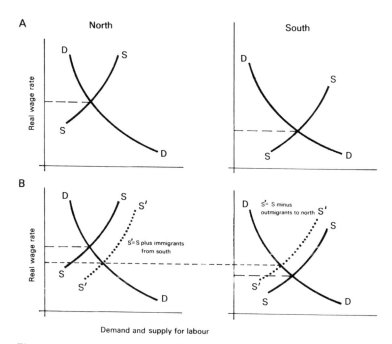

Figure 4 The equilibrating effects of labour migration in a two-region economy.
A. Wage rates before migration. B. Wage rates after migration.

Source: adapted from Armstrong and Taylor, 1978, Figure 3.1.

perfectly competitive world in which the prices of factors of production reflect their relative scarcity and in which there are diminishing, rather than increasing, marginal returns to production factors. It is also a world in which economic adjustments are instantaneous. The reality of analysis will be addressed later in the chapter, but significantly, *if* it is further assumed that labour participation rates are equal between regions, transfer costs are non-existent and labour and capital are freely mobile between regions and completely informed about relative prices, then the spatial equilibrium which Ohlin identifies is characterized by *equal* average *per capita* incomes in each region.

August Lösch and hierarchical order in the ideal economic region

While Ohlin examined the mutual interdependence of prices and outputs in discrete and pre-defined 'regions', August Lösch, in his book *The Economics of Location*, tried to determine what general equilibrium would look like in continuous geographic space. As Stolper writes in the foreword to that classic text, this was the first attempt 'to present a full general equilibrium system describing in abstract the interrelationship of all locations' (Lösch, 1954, p. ix).

In undertaking this task, Lösch explicitly was concerned to provide information which would be valuable in the formulation of public policy. He was thus less interested in the *explanation* of actual location patterns in the world, but rather in the determination of what he called the 'rational' location. As he put it in his own famous words:

> No! The real duty of the economist is not to explain our sorry reality, but to improve it. The question of the best location is far more dignified than determination of the actual one.　　(Lösch, 1954, p. 4)

But what exactly is the 'best' location, and why are particular locations said to be 'rational'? The norm which he prescribed, with minor qualifications, was the state of spatial equilibrium. His theoretical effort was thus directed to determining, through an abstract model, the nature of this equilibrium. Economic policy, he wrote, must vary in individual cases. But 'it is the business of policy to achieve the basic forms of the model and make good the assumptions under which it operates' (p. 358); and moreover, 'wherever something new is being created, and thus in settlement and spatial planning also, the laws revealed through theory are the sole economic guide to what should take place' (p. 359).

Lösch suggests that general spatial equilibrium is characterized by five conditions:

1 The location of every individual must be as advantageous as possible, and so entrepreneurs must have located production in the most profitable places and consumers must have maximized their utility.
2 The points where production occurs must be so numerous that the entire area is occupied, and so all the population is served.
3 There must be no abnormal profits.
4 Areas of supply, production and sales must be as small as possible.
5 At the boundaries of market areas consumers must be indifferent to which of two neighbouring production points they get their supply from.

He lists a set of equations which define these conditions and then graphically portrays what he calls the 'economic landscape', the location of market areas and production centres, of transport lines and of cities.

To simplify the determination of the economic landscape at equilibrium he assumes that 'economic raw materials are evenly and adequately distributed over a wide plain which is homogeneous in every other respect and contains nothing but self-sufficient farms that are regularly distributed' (p. 105), and then asks what will happen if the inhabitants on the plain decide to produce manufactured goods over and above their subsistence needs. How many producers will there be? What is their location, and scale of output?

He starts by considering one commodity – beer. The consumers on the plain are assumed to pay the transport costs involved in buying beer, and thus the further away from the point of production, the greater the price. Assuming a given demand curve for beer (Figure 5A) and a given rate of transport, it is possible to describe the quantity of beer demanded at various distances from the producer (Figure 5B). As the diagram shows, there is a certain distance beyond which consumers will be unwilling to consume beer.

But is it worthwhile for someone to begin beer production in these conditions? It all depends on the costs of production at different scales of activity and the revenue which may be earned at different prices. From the area under the spatial demand cone in Figure 5C, it is possible to calculate the total revenue which is achieved at a given price and the average revenue per unit of production. The average revenue which the beer producer will get at various possible prices may then be calculated. If the price goes up, then the demand cone will contract, and if the price comes down, the demand cone will expand, and as a result the average revenue curve slopes down to the right (Figure 6A).

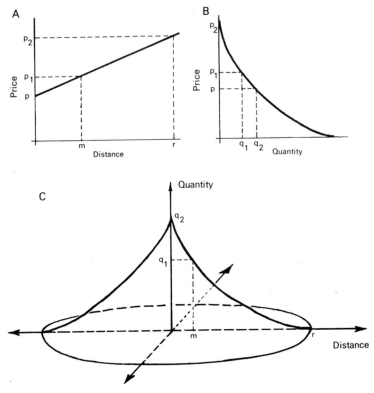

Figure 5 The demand for beer in geographical space. A. Price to the consumer at various distances from the producer. B. The demand curve for beer. C. The spatial demand cone – quantity demanded at various distances from the producer.

Source: adapted from Berry, 1968.

As long as average revenue at any given scale of activity exceeds average costs, then profitable production is possible (Figure 6B). But as long as profits are made, more and more people will start brewing beer. At the start, the market areas surrounding each selling-point will be circular, reflecting the maximum distance that consumers are willing to travel for beer. But as more and more producers crowd on to the plain, market areas will start to overlap and as consumers, in order to maximize their utility, will travel to the nearest seller, market areas will be hexagonal. As a producer's market area starts to shrink, so the area under the demand cone at a given price becomes less, and the average revenue curve slopes more steeply. New producers will continue to start beer production as

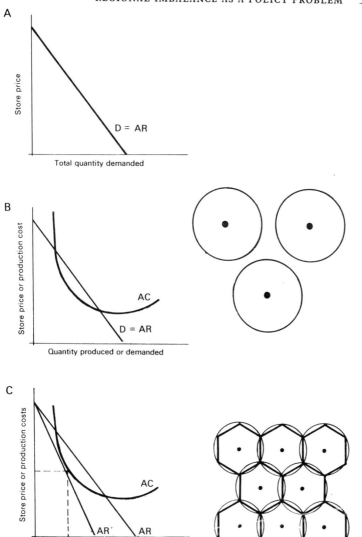

Figure 6 The equilibrium pattern of beer production. A. The aggregate demand curve, assuming a single producer and no spatial competition for consumers. B. Average production costs and revenues, assuming no spatial competition for consumers. C. Long-run equilibrium, with many producers and hexagonal market areas just large enough to ensure that $AC = AR^1$.

Source: adapted from Berry, 1968.

long as profits can be made and the whole system will reach equilibrium only when average costs just equal average revenue (Figure 6C). The result, which as in general equilibrium analysis is an instantaneous solution, is a network of hexagonal market areas for beer production completely filling the plain.

If more commodities are produced for the consumers on the plain, it is possible to visualize a series of such networks of market areas, all with a different hexagonal mesh which is determined by production costs, transport costs and elasticity of demand. In determining the general equilibrium, Lösch rejects the ideas that these nets of hexagons 'can be thrown at will over our plain' (p. 124) and instead co-ordinates their location so that all of them have at least one centre in common (the regional metropolis) and then rotates them around the centre until the greatest number of production locations coincide. This operation clearly has *no* relationship whatsoever with real world processes, but may be regarded as the graphical equivalent of solving the set of simultaneous equations which describe the conditions for equilibrium. The resulting economic landscape, which is called the 'ideal' economic region, is regarded by Lösch as a 'precarious emergency bridge' in the elaboration of spatial economic theory (Figure 7).

At equilibrium, in Lösch's scheme, there is a hierarchy of *central places*, that is centres providing manufactured goods and services to the surrounding population. It is a hierarchy in the sense that there are many places providing a small range of local services and a few places providing a large range. And significantly, even though Lösch elaborates his analysis on a completely uniform plain without any resource differentials, the equilibrium is characterized by important spatial disparities. Some parts of the plain – the 'city-rich zones' as Lösch calls them – have more central places, producing more goods, than other parts – the 'city-poor' zones (Figure 7).

How the population, which was initially distributed evenly over the plain at the outset, will be redistributed as these centres crystallize is not considered by Lösch, and has provided a line for much criticism (see Isard, 1956a). But if there is a regular relationship between the functional range of activity in a centre and its population size, then Lösch's model specifies the distribution of relative city sizes at equilibrium.

There are many other ways in which the nature of general spatial equilibrium may be defined (see Bramhall, 1969, for a good introduction), but the contrasting models of Ohlin and Lösch illustrate some of the difficulties which inevitably arise if spatial equilibrium is used as a norm to define a spatial pattern as a social and economic problem.

For a start, it is apparent that equilibrium, or 'balance', is *not* equivalent to equality. It is true that in Ohlin's framework, if various assumptions

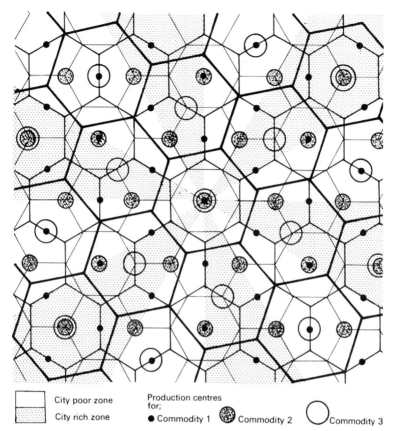

Figure 7 The equilibrium spatial arrangement of market areas and production centres with three different commodities.

Source: adapted from Isard, 1956a, p. 270.

are made, then spatial equilibrium will be characterized by equal average *per capita* incomes in different regions. But one of the most important conclusions of Lösch's work is that even if natural resource differences are eliminated, there will be systematic disparities in the spatial arrangement of productive units at equilibrium. As he dramatically puts it when he describes the final result of his analysis:

> we suddenly have crowds of economic areas on a plain we deprived of all spatial inequalities at the outset.   (Lösch, 1938, p. 101)

This means that there is no simple test for identifying spatial equilibrium and that the mere existence of regional economic disparities does *not* signal a state of disequilibrium.

I emphasize this point not because I believe that regional theorists are all guilty of this fallacy – although the term regional balance is sometimes interchangeable with regional equality in the literature – but because it makes the use of equilibrium as a norm for diagnosing a problem particularly difficult. For, in order to determine whether a spatial pattern in reality deviates from the equilibrium norm, it is necessary to relax the restrictive assumptions of the models which specify equilibrium so that they correspond more closely to conditions pertaining in reality. But how can one do this in practice? What, for example, does spatial equilibrium look like in Brazil or India? And if it cannot be specified, is it meaningful to say that those countries are characterized by 'regional imbalance'? Regional *disparities*, perhaps; or regional *inequality*. But not regional *imbalance*.

This problem considerably restricts the practical utility of using spatial equilibrium as a norm in the assessment of spatial patterns, but there are ways of circumventing it, as will become apparent in the section which begins at p. 42. Let us for the moment disregard the difficulty and proceed under the assumption that a condition of regional imbalance can be identified. The argument that this condition is a policy problem then rests upon two further propositions: first, that the market mechanism by itself will not move an economy towards spatial equilibrium; and second, that the achievement of spatial equilibrium is desirable. The next part of the chapter will examine these propositions.

GUNNAR MYRDAL AND CUMULATIVE CAUSATION

Most regional theorists agree that equilibrium in a space economy is unlikely to be achieved purely through the operation of market forces. Gunnar Myrdal, another Swedish social scientist, was one of the first to expound this view and indeed wrote:

> That there is a tendency inherent in the freeplay of market forces to create regional inequalities, and that this tendency becomes more dominant the poorer a country is, are two of the most important laws of economic development and underdevelopment under *laissez-faire*.
> (Myrdal, 1957, p. 34)

The key to Myrdal's argument is the concept of *circular and cumulative causation*. He wrote that 'the notion of stable equilibrium is normally a false analogy to choose when constructing a theory of changes in a social system' (Myrdal, 1957, p. 12), and suggested that a change in some variable in a social system does not induce *countervailing* changes which move the system back to equilibrium but instead induces *supporting* changes which move the system further away from the initial state. Social systems are thus not self-equilibrating, but rather characterized by a process of circular and cumulative causation.

Myrdal first evolved this notion in analysing the economic and social status of the black population of the USA, but then applied it to the explanation of regional economic inequalities. He suggested that once a development starts in a particular centre, for whatever reason, then that region develops its own momentum of growth through the process of cumulative causation. Thus, for example, the location of a new industry in a region can set off a train of effects which will attract further new industry (Figure 8).

This momentum of growth is then further 'sustained and fortified' through interaction between the growing centre and other parts of the country. Trade and factor mobility, far from having equalizing effects as Ohlin suggests, rather have 'backwash effects' on the lagging regions in the sense that they retard their growth and widen the economic gap between the regions. Through migration, the poorer regions lose their most enterprising and youngest workers; the banking system siphons off the savings of people in the poor regions and reinvests them in the richer

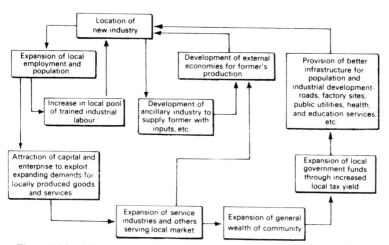

Figure 8 Myrdal's concept of cumulative causation: an example of industrial expansion in a region.

Source: Keeble, 1967, Figure 8.4.

regions; and freer trade tends to bankrupt small and traditional industries in the poorer regions as they cannot compete with the industries in
the growing regions which are working under conditions of increasing
returns to scale. In this way, Myrdal argues that continuous growth in
one region occurs 'at the expense of other locations and regions' (p. 27).
These localities may be stagnant, or even in decline, for they too are subject to cumulative forces, some of which are social rather than narrowly
economic, but all of which promote a momentum of economic contrac-
tion.

The momentum of growth in what Myrdal calls the centres of economic expansion may have positive 'spread effects' on the economy of
other regions, for example, through an increased demand for their raw
materials. The net effect of interregional interaction then depends on the
combined impact of backwash and spread effects. This complicates the
analysis, but Myrdal is adamant that 'in no circumstances do spread
effects establish the assumption for an equilibrium analysis' (p. 32).
Backwash and spread effects may cancel each other out but 'this balance
is not a stable equilibrium for any change in the forces will start a cumulative movement upwards or downwards' (p. 32).

Myrdal hypothesizes that the relative strength of backwash and spread
effects varies according to the level of development of a country suggesting that spread effects are stronger in more developed countries. This is
attributed to the fact that higher levels of education, improved transport
and communications and 'a more dynamic communion of ideas and
values' (p. 34) accompanies development and reduces obstacles to the
operation of spread effects. And thus Myrdal concludes 'the free play of
market forces in a poor country will work more powerfully to create
regional inequalities and to widen those which already exist' (p. 34).

JOHN FRIEDMANN'S CASE FOR REGIONAL POLICY (1966)

As I noted in the Introduction, Myrdal's work is generally taken to be
the starting-point for the elaboration of regional development theory.
His ideas attracted much attention (see Keeble, 1967) and still furnish a
basic framework for analysing regional economic disparities. One of the
scholars to develop his argument was John Friedmann, who in 1966
made a case for regional policy in developing countries which extended
Myrdal's analysis by linking it with prevailing ideas about what 'development' is, and with concepts drawn from location theory.

Friedmann's case centred on 'the spatial transformations engendered
by economic growth' (p. 6). Taking 'development' in Rostow's terms as
a process of change from an agricultural to industrial and post-industrial

society which occurs in a similar series of stages in all countries, Friedmann suggested that regional policy becomes a critical policy issue in 'transitional societies', those moving from an agrarian to an industrial economy. In pre-industrial economies, those in which industry makes up less than 10 per cent of GNP, regional policy is 'inappropriate' and the main policy emphasis must be upon 'creating pre-conditions for economic development'. In industrial economies, those in which industry makes up 25–50 per cent of GNP, regional policy is 'vestigial', only concerned with alleviating problems in depressed areas and making adjustments to common market organizations. But in the transitional phase, during take-off in Rostow's terminology, regional policy is 'critical' (Table 1).

Friedmann develops a simple model of the spatial transformations associated with national development to explain why this is so. The sequence of changes is played out on 'a previously uninhabited area colonized from the sea' (p. 8). The first phase is one of initial settlement along the coast, exploration and occupation of interior regions. A colonial economy based on agriculture, cattle raising and mining is established, with some of the early settlements growing into commercial centres and one becoming an administrative centre. Once this colonial economy is established, a number of distinctive regional economies exploiting different local resources may be discerned. The main spatial changes which occur during this phase reflect changes in the pattern of export demand, with different regions favoured for settlement and investment in succession as resources are exploited. At the same time administrative and service centres develop, but they are geared towards their respective regional economies and do not form an interdependent *system* of cities. Towards the end of this phase, the imaginary country receives independence, but at that time it 'will appear to be composed of a congeries of relatively autonomous regional economies and socio-cultural subsystems, each with its own administrative and commercial centres and traditional centres of export' (p. 9).

Industrialization, which begins in the next phase, effects dramatic shifts in the spatial pattern. It

> typically leads to a concentration of investments upon one or two areas, while much of the remaining territory becomes locationally obsolete. A dualistic structure is thus imprinted upon the space economy, comprising a 'centre' of rapid intensive development and a 'periphery' whose economy, imperfectly related to this centre, is either stagnant or declining.   (p. 9)

The centre, in this dualistic structure, is a single *core region*, which is 'one or more clustered cities together with an encompassing area that

Table 1   Phases of national development and regional policy

Type of economy	Pre-industrial†	Transitional	Industrial	Post-industrial
Industry as share of GNP, 1950–5*	0–10%	10–25%	25–50%	declining
Importance of regional policy for national economic growth	inappropriate	critical	vestigial	shift to a new focus
Policy emphasis	creating pre-conditions for economic development	creating a spatial organization capable of sustaining transition to industrialism	depressed area problems; area redevelopment; spatial adjustments to common market organization	urban renewal; spatial order and circulation within metropolitan regions; open space and amenities of landscape
Examples of countries in each category	Tanganyika Paraguay Bolivia Afghanistan Cambodia Burma	Venzuela Brazil Colombia Turkey India Pakistan Iraq Mexico	France Italy W. Germany Japan Israel UK Canada Australia	USA‡

* Hollis B. Chenery, 'Pattern of industrial growth', *American Economic Review*, I (4), September 1960, Table 1.
† Estimated. See Everett Hagen, 'Some facts about income levels and economic growth', *The Review of Economics and Statistics*, 42 (1) February 1960, Table 1.
‡ The turning point, it appears, was 1953, when manufacturing industry accounted for 32.1 per cent of the national income. The corresponding share of manufacturing for the average of the years 1960 to 1962 was only 28.6 per cent. Cf. US Department of Commerce, Bureau of the Census, *Historical Statistics of the United States*, Series F 22–33; Washington, DC: US Government Printing Office, 1960, and *Survey of Current Business*, July 1963, Table 7.

Source: Friedmann, 1966, p. 7.

may be conveniently delimited by the extent of daily commuting or, alternatively, by the distribution of agricultural activities that furnish sustenance to central urban populations' (p. 41). And the spatial pattern is characterized as one of *primacy*, 'the domination of the space economy by a single urban region' (p. 35).

By analogy with the world scale, Friedmann suggests that the relationship between centre and periphery *within* countries during the transition to an industrial economy is a colonial one. The powerful region 'reduces the rest of the space economy to the role of a tributary area' (p. 99). The periphery is 'drained of its resources, manpower and capital' (p. 99). The primate cities 'tend to feed upon the rest of the nation'. Instead of generating a new economic order and new wealth, 'they feast on what may be extracted by the sweat of poor, provincial labour' (p. 35). Labour, capital, entrepreneurship and foreign exchange all thus flow towards the centre and the periphery's position is further aggravated in that the secular trend in the interregional terms of trade tends to be against primary production.

In the long run, when the nation has passed through the take-off phase, matures industrially, and enters an era of high mass consumption, interregional inequalities will diminish as the primacy of the single core region is reduced, and an interdependent system of cities, which resembles Lösch's economic landscape, is established. But the sequence of stages in the spatial organization of an economy which *ideally* every economy passes through as it grows (Figure 9) takes a long time. There is no automatic tendency of regional income convergence towards the spatial equilibrium which Ohlin's work would suggest. Rather, 'disequilibrium is built into transitional societies from the start; the technological revolution is permanent, changes in demand and supply conditions are so rapid and their consequences of such magnitude that they can scarcely be considered marginal' (p. 14). Indeed, once the dualistic centre-periphery structure is established, 'the unrestrained forces of a dynamic market economy appear to be working against a convergence of the centre and periphery' (p. 18).

It is 'because normal equilibrating forces are too weak to rectify the centre-periphery imbalance within a reasonable period' (p. 99) that regional policy must be introduced in transitional economies. For while changes in spatial structure are a function of economic growth, growth is itself conditioned by spatial structure. As Friedmann puts it, 'Interregional balance and an hierarchical system of cities are essential conditions for national development' (p. 37). A lasting centre-periphery relation

> leads to extreme inequities in welfare among regions . . . encourages the underutilization of natural resources . . . is conducive to the inefficient location of industry . . . has politically destabilizing effects . . . contributes to the problems of rapid concentrated urbanization at a single centre . . . and tends to restrict development of a consumer market on a national scale. (p. 99)

Friedmann thus raises the spectre of a poverty trap: the growth of the economy is restrained by the existence of the 'dualistic' centre-periphery

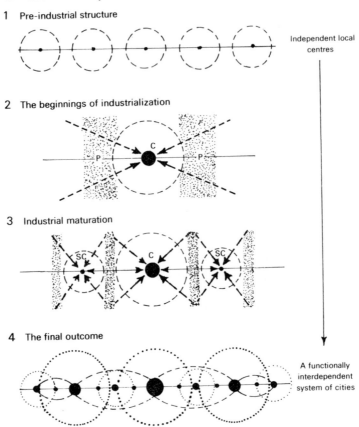

Figure 9 The stages of spatial organization.

Source: adapted from Friedmann, 1966.

structure, and the 'dualistic' centre-periphery structure persists because the economy does not grow. It is a trap which is likely to be exacerbated by political pressures from less developed regions which may threaten the stability and territorial boundaries of the nation state. But it is a trap that can be escaped − through planning intervention. And that is precisely where regional policy comes in. Its *critical* role is 'to create a spatial organization capable of sustaining the transition to industrialization' (p. 7).

SPATIAL EQUILIBRIUM AND SPATIAL INTEGRATION

Like Myrdal, Friedmann emphatically rejects the view that the 'invisible hand' of the market will ensure the attainment of spatial equilibrium, and even writes of 'the bankruptcy of the equilibrium model as a basis for policy prescription' (p. 18). But this statement conceals a deeper reliance on the spatial equilibrium model which becomes apparent when Friedmann attempts to specify what 'a spatial organization which sustains the transition to industrialism' actually is.

It is certainly *not* a centre-periphery structure for that leads to the misallocation of investment and under-utilization of natural resources which strangles growth. But why is that so? One answer would be that the relationship between the dominant core region and the periphery is 'imperfect'. But this does not take the argument forward, for a 'perfect' relationship in this context is presumably one in which resources are not misallocated or under-utilized. Friedmann does say that the centre-periphery structure is unfair, and it is likely to promote political grievances, to which the central government may respond by redistributing resources 'in an unprincipled way' (p. 13). But one searches Friedmann's text in vain for the economic case *why* the centre-periphery structure may strangle growth. Indeed, other parts of his book complicate the picture further for he asserts that the concentration of investment in a few localities allows the realization of agglomeration economies, and thus creates the potential for even greater growth.

The basic reason why 'the transition to industrialism' is hindered by the centre-periphery structure seems to be that the centre-periphery structure *lasts*. Its persistence provides *prima facie* evidence for the misallocation of resources because it does not correspond to what Friedmann imagines spatial equilibrium is, and because, at spatial equilibrium, resources *are* optimally allocated. It is for this reason, one must presume, that he writes that interregional balance and a hierarchical system of cities are *essential conditions* for development.

I say presume, for Friedmann never explicitly states this. But the point becomes clearer when one considers the goals to which regional policy should be directed. Friedmann cannot specify the optimal spatial pattern at any given moment in terms of its short-run and long-run effects on growth. However, he is certain about *the direction of improvement*:

> The goal of integration is essential for a nation initiating its drive to industrial maturity. It has in view the breakdown of a pattern of regionalized economies partly closed to commerce with one another and holding on a steady course toward an interdependent national system, based on the principle of comparative advantage.   (pp. 55–6)

To escape the poverty trap which the centre-periphery structure presages, a deliberate regional policy should aim for:

1. the gradual elimination of the periphery on a national scale by substituting for it a single interdependent system of urban regions, and

2. the progressive integration of the space economy by the extension, on a national scale, of efficient commodity and factor markets.

(p. 54)

The 'imperfect' relationship between centre and periphery should thus be replaced by 'full integration of the space economy' (p. 55), for the resources will then be properly allocated.

The term 'spatial integration' is as elusive as the term 'regional balance', having positive political and social overtones. But if the objective of 'full integration of the space economy' is more than empty rhetoric, then in essence the policy which Friedmann proposes must be *to make the real world correspond more closely to the conditions which economic models suggest are necessary for the attainment of spatial equilibrium.* In doing so, Friedmann neatly sidesteps the difficulty of defining spatial equilibrium, but at the same time he adopts a confusingly ambiguous attitude to spatial equilibrium models. On the one hand, he rejects the model as an adequate explanation of real world process, while on the other hand he accepts the model as a guide for judging existing spatial patterns and guiding them in the future. Thus the equilibrium model is 'bankrupt' for him in the sense that it implies that planning intervention is unnecessary. But it nevertheless provides *the* underlying guide for policy.

Friedmann's argument illustrates well the *implicit* way in which spatial equilibrium is used in regional development theory as a norm to diagnose spatial patterns as social and economic problems. But the simultaneous rejection of spatial equilibrium as an explanatory tool and acceptance as a normative device is not *necessarily* inconsistent. For the pattern which is found at spatial equilibrium may well be a desirable and attainable state. Whether or not it is will be considered in the next section.

THE IRRELEVANCE OF SPATIAL EQUILIBRIUM AS A NORM

At this point the argument becomes more complex. We must show that 'regional balance' in the sense of general spatial equilibrium is in fact *neither* desirable *nor* attainable, and thus that it is irrelevant as a norm for diagnosing spatial patterns as socio-economic problems and for guiding public policy. But the argument cannot proceed merely by objecting to the lack of 'realism' of spatial equilibrium models. It must question the *logical* basis of the idea that market forces operating in a space economy can achieve an equilibrium which is optimal.

The severity of the assumptions of spatial equilibrium models does, of course, make it difficult to compare the real world with the model solution, but the assumptions can be relaxed and so be much more realistic than those which underpin the simple spatial models of Ohlin and Lösch which I have presented in this chapter. It would, for example, be possible to distort the regularity of Lösch's isotropic plain.

The way that time is treated in static equilibrium models may seem to render them particularly irrelevant for planning *development* as, by definition, the exogenous variables, such as production technology, transport costs and tastes, are always changing. The rate of change may be so fast that an economy is always 'lurching from one out-of-equilibrium position to another', to use Joan Robinson's marvellous phrase. But within a comparative statics framework, it is possible to specify spatial equilibrium at various levels of development and then, as Lösch (1954) puts it, 'the state can shorten the costly groping of an uncontrolled economy towards equilibrium by acquiring an idea of how it is likely to turn out, and then encouraging an appropriate development' (pp. 333–4). And if necessary, a dynamic equilibrium path can be determined on the basis of given rates of change in the exogenous variables.

The charge that spatial equilibrium models 'lack realism' is thus insufficient for it is possible to build ever more complex models. But more significantly, if the only weakness of the model is that its assumptions are 'unreal', it may be argued that this is not a weakness in the model but rather *a weakness in the real world*. The 'unrealism' of the model can thus be turned into a policy prescription. Policy should be directed towards making sure that the conditions in the model *do* apply in the world, that is, policy should 'lubricate' market forces – ensuring that all economic factors have perfect information; increasing factor mobility and enabling adjustment to change; creating conditions of perfect competition. From this perspective, the 'unreality' of the model disappears for the world is *made* to behave 'perfectly'.

This viewpoint, and spatial equilibrium models in general, can only be successfully challenged at the level of their logical coherence. It is necessary to demonstrate that spatial equilibrium is *not* an optimum, and that it is *logically* impossible to attain it in a space economy even when the market mechanism is 'fully lubricated'. Let us begin by addressing the question: in what sense is spatial equilibrium optimal?

We may approach this question by examining, first, the nature of general equilibrium which is achieved without any consideration of space. It is worth noting at the outset that this is a purely economic optimum which values the goods produced by an economy in terms of the preferences which individuals have and express in the prices they are willing to pay for different goods. Lösch's isotropic plain will be crowded with a network of opium dens if that is what consumers demand, whether or not the consumption of opium is considered socially desirable. Furthermore, no account is taken of the pattern of resource allocation which is ecologically best, or even, to take the argument to an extreme, what is strategically best in a country threatened by war (Lösch, 1954, p. 344).

This said, however, general equilibrium is *Pareto optimal* in the sense that resources are allocated in a way which maximizes the social product as measured by the value of total output, and no individual can improve his or her position without making another individual worse off. The achievement of a *Pareto optimum* may conceivably be considered desirable, but it is important to stress its implications, particularly in terms of distributive justice. The key point is that the *Pareto optimum* is 'optimal' relative to a given distribution of money income, and this distribution can be highly unequal. To use an example from Amartya Sen, if a cake is divided between ten people such that one gets nine-tenths of the cake and the rest share the remaining one-tenth equally among themselves, that distribution is *Pareto optimal*, because any change that makes someone better off is going to make someone else worse off. Indeed, any division of the cake is *Pareto optimal*.

It may be seen, then, that the *Pareto optimum* is an 'optimum' only in a very restricted sense. It maximizes the social product in relation to a given structure of demand, which may be dominated by a small stratum of rich people. And using many criteria of 'fairness', it could be described as an inequitable solution. But when a spatial dimension is added to the analysis even more caveats arise. For there is good reason to believe that *spatial* economic equilibrium is not even *Pareto optimal*.

The first reason for this is the existence of externalities. These exist when an activity generates side-effects which are not reflected in costs and prices. They may be negative, for example, the extra traffic congestion generated by the location of a new industry in a town; or positive, for example, the cost savings which other firms engaged in manufacturing activity in the town may gain because of the proximity of the new industry and the general increase in the level of economic activity. But they invariably exist as a *spatial field* of effects, as is perhaps best illustrated by the atmospheric pollution caused by a factory. The presence of externalities seriously weakens the argument that the invisible hand of the market will lead to an optimum, for the market mechanism cannot allocate resources efficiently when externalities are present. Yet, because their incidence varies between locations, they will invariably be taken into consideration when decisions are made in a space economy.

The spatial configuration of external effects and their impact on location decisions has been analysed most fully at an urban scale (see, for example, Harvey, 1973, chapter 2), and it may be argued that they are of less relevance when questions of the *interregional* allocation of resources are concerned. But whether or not this is true, there is a second reason why spatial equilibrium, if it can be attained, is not likely to be *Pareto optimal*. It is because it is impossible to have perfect competition when there are transport costs between locations. Once consumers have to pay extra transport costs to bypass a particular producer, that producer may 'raise prices without losing all their custom, extract monopoly profit and indulge more easily in various forms of price discrimination' (Massey, 1973, p. 193).*

In the present era when the international and national economy is dominated by large-scale corporations, such spatial monopolies may seem trivial. But they seriously undermine the prescriptive utility of spatial equilibrium. As Mills and Lav (1964) have demonstrated in examining the implications of free entry in Lösch's model, firms produce less than what is *Pareto optimal*, and also that output could be produced and distributed more cheaply if entry was restricted and firms larger. A similar conclusion is reached by Beckmann (1972), who asserts that average consumption may be maximized by *controlling* prices and allowing free entry to reduce profits to zero.

The presence of market distortions implies that, in a spatial context, equilibrium is not even *Pareto optimal*. However, the view may be adopted that even if all the conditions for *Pareto optimum* cannot be achieved, an attempt should be made to establish as many conditions as possible, so that an economy 'improves' in the right direction. Intuitively this is attractive, but it ignores what economists have called 'the theory of the second best'. This states that there is no *a priori* presumption that a movement towards the best position represents a movement to a better position. It has not been applied in the evaluation of spatial distributions, but as it holds for an economy in general, it is safest to assume, until demonstrated otherwise, that the fulfilment of some of the conditions for spatial equilibrium will *not* necessarily make an economy better off than their non-fulfilment.

The conclusion that the spatial equilibrium which is attained through the free play of market forces is not an optimum seriously weakens the case for using it as a norm for evaluating spatial patterns. But the observation that there cannot be perfect competition over space points towards an even more basic difficulty with equilibrium thinking. For it suggests, as Richardson (1969) has observed, that general equilibrium is *inconsistent* with the implications of the space economy.

Perfect competition assumes the independence of individual decisions, but *as soon as a spatial dimension is added to an economy*, it is

* Much of the argument in this section is drawn from this source.

apparent that decisions are interdependent in the same way as they are under conditions of oligopoly. Imagine, for example, two ice-cream vendors on a beach along which people are evenly distributed. Assume that everyone on the beach will buy an ice-cream, but will always buy from the nearest vendor, and that vendors try to maximize sales revenue. Suppose, as in Figure 10, that the two vendors start the day by locating themselves at the quarter-points of the beach, a position which in fact would minimize the total distance walked by all the ice-cream consumers on the beach. But this position is not stable, for in trying to maximize sales revenue, vendor *A* will try to poach more of *B*'s market, *B* will retaliate by shifting location, and the only stable equilibrium will be when both vendors position themselves at the centre of the beach. It can be demonstrated that at the equilibrium solution the average distance walked by consumers is doubled, which is an important conclusion in itself. But imagine what happens if there are *three* ice-cream vendors. Their locational interdependence in terms of market share means that there is in fact *no stable solution*.

This example may seem frivolous, but it is of major importance for it applies equally to more complex problems. Over twenty years ago, Koopmans and Beckmann (1957) attempted to determine an efficient assignment of indivisible resources between a set of locations and found that it was impossible for a decentralized price system to lead to a stable

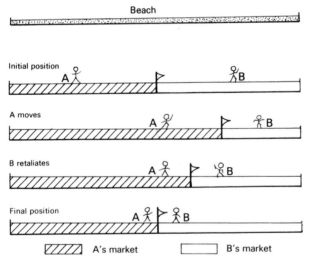

Figure 10 The location of ice-cream vendors on a beach.

Source: adapted from Alonso, 1964; original example, Hotelling, 1929.

spatial pattern of economic activity. There was always an incentive for an entrepreneur to seek another location than the one in which his or her establishment was already located. Koopmans and Beckmann delayed publishing their article for a few years because they found its results 'perplexing' and 'negative'. But in what sense is this so? It is precisely because their results imply that the aggregate of locationally interdependent individual decisions *cannot* be guaranteed to produce an equilibrium. The market thus cannot even attain the state which is supposed to be optimal.

The existence of locational interdependence is not only apparent in the way that markets are shared, but also in the ability of firms to achieve *agglomeration economies*. These are a type of externality and may be defined as 'the cost savings to a firm accruing because of the scale of industry in a particular conurbation or region, and the resultant ability of the firm to share external expenses with others' (Keeble, 1976, p. 59). Agglomeration economies are an important influence on locational decisions, and they can in no sense be regarded as 'imperfections'. But once they are allowed in the space economy, the whole notion of equilibrium becomes untenable. For the achievement of equilibrium is posited on the assumption that economic changes are created by changes in the *exogenous* variables. The presence of agglomeration economies, and indeed any increasing returns to scale, means that the forces for change are *endogenous*. If this is so, then 'the actual state of the economy during any one "period" cannot be predicted except as a result of the sequence of events in the previous periods which led up to it' (Kaldor, 1972, p. 1244). The economy is not equilibrating, but characterized by progressive and cumulative change.

This is precisely what Myrdal was arguing. But the implication of his argument that the market mechanism will fail to achieve an equilibrium solution is *not* that this is due to 'imperfections' in the real world; but rather that it is *logically impossible* to attain an equilibrium solution which maximizes welfare. Spatial equilibrium is therefore not just 'a false analogy' for the analysis of spatial patterns, but also an inadequate guide for regional policy. In these terms, regional imbalance is *not* a policy problem. There is no state of balance. And if there were, it would not be an optimum.

2

Growth, income distribution and spatial inequality

The argument thus far suggests that it is fallacious to use spatial equilibrium as a norm to identify 'imperfections' and as a basis for policy prescription. But the abandonment of equilibrium thinking does not imply that 'imperfections' cannot be identified at all, for it is possible to evaluate spatial patterns as problems using other norms. And in fact, the technical case for regional policy, when it is *explicitly* stated, usually does not talk in terms of spatial disequilibrium, but rather the efficiency and equity of spatial distributions.

This chapter examines the main arguments which have been made to show that regional disparities in development, the size of national metropoli and rural-urban disparities are either inefficient, or inequitable, or both. 'Efficiency' and 'equity' may be specified in various ways. But the desirability of achieving both rapid growth and a fair income distribution is a dominant theme in all development planning rhetoric, and the feasibility and ways of achieving it have preoccupied theorists and policy consultants in the development field throughout the 1970s (see Chenery *et al.*, 1974). And so here an *efficient* spatial pattern will be taken to be one that maximizes the national growth rate, and an *equitable* spatial pattern as one that promotes a fair distribution of income.

THE TRADE-OFF BETWEEN AGGREGATE EFFICIENCY AND INTERREGIONAL EQUITY

The most common justification for policies to reduce regional disparities in 'development' is that such disparities are inequitable. Just as it is said that all people should have an equal share in the benefits of 'development' whether they are rich or poor, so it is argued that all people should have an equal share regardless of *where* they live. A spatial pattern in which 'development' is concentrated in a few places can thus be diagnosed as a problem in that it is unfair, and policies should be introduced to ensure more 'even development'.

In the theoretical literature, this common-sense view is refined by adding that policies which reduce the spatial concentration of investment will lead to a less efficient location pattern for economic activities. Interregional equity can thus only be achieved at the expense of the national growth rate. If this is so, there is a conflict between maximizing growth in the poorer regions and maximizing growth in the 'nation' as a whole, and the formulation of a policy to reduce regional disparities in development can be seen as a question of deciding the trade-off between aggregate efficiency and interregional equity.

The case that such a trade-off exists is most forcefully put by theorists who have applied industrial location theory to developing countries (see, especially, Alonso, 1968). It is said that manufacturing investments, particularly in the 'early stages of development', must be concentrated in a few localities in order to maximize their efficiency. This is in order to take advantage of agglomeration economies and reduce risks of dislocation of supplies. In addition, according to Alonso (1975), most industries in 'newly industrializing countries' are infant industries and the primate city provides 'the most hospitable seedbed' (p. 82). Thus *in the short run*, the pursuit of interregional equity through policies designed to disperse industry is likely to reduce the growth rate.

In the long run, so the argument goes, some major structural transformation in the space economy *may* be necessary to sustain growth. The continuing concentration of manufacturing investment in a few localities can restrict effective demand within a country and leave some natural resources unexploited. If this is true, the maximization of the national growth rate *in the long run* may be in conformity with the adoption of *immediate* measures to improve interregional equity. But judging the exact timing of such measures is a difficult task. For, although at first the concentration of manufacturing activities will increase regional economic disparities, benefits can begin to 'trickledown' to poorer regions 'naturally' with the growth of the economy. Thus it is possible that *in the long run*, the immediate and wholesale pursuit of aggregate efficiency will lead to the achievement of greater interregional equity sooner.

How sound is this argument? Whether spatially concentrated growth will have 'natural' trickledown effects on surrounding areas is a major subject of debate within regional development theory, as we shall see in Part Two of the book. But I do not wish to go into this argument here, nor to attempt to assess the long-term efficiency and equity implications of spatial patterns. For although the inclusion of a time dimension is necessary in any adequate analysis of the trade-off between aggregate efficiency and interregional equity, there are deep *logical* problems in the way that the trade-off is presented, which apply to both short-run *and* long-run analyses. And the existence of these logical problems implies that policies to reduce regional economic disparities are *not* necessarily bought at the expense of aggregate efficiency, and that the pursuit of interregional equity is *not* necessarily a desirable goal.

The first logical problem is that judgements about the efficiency implications of spatial patterns are based on underlying assumptions about how growth occurs. These assumptions are implicit, but the *a priori* expectation that there is a trade-off between aggregate efficiency and interregional equity depends upon them. In the argument summarized above, it is broadly assumed that growth will be maximized through rapid industrialization. This may be correct, but there are many who would contest it. And even if it is correct, there are various industrialization strategies and the most efficient location pattern for industry, and hence optimal degree of industrial concentration, will vary between them. The conclusion that 'the efficiency goal is best served by a policy that permits concentration, at least in the short run' (Alonso, 1968, p. 629) is thus conditional on the most efficient growth strategy.

This point may be amplified by introducing some ideas of Albert Hirschman (1958). In his book *The Strategy of Economic Development* he argues that the governments of developing countries should deliberately foster sectoral bottlenecks with a big investment push in a few leading industrial sectors. The details of his argument will be considered more fully in the next chapter. But what is signficant here is that once such a strategy is advocated, then a particular spatial pattern of investment becomes most desirable. And it is on this basis that Hirschman confidently asserts:

> There can be little doubt that an economy, to lift itself to higher income levels, *must* and will first develop within itself one or several regional centres of economic strength . . . interregional inequality of growth is an inevitable concomitant and *condition* of growth itself.
>
> (p. 183, emphasis added)

If it were argued that the growth rate would be maximized through investment in agriculture and small light industry, then it would be impossible to come to as forceful a conclusion as Hirschman's. Though again, there may be particular types of agricultural development strategy which would be better achieved by intensive concentration of resources in a few areas.

The *a priori* expectation that there is a trade-off between aggregate efficiency and interregional equity must therefore be tested in individual cases. But even if it can be shown that the national growth rate is, or is not, adversely affected by measures which increase interregional equity, this does not mean that such form of equity is a desirable goal.

To demonstrate why, it is necessary, first, to specify precisely what 'interregional equity' is. This issue has not received the close attention of regional theorists. Reiner (1964) provides an interesting discussion of the different ways in which a national planning body may operationally define equity in regional investment decisions. And Harvey (1973, chapter 3), before his intellectual switch to Marxian analysis, established an elaborate set of principles by which 'territorial social justice' may be 'justly arrived at'. But in general, regional theorists have equated interregional *equity* with interregional *income equality*. As Richardson (1979, p. 162) notes, 'Most analyses use average *per capita* incomes within a prescribed geographical area as the basic indicator, then typically use measures of dispersion among regions or ratios to present the state of interregional equity.'

Let us accept this definition of equity and leave aside the simplifications which it entails. For even if we elaborate a more complex definition, we will still face the same problem in measuring 'interregional equity'. And that problem inevitably arises because there are no standard spatial units which may be defined as the *right* regions for measuring the differences which indicate inequity. This means that whether or not greater 'interregional equity' is being attained in a country *depends on the regional boundaries which are selected.*

Suppose, for example, a policy to promote industrial dispersion is adopted in a country in order to achieve greater 'interregional equity'. A growth centre strategy which guides industrial investment to a few localities is pursued and it has the effects on average regional *per capita* income as illustrated in Figure 11. Has the policy been successful? A statistical measure of the dispersion of incomes among the regions would show exactly opposite results from one set of regions to the other. But which set of regions is correct? There may be a *political* justification for adopting a particular set of regions, if the aim is to placate regionalist movements expressing grievances about their neglect by showing evidence that 'their' region is doing better. But the only *technical* justification why one set of regions may be preferred to another is that an improvement of interregional equity measured *for those regions* represents an improvement in social equity.

And this points to the most fundamental weakness in the view that regional economic disparities should be reduced for the sake of equity, and that greater interregional equity is a desirable goal. For it only makes sense in technical terms if there is a relationship between *spatial* (in this case, interregional) equity and *social* equity. Such a relationship doubtless exists. But to assume that a reduction in interregional inequality is equivalent to a reduction in interpersonal inequality is to commit what

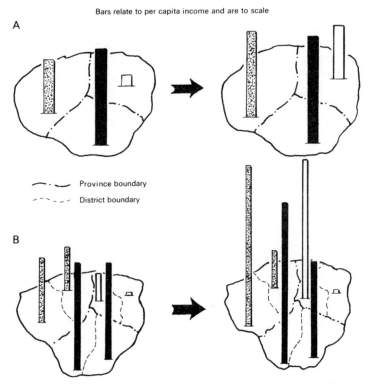

Figure 11 'Regional' *per capita* incomes in a hypothetical country. A. The pattern of inequality with provinces as regional units. B. The pattern of inequality with districts as regional units.

logicians call an ecological fallacy – that is, to infer that the average conditions in an area apply to all individuals in that area. In fact, available evidence shows that policies to promote rapid growth in poorer regions may result in a more unequal income distribution within those regions (Barkin, 1972; Gilbert and Goodman, 1976). And the effects of such policies on the income distribution of the whole country are unknown.

The pursuit of interregional equity as a policy goal has been characterized as substituting 'place prosperity' for the more fundamental goal of 'people prosperity' (Winnick, 1966). The reduction in disparities in average regional *per capita* incomes will certainly affect total income distribution. But as Hoover (1975) has noted, 'Attacking human hardship and lack of opportunity through place prosperity might be like using a shotgun to kill flies' (p. 260). In the absence of analyses of the relationship between spatial equity and social equity, the pursuit of interregional equity becomes a meaningless goal. Regional disparities in development may well be a dimension of inequity within society. But the reduction in regional economic disparities is not necessarily a way of achieving greater equity.

Thus in formulating a case for the reduction of such disparities in terms of a trade-off between aggregate efficiency and interregional equity, both the hypothesized adverse effects on national growth performance and the expected social gains in terms of equity may be largely illusory.

THE LARGE CITY PROBLEM

The idea that the big metropoli of developing countries are *too* big is as prevalent as the view that reductions in regional economic disparities will promote equity. Rapid urbanization is associated with a familiar catalogue of social and economic 'problems' – the spectacular growth of shanty-towns; inadequate water supply and sewerage infrastructure; high rates of unemployment and the proliferation of casual workers eking out a marginal existence in petty production and trading; crime; traffic congestion. These 'problems' are most visible in the largest cities, and it seems intuitively obvious that they have been exacerbated by the concentration of urban growth in the largest cities and that they may be ameliorated by deliberate policies to channel rural–urban migration into medium sized cities and small towns. But the theorists who have examined the efficiency and equity of city size are divided on the issue.

It is worth noting at the outset that much of the debate has centred around the concept of an *optimum city size*, which is defined by comparing the costs and benefits of individual cities of different sizes. From a broader perspective, some writers have discussed the notion of an *optimum city size hierarchy*, in which case the size of large metropoli is not being evaluated in absolute terms, but rather relative to the size of other cities in the country. A more sophisticated view could examine not just the size of cities, but also their growth rate (Townroe, 1979). But whether such an elaboration of theory would yield more meaningful results is doubtful. For, as I shall argue, any attempt to relate city size to economic growth and income distribution is likely to contain logical flaws, whether it is static or dynamic.

The optimum city size debate

The idea that there is an optimum city size and that market forces are likely to create cities which are bigger than the optimum is most forcefully argued with hypothetical diagrams which assume that a city can be treated as an aggregate productive unit just like a firm, and that it is therefore possible to determine average cost and average product curves for cities of different sizes (see Alonso, 1971). It is assumed, usually by reference to the operating costs of municipal facilities such as police services, water supply and economic infrastructure, that average costs *per capita* rise with city size, but that at the same time productivity increases with city size, and so average product *per capita* (and therefore gross income *per capita*), also rises (Figure 12). Given that the shape of the curves is the same as those illustrated, there is a unique point, *P*, where net *per capita* income of the urban inhabitants is maximized. This is usually taken as the optimum city size.

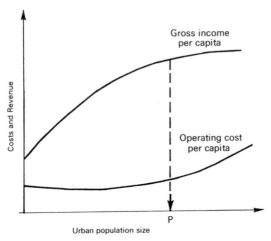

Figure 12 The optimum size of an urban agglomeration.

Source: McCrone, 1969.

Cities are expected to grow beyond this point because it is assumed that there is a divergence between the *private costs*, borne by entrepreneurs, and *social costs*, borne by the urban community. Such divergence arises through externalities. In Figure 12, for example, if infrastructural costs are borne by the municipal authority and the costs of traffic congestion, increased atmospheric pollution and increased crime borne by all house-holds in the community, while entrepreneurs reap the agglomeration economies which lead to higher productivity, it may be expected that the city will become 'too big'.

It is important to note that this expectation rests upon assumptions about the way cities grow, in particular, that as productivity rises, incomes will rise and that as long as incomes are rising, the urban population will grow. But further, the very existence of the optimum depends upon the shape of the curves. If the average cost curve is flat and there is no downturn in the average product, then there is no optimum. Net income *per capita* just rises as city size increases. Thus in order to sustain the argument that there is an optimum city size, it is necessary to demonstrate that the curves are shaped roughly as they are in the hypothetical model.

This raises a myriad of empirical difficulties. The first problem is to delimit 'the city'. City size is measured in terms of population and therefore to determine the size of a city requires a working assumption about its areal extent. Municipal boundaries provide the easiest one, and often population statistics can only be obtained for cities defined in that way. But it may be argued that such administration boundaries do not coincide with the real extent of the city as a working economic unit. The phenomenon of urban sprawl has meant that official legal boundaries are often outdated with new suburbs beyond municipal jurisdiction. And it has even been suggested that with the increasing mobility of the population in western Europe and the USA the very concept of a city as a distinct spatially defined settlement no longer holds and it is more meaningful to talk of a 'non-place urban realm' (Webber, 1964).

If cities can be spatially defined, then the next problem is to measure costs and product *per capita*. Most work has focused on the unit operating costs of public services and inter-urban variations in income *per capita*, which are supposedly an indicator of urban productivity. The results of these investigations have shown that income *per capita* is higher in larger cities, even taking account of differences in the cost of living and using statistical methods to eliminate the confounding effects of different occupational structures in different sized cities (Hoch, 1972; Ternent, 1976). Similarly, although there are wide variations in results, some studies have identified a broad band of city sizes where the operating costs of public facilities are minimized (see Button, 1976, Table 6.1).

These results support the diagrammatic representation, but it may be objected that they represent a narrow view of the costs and benefits of city size. What of traffic congestion, crime, air pollution, the 'bright lights', variety of consumer choice? . . . the reader may complete the list as he or she wishes. Once the perspective is widened, it becomes necessary to gather information on a whole series of costs and benefits, some of which are monetary, some non-monetary, and all of which are difficult to measure. Furthermore, to derive an optimum city size it is necessary to aggregate them into a single measure of net benefits. This can be done, but it must be based on the researcher's own assumptions of, say, the relative costliness of air pollution and crime. And if the distributional effects of city size are to be measured, then costs and benefits must be aggregated for different groups according to their goodness or badness.

It is for this reason that Richardson (1973b) has written:

> The dilemma of optimal city size protagonists is that in order to obtain a determinate solution they are forced to take either a restrictive view of the problem which means that the scope of the analysis is inadequate or incomplete or they make their focus more comprehensive in which case their task becomes impossible. (p. 121)

This casts serious doubt on the validity of any hypothetical curves which are postulated. But all attempts to estimate an optimum city size are doomed to failure for a deeper reason. It is that *correlation* between costs and benefits and city size cannot be assumed to mean *causation*. Again, as Richardson notes:

> City size may in at least some cases be an intervening variable that forms a statistical link between one variable and another and may stand as a surrogate for one of them but is not the real independent variable itself. If this were so it could mean that an analysis of the economics of city size is littered with misspecified problems.
> (Richardson, 1973b, p. 8)

Take the growth of shanty-towns, for example. Is this a problem *of* large cities, somehow caused by their largeness, or is it a problem of the organization of the housing market, which happens to be particularly visible *in* large cities? Clearly the size of a city can have effects on the way its housing market operates, but the whole optimum city size debate is predicated on the assumption that the problems *in* large cities are actually problems *of* the largeness of those cities, and so it is possible by limiting the size of cities to avoid the problems. Unfortunately, if the problem is rooted in the broad political and economic processes of society, then such a strategy is likely merely to relocate it. Building up a tier of medium sized centres which can act as alternative destinations for rural–urban migration, for example, may halt the growth of shanty-towns in the large metropoli, but at the same time foster their growth in the new intermediate centres.

The distinction between problems *of* large cities and problems *in* large cities has been recognized in the optimum size debate, but its significance does not seem to have prevented further empirical research and argument. Its implication is that all empirical attempts to estimate an optimum city size through measuring the costs and benefits of cities of different sizes are misconceived.

Urban primacy from a national perspective

One of the fallacies of optimum city size analysis has been to assume that the observed empirical regularity between income *per capita* and city size means that large cities are more productive. Such a conclusion ignores rural–urban relationships, and the possibility that part of the product of large cities is appropriated from elsewhere.

As Wingo (1972) has pointed out, the method of comparing costs and benefits in cities of different sizes adopts a *metropolitan perspective* on the problem, and does not say whether the greater productivity of the largest cities contributes to the aggregate efficiency of city-with-region and even the 'nation' as a whole. The metropolitan perspective is, according to Wingo, 'of interest to city planners and imperialists' (p. 18), a pregnant juxtaposition of categories. In order to undertake a comprehensive evaluation of the large city problem it is necessary to adopt a *national* perspective.

One way of doing this is to present the large city problem as a trade-off between aggregate efficiency and interregional equity, in exactly the same way that the question of regional disparities is discussed (Mera, 1973). The trade-off arises because, on the one hand, large cities supposedly promote agglomeration economies and therefore any policy of urban dispersal is likely to slow down the rate of growth. On the other hand, the growth of medium sized cities in less developed regions is seen as a method of reducing interregional disparities in *per capita* income.

Again, although it is perhaps becoming tedious by now, we must note that this conclusion rests on assumptions about the relationship between urban growth and regional development. Furthermore, as argued in the first section, interregional equity is not necessarily synonymous with social equity. It may be, as Richardson (1972) has argued, that in larger cities 'the burden of social costs falls on those too poor to evade them, while the benefits of urban productivity are not equally shared but accrue to owners of urban land, business corporations and other monopoly groups' (p. 46). But there has not been sufficient work to demonstrate how processes of differentiation vary in different types of cities.

A second, and more common way, of examining the large city problem from a national perspective is to try to assess the effects of different *city size distributions* on growth and income distribution. In doing so, the large city is not evaluated as being 'too large' in itself, but relative to other cities in the country. When such a shift in perspective is made, all the difficulties defining city size remain, but the theorist has the added problem of identifying different kinds of hierarchical distribution of cities. In all countries, there are fewer large cities than small cities, but how may the size distribution of Zambia and Sierra Leone, for example (Table 2) be distinguished, and how may their effects on efficiency and equity be evaluated?

Table 2 Contrasting city size distributions

	Zambia (1969)		Sierra Leone (1963)	
Over 200,000	Lusaka	238,100	—	
100,000–200,000	Kitwe	179,300	Freetown	157,613
	Ndola	150,800		
	Mufulira	101,200		
50,000–100,000	Chingola	92,800		
	Luanshya	90,400	—	
	Kabwe	67,200		
10,000–50,000	Livingstone	43,000	Bo	26,613
	Chililabombwe	39,900	Kenema	13,246
	Kalulushi	24,300	Makeni	12,304
	Chipata	13,300	Lunsar	12,132
	Choma	11,300	Koidu	11,706
	Mongu	10,700		
5,000–10,000	Mazabuka	9,400	Yengema	7,313
	Kasama	8,900	Magburaka	6,371
	Mansa	5,700	Segbwema	6,258
	Mbala	5,200	Bonthe	6,230
	Chambishi	5,000	Jaiama NY	6,064
			Port Loko	5,809
			Yomandu	5,469
			Kailahun	5,419
			Barma	5,280
			Blama	5,073

In the literature, the optimal city size distribution which has been taken as the norm by which to measure whether the largest cities are too large is the *rank-size distribution*. Technically this is given by the formula:

$$P_i = P_1/i^q$$

where P_i is the population of i-th city in the series 1, 2, 3 . . . n in which all cities in a country are arranged in descending order by population, and P_1 is the population of the largest city. The exponent q may be determined empirically, but in some cases it is more or less equal to 1, and then the population of the second city is half the population of the largest, the population of the third city one-third the population of the largest, and so on. When this relationship holds, the city size distribution is said to conform to the *rank-size rule*.

When the hierarchical distribution of cities in a country follows a rank-size distribution (whether it conforms to the rank-size *rule* or not), there is always a regular relationship between the size of a city and its rank, which is constant throughout the hierarchy. If $q = 2$, for example, the second city should be one-quarter the size of the first, the third city one-ninth, the fourth one-sixteenth, and so on. When any such regular geometric progression is plotted on logarithmic paper, it appears as a straight line, and this has been used as one simple test for the existence of such a distribution, and also for the identification of a second type of city size distribution which deviates from the norm – the *primate city size distribution*. (Figure 13). In this distribution, there are less medium sized cities than in the rank-size distribution and if the latter is taken to be a norm then it may be said that there are 'too few' medium sized centres, or the primate (biggest) city is 'too large'.

But why should the rank-size distribution provide a norm? Which rank-size distribution is optimal? Is it best if a city size distribution conforms to the rank-size rule? And if it does, how does such a distribution promote efficiency and equity? It is debatable whether these questions are answerable, particularly since the effects which the hierarchical distribution of cities are supposed to engender must vary with the *spatial* distribution of cities. Yet it is frequently asserted that in developing countries there are too few medium sized towns. Johnson (1970), for example, writes that 'The raising of average incomes in underdeveloped countries will require town-building programmes and until this task of spatial restructuring is understood, resources will continue to be wasted in fruitless efforts to find some quick and easy route to modernization' (p. 177). And Rondinelli and Ruddle (1978) have argued that equitable growth cannot be achieved without 'balanced spatial development' (p. 52). As they put it:

> The problem is that in many countries essential components of the spatial hierarchy, especially at the middle levels, are missing, under-developed or poorly distributed and that the linkages and interactions among settlements are absent or not well-developed. The majority of the population, especially the rural poor, live in scattered villages too small to support basic services and facilities and too isolated to benefit from the growth of large urban places.   (p. 76)

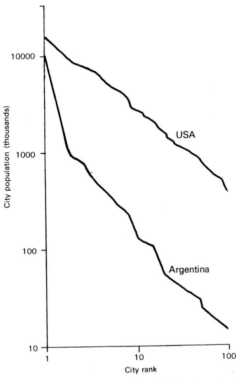

Figure 13 Contrasting city size distributions. A. USA (1960) – approximately rank-size rule. B. Argentina (1960) – primate city size distribution.
Source: adapted from Berry, 1971a, Figures 2 and 18.

The arguments which underlie such assertions are very vaguely presented. Johnson, for example, sometimes reverts to organic analogies: 'Just as a happy conjuncture of the right soil, the right rainfall, the right temperature and the right amount of sunshine can produce grapes that yield a vintage wine, the proper spatial organization of the landscape can provide incentives that will induce people to do their very best to maximize the productive capacity of an economic region' (pp. 74–5). But two clear justifications emerge. First, the reduction of primacy is associated with 'development'; and second, a rank-size distribution is associated with an integrated space economy.

One of the first attempts to examine the changes in a city size distribution in a country over time was made by Zipf (1949) for the USA. He plotted data for ten-year periods between 1790 and 1930 and found that the urban hierarchy conformed more and more closely to a rank-size distribution. In 1940, it was even in line with the rank-size rule, the population of New York, the largest city, having a population of 11,690,000, while Boston, the fifth ranking city, had a population of 2,351,000, which was just 13,000 more than the rule predicts (Isard, 1956a).

This observation prompted the hypothesis that the reduction of primacy was associated with 'development', and during the 1960s and early 1970s various studies examined this relationship through cross-national comparison of city size distribution and the level of development. The pioneering work was done by Berry (1961) who proposed a 'developmental model of city size distributions', from a primate city size distribution which is associated with 'over-urbanization and superimposed colonial economies in underdeveloped countries or with political-administrative controls in indigenous subsistence and peasant societies', to a rank-size distribution 'associated with the existence of integrated systems of cities in economically advanced countries' (pp. 138–9). Unfortunately, his evidence did not support the conclusion that the reduction of primacy was a concomitant of development. Instead he found, by comparison of thirty-eight developing countries, that:

> Countries with rank-size distributions include urban-industrial economies (Belgium, United States), larger countries (Brazil) and countries with long histories of urbanization (India and China). . . . Primacy characterizes small countries with simple subsistence economies (Thailand) or is associated with the presence of an empire capital (Portugal). (p. 149)

The complexity of the pattern, also confirmed by other studies (Linsky, 1965; Vapnarsky, 1969), would perhaps suggest that attempting to correlate primacy and development was futile, but in a notable contribution, El Shakhs (1972) overturned Berry's conclusion.

Significantly, El Shakhs adopted a different method of measuring primacy to that of Berry, and instead of plotting city sizes as frequency distributions, he calculated a statistical index which measured the relative sizes of cities in a hierarchy and which varied neatly between two hypothetical extremes, 0 where all settlements are equal in size, and 1, 'pure primacy', where all the population is concentrated in one settlement.

El Shakhs computed this index for seventy-five countries in the world and relating the degree of primacy to level of development, he found that:

> 1 there is a significant association between the degree of primacy of distributions of cities and their socio-economic level of development, and

2 the form of the primacy curve (or its evolution with development) seems to follow a consistent pattern in which the peak of primacy obtains during the stages of socio-economic transition with countries being less primate in either direction from that peak.   (p. 30)

This conclusion, basically inferred from the evidence in Figure 14, was backed by historical analyses of the pattern of change in the USA and Great Britain.

Ignoring the fact that this conclusion was conditional on the method of measuring the city size distribution, let us consider the logic of inferring from such data that the large cities of developing countries are 'too' large and that a tier of medium sized centres should be established to sustain development. The argument is very similar to the one which has been used to suggest that a country is *over*-urbanized. That concept, which was fashionable in the early 1960s (and is still used by some regional theorists), rests on the notion that for a given level of development of non-agricultural activities (measured by the proportion of the total population of a country working in those sectors of the economy) there is a *normal* level of urbanization (measured by the proportion of the population living in urban centres). If a country had a larger urban population than the norm predicted, then that country was said to be over-urbanized, and attempts should be made to slow down the rate of urban growth.

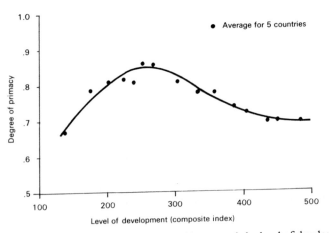

Figure 14 The relationship between primacy and the level of development.

Note: sample of 75 countries, divided into 15 groups of 5, according to level of development.

Source: El-Shakhs, 1972.

The norm by which this was decided was set either by looking at the pattern which prevailed when the now-rich western countries were first industrializing, or by taking a cross-section of countries at various levels of development and drawing a regression line between levels of urbanization and extent of non-agricultural employment. Non-agricultural employment is supposedly an indicator of industrialization, and the logic behind the concept of over-urbanization is that if more people are living in cities than is 'normal' for a certain level of industrial development, then the extra people are unproductive.

The fundamental problem with this argument is how the norm is set. As Sovani (1964) points out, there is no *theoretical* reason why the development experience of the now-rich countries should provide the norm and so one could equally well argue that the countries of Africa, Asia and Latin America today are not over-urbanized, but rather that North America and western Europe in the nineteenth century were *under-urbanized*! The norm rests on a Eurocentric perspective and the assumption that there is a unilineal development path through which all countries pass. This assumption abstracts from history, ignoring the great technological changes which have occurred over the last two hundred years, and ignores the different relative position of different countries in the international economy. As such, and as Sovani cogently argued, the definition of over-urbanization is unsatisfactory.

In some ways, advocates of a rank-size distribution of cities in developing countries have merely transformed the notion of over-urbanization. Instead of relating urbanization and industrialization at various levels of development, they relate the hierarchical pattern of urbanization to development to see if the *largest city* is 'over-grown'. And just as the arguments about 'over-urbanization' are unsatisfactory, the arguments which posit that a particular city size distribution is necessary to sustain development because of the development experience of the now-rich countries, or because a statistical regularity describing the relationship between primacy and 'development' may be discovered, must similarly be rejected. They raise a contentious empirical observation that the presence of a tier of medium sized cities was a *concomitant* of development to a prescriptive judgement that they are a necessary *condition* for development without any theoretical justification.

But the literature is not totally devoid of theoretical analysis, for it is asserted that a rank-size distribution is associated with an integrated space economy. This association has been proven *mathematically* by Berry (1971a). His proof shows that whenever the growth rate of cities is the same for each size class of cities, then over time a rank-size distribution of cities will emerge. Berry then argues that such a city growth pattern will only occur if all the cities are linked in a system and so the rank-size distribution is characteristic of an 'integrated, developed polity' (p. 116).

But such a mathematical proof is inconclusive for it denies the possibility that the rank-size distribution could be the result of other processes (government *fiat*, for example), and does not show how integration promotes development. As I noted in the previous chapter, the term 'integration' is used very loosely within the literature, but in the final analysis, what it means, and why it is deemed to promote growth, or even equitable growth, is that the price system, in a spatial context, is working 'properly'. That is, resources are being allocated where they yield greatest marginal returns. The rank-size distribution is thus associated with a particular type of integration.

The reader may be wondering how the mere manipulation of the settlement pattern to achieve an ideal hierarchical and spatial distribution of cities would engender such changes in economic organization. But this is precisely the argument which E. A. J. Johnson launches in his book *The Organization of Space in Developing Countries* (1970). Johnson, an economic historian, believed that economic development must be founded on agrarian change, and in particular the growth of marketed surplus. This, in turn, required, and was facilitated by, the existence of a particular hierarchical and spatial distribution of cities. As he put it:

> The more contexts in which the phenomenon is studied, the clearer it becomes that development is a function of agrarian commercialization and that the rationalization of agrarian conduct under a pecuniary stimulus calls for a network of conveniently located central places where efficient exchange of goods and services can occur.   (p. 28)

The argument, which is based on assumptions about the way that farmers respond to price incentives, hinges on the organization of rural–urban marketing systems. If a primate city size distribution is found, the marketing activities will tend to be monopolistic, organized by urban traders who depress prices and leave no incentive for increasing production. 'The rationalization of agrarian conduct', as he calls it, requires accessible market centres, and 'until more and better market centres are developed there is no escape from the web of chronic adversity' (p. 173).

This is a brave attempt to postulate a mechanism whereby different city size distributions are related to growth, and it does have some basis in that local- and long-distance trade are often differently organized, and in a country with a primate city size distribution a greater proportion of rural–urban trade will be carried out over long distances (see Smith, 1976). But there have been enough marketing studies in developing countries to show that monopolistic pricing is not merely a function of the physical accessibility of farmers to markets, and such accessibility alone cannot be guaranteed to ensure fair prices. And even if the marketing system is working well, the relations of production may mean that competitive prices do not lead to growth, and certainly not equitable growth.

It is possible to circumvent the problem of explaining how a particular city size distribution has magical effects on economic organization of trade by broadening the perspective, and arguing that the problem is not just the way in which the urban population is distributed, but also the functions which towns of different sizes perform within the economy and also the way that they are interrelated. This, it must be said, is clear in Johnson's work when he shifts from analysis to prescription. And it is the perspective which Rondinelli and Ruddle (1978) adopt in their book *Urbanization and Rural Development: A Spatial Policy for Equitable Growth*, which builds on Johnson's argument.

Rondinelli and Ruddle advocate a 'balanced spatial system', that is, one in which there is a 'proper' hierarchy of centres which are well-articulated among themselves and with their rural hinterlands. The large city problem, then, is not just the absence of medium sized towns, but also the absence of what they call 'linkages'. From their perspective, a well-articulated space economy is said to promote the emergence of a rank-size distribution and such a distribution fosters 'appropriate' linkages. Spatial policy must be directed towards creating not just the ideal urban hierarchy, but also the ideal functional relationships between urban centres, and between centres and their hinterland.

But what is the ideal? And why is it 'proper'? The word 'balance' should alert the reader. For the functional hierarchy which Rondinelli and Ruddle propose is in the mould of the hierarchical order of Lösch's ideal economic region. There are deviations, according to the distribution of different types of industry. But ultimately, if one ignores the simple use of historical analogues relating primacy to development and also unsubstantiated assertions about the beneficial effects of particular settlement patterns and patterns of spatial interaction, the only justification for the proposed pattern is that it approaches the form of the equilibrium economic landscape. Thus, the most elaborate attempts to analyse the large city problem from a national perspective fall back upon the fallacies of equilibrium thinking.

THE THESIS OF URBAN BIAS

The use of spatial equilibrium as a norm to diagnose spatial problems and a guide for public policy to alleviate those problems is also evident in discussions of rural-urban inequality. In some analyses services are said to be 'over-concentrated' in the cities, or there are 'gaps' in the proper array of services which are ideally found in settlements of different sizes. 'Rural-urban balance' may be achieved once the spatial and hierarchical distribution of services conforms to the pattern of maximum packing-in of service distribution points predicted by central place theory, when no areas are left unserved and all service units are economically viable (Wanmali and Khan 1970).

Rather than review such arguments in detail, I shall focus here on Michael Lipton's thesis of urban bias which is elaborated most fully in his book *Why Poor People Stay Poor* (1977). Lipton is not a regional theorist, but his thesis posits the view that resource allocations between rural and urban areas have been biased away from that which is most efficient and equitable towards urban priorities. The validity of this assertion, and Lipton's explanation of how and why urban bias occurs, have been the subject of much criticism (see, for example, Griffin, 1977; van Arkadie, 1978; Currie, 1979; and Byres, 1979, among others), particularly as he raises the thesis to the status of a master hypothesis *explaining* world poverty. The argument in its entirety need not concern us here. But Lipton's discussion of how urban bias may be identified is the most sophisticated attempt to evaluate the efficiency and equity implications of rural–urban disparities, and can be usefully set alongside the debates within regional development theory about the trade-off between aggregate efficiency and interregional equity, and about the large city problem.

Unlike much of the literature within regional development theory, Lipton takes great care to specify what efficiency and equity are. 'Bias' is not simply that more resources go to urban centres rather than rural areas, but that the pattern of allocations *has slowed down the rate of growth* and, at the same time, *increased welfare disparities*. Using a hypothetical diagram (Figure 15), Lipton shows how the most efficient and the most equitable rural–urban resource allocation may be different, and so that there may be a grey area where allocations are rural-biased from an efficiency viewpoint, but urban-biased from an equity viewpoint. But he asserts that in most developing countries resource allocations are unequivocally urban-biased away from both what is most efficient and what is most equitable towards urban centres.

Lipton has a common-sense view of equity which takes a fair distribution to be one in which areas and sectors should receive resource allocations in proportion to their population. For example, inequity is evident in that 'less than 20 per cent of the investment for development

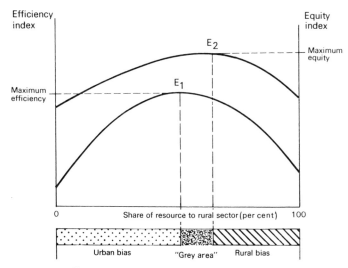

Efficiency index

Equity index

E_2

Maximum equity

Maximum efficiency

E_1

0   Share of resource to rural sector (per cent)   100

Urban bias   "Grey area"   Rural bias

Figure 15 Efficiency, equity and rural-urban resource allocation.

Source: adapted from Lipton, 1977, p. 45.

has gone on the agricultural sector, although over 65 per cent of people living in less developed countries and over 80 per cent of the really poor depend for a living on agriculture' (p. 16). But the overall analysis is much more sophisticated than the discussions reviewed in the earlier part of this chapter in that he asserts that urban bias is not merely a question of resource allocations between urban and rural areas, but also *within* them. Thus, an allocation of fertilizer supplies, totally within rural areas, may be urban-biased if it is directed towards the large-scale farmers who will increase their output for the urban markets rather than towards the small-scale farmers whose consumption level is hovering around minimum subsistence needs. Further, the welfare effects of urban bias are not merely seen to derive from economic disparities between urban and rural *areas*, but also from the fact that the distribution of income between *persons* is more equal within rural areas and so a shift in resources between town and country is not only going to reduce spatial disparities, but also social disparities. Indeed, Lipton goes as far as to argue that rural–urban inequality is causally interrelated with both intra-rural and intra-urban inequality, and so 'an initial assault on rural–urban inequality is likely to be *strategic* in a campaign to shift the benefits of growth to the poor as a whole' (p. 171, emphasis added).

The massive edifice of Lipton's analysis (it runs to some 350 pages) rests like all attempts to relate growth, income distribution and spatial differentiation, upon the more or less arbitrary definition of some spatial unit, which in this case is the definition of a town. Lipton draws the dividing-line between 'urban' and 'rural' by specifying that the former includes all settlements with more than 10–20,000 people, and the latter includes all other areas. There seems to be no logical reason why this size range is chosen. 'Urban' settlements could equally well be taken to be those places with more than 5000 people (which is the census definition in many countries), or places with more than 50,000, which usually have a fuller array of facilities and a more complex occupational structure. Ideally, the 10–20,000 cut-off point would be chosen as it has relevance to the way that the mechanisms of urban bias operate. But Lipton does not make this connection, and indeed, if one accepts the assertions of some regional theorists, that productive investment and provision of social and economic infrastructure in small towns of about 50,000 inhabitants will have spill-over effects in the surrounding areas which raise rural output and incomes, then the dividing-line between 'rural' and 'urban' which Lipton chooses is likely to be highly misleading.

Leaving aside this possibility, the fact that Lipton uses a *spatial* definition of urbanity raises thorny empirical problems when it comes to identifying 'urban bias'. For, as with the notion of an optimum city size, the idea of urban bias rests upon the proof that efficiency and equity vary with different rural–urban resource allocations in a manner similar to that illustrated in the hypothetical diagram (Figure 15). The problem is how can such proof be furnished.

In order to demonstrate the inefficiency of resource allocations in developing countries, Lipton compares the extra output which may be achieved through an extra unit of capital investment in *agriculture* and *non-agriculture*. His results for a variety of countries reveal that urban bias is indeed widespread: 'In less developed countries as a whole, an extra pound's worth of extra capital seems to be associated with about twice as much extra output in the agricultural sector as elsewhere in the economy' (p. 189). This is why it is said that 'the rural sector contains . . . most of the low-cost sources of potential advance' (p. 13).

A similar sectoral approach is adopted to demonstrate the inequity of resource allocations. Lipton notes the results gathered from survey data of income and consumption which show that 'the gap between rural and urban consumption is indeed surprisingly small' (p. 148), but prefers to use data on output per worker in agriculture and non-agriculture to identify the rural–urban welfare gap. The evidence quite starkly shows that output per worker is much higher in the latter (Table 3), and this is

Table 3 Output per person disparities: the ratio of non-agriculture to agriculture (selected countries)

Africa (1970)		Asia (1970)		Caribbean and Latin America (1970)		Industrial West (10–30 years after growth accelerated)	
Zambia	34.9	Thailand	6.7	Chile	4.4	Sweden 1863	2.7
Libya	24.4	Iraq	4.0	Jamaica	4.2	Netherlands 1860	1.7
Tanzania	10.9	Malaysia	3.8	Venezuela	4.0	Germany 1857	1.7
Ivory Coast	9.5	Pakistan	3.2	Paraguay	2.4	Italy 1898	1.6
Sudan	7.8	India	3.1			Great Britain 1801	1.1
Malawi	7.3	Taiwan	3.0			Denmark 1872	1.1
Sierra Leone	6.0	Iran	2.8			France 1830	1.1
Tunisia	5.7	Indonesia	2.4				
Uganda	5.5						
Nigeria	2.0						

The figures show domestic output per person outside agriculture as a multiple of that in agriculture. It is assumed that the ratio of workers to persons is not very different between the two sectors.

Source: Lipton, 1977.

presumed to show the difference between potential purchasing power per head in rural and urban areas, and thus to demonstrate the existence of a 'rural–urban welfare gap'.

As Byres (1979) has noted, Lipton argues by illustration rather than systematic comparison of countries following different development strategies, and so his conclusion that the thesis of urban bias is the key to understanding patterns of *world* poverty is ill-founded. However, more important for the present argument is the possibility that the reallocation of resources to rural areas, although it may maximize growth and reduce welfare disparities in the short run, may not be the best way to achieve these goals in the long run. Lipton unequivocally rejects the idea that the invisible hand of the market will automatically lead to a rural-urban equilibrium in which resources are properly allocated. But he fails to address the argument that investment in capital goods industry, which in the terms of the thesis would be 'urban', can have cumulative multiplier effects which not only increase the level of output but also the rate of increase in the level of output (Byres, 1979). This argument may be contested, and indeed was the crux of the so-called Soviet Industrialization Debate of the 1920s. But whether it is correct or not, the validity of Lipton's method of identifying inefficiency in resource allocation rests on the assumption that it is wrong. The thesis of urban bias, therefore, just like the argument that interregional economic inequalities are a necessary condition for growth, is rooted in a particular view of the best development strategy.

It is perhaps not surprising that Lipton has to resort to sectoral comparison in order to make global judgements. He would be unable to get data otherwise. But in using *sectoral* data to show that resource allocations are biased towards urban *areas*, Lipton further assumes that allocations to non-agriculture and agriculture are coincident with allocations to places with over 10–20,000 people and allocations to other areas. Agriculture may be equated with 'rural', but it is patently fallacious to assume that 'non-agriculture' allocations only occur in urban centres.

Similarly, in discussing the use of output per head data as a measure of inequity, he rightly points out that 'the worker does not get the full product of his labour in either sector, some goes to the owners of capital and land who may or may not be the same people as the workers' (p. 154). The disparity thus measures the *potential* welfare created by outputs inside and outside agriculture. In order to reach the conclusion that rural–urban allocations are inequitable, he argues that output is more equitably distributed in rural areas than urban centres. But the evidence for this is weak, and in order to sustain the argument, he starts to shift the definition of 'urban' and 'rural', suggesting that some of the people living *in* urban centres are in fact 'fringe-villagers', part *of* the rural sector, and some of the people living *in* rural areas are in fact 'crypto-urbanites', part of the urban sector. Thus the argument not only requires that 'non-agriculture' is equated with 'urban' and 'agriculture' with 'rural, but also that the spatial definition of urbanity is modified to include a social dimension.

The way that Lipton presents the evidence suggests that the problem has been misspecified. Ignoring the caveat about long-term effects noted above, it may be concluded from the evidence that there is anti-agricultural bias, or industrial bias. Or it may be suggested that 'on the one side we have urban capitalists, members of the bureaucracy and professions, the urban labour aristocracy and the large landowners, and on the other side we have the small farmers and tenants, landless agricultural workers and members of the so-called [urban] informal sector' (Griffin, 1977, p. 109), and that resource allocations are biased to the former classes. But the phenomenon of urban bias merely reflects the location of industry and particular social groups *in* towns.

The reason why Lipton persists with a spatial rural–urban dichotomy while all the evidence used applies to other economic and social divisions is that his overall thesis is that urban bias arises because of the conflict between 'rural' and 'urban' classes. These groups supposedly have a communality of interest which transcends all other divisions in society. As he puts it, 'The most important class conflict in poor countries of the world today is not between labour and capital. Nor is it between foreign and national interests. It is between the rural and urban classes' (p. 1). The questionable validity of this assertion need not detain us here, for our major concern is the way in which the efficiency and equity of spatial patterns may be assessed. What is important is that the most sophisticated attempt to argue that rural-urban inequality reduces the rate of growth and increases disparities in welfare cannot be sustained with a *purely spatial* definition of the rural and the urban.

THE NATIONALIST RHETORIC OF SPATIAL REORGANIZATION

Before concluding this discussion of the efficiency and equity of spatial patterns, it is worth highlighting one general framework within which all the preceding arguments are sometimes presented. The framework is a nationalist one which asserts that the spatial patterns of economic activity and population in developing countries are the outcome of investments designed to serve the ends of colonial exploitation, and that they are now dysfunctional for 'self-centred' national development.

Colonial spatial structure hinders national growth and the achievement of an equitable income distribution, and spatial reorganization is required to meet national needs (see, for example, Logan, 1972; Mabogunje, 1980; and, from a different perspective, Slater, 1975).

As will become evident in chapter 4, present-day spatial patterns in many developing countries are rooted in their colonial history. Transport networks were designed to facilitate the import and export of produce, and for military control; provincial and district boundaries were demarcated to ensure a cheap and effective colonial administration; and the resources which were initially exploited were those in demand in the colonial metropole. The present patterns of regional economic disparities and of urban settlement were crystallized in the colonial era.

But is it possible to infer that these patterns now hinder the achievement of equitable national growth? The answer must be *not necessarily*. There are some patterns, for example a dendritic transport network, which can be said to have negative effects. Such a network has a tree-shape in which all the branches converge on the major ports, and in the absence of cross-links between the branches, all movement across a country has to go through the ports. In this way, transportation costs are increased. But other patterns are difficult to assess. An urban centre, which first grew as a colonial entrepôt, may now act as an important service centre for the surrounding rural population. That it was located to serve a colonial design does not mean that it is now misplaced. 'Spatial reorganization' implies that new infrastructural investments should be made in areas in which the colonizers were not interested, instead of incremental investments in the locations where there is an existing momentum of capital accumulation. Whether such a strategy will promote greater growth and equity or not has to be analysed, not asserted through rhetoric. A spatial pattern cannot be branded as 'bad' merely because its origins lie in the colonial era, and equally, another pattern cannot be said to be 'good' merely because it represents a reorganization of the earlier, colonial spatial pattern.

CONCLUSION

The only conclusion that is possible from any rigorous analysis of the technical arguments which have been made to show that regional disparities in development, the size of national metropoli, and rural-urban disparities in development are social and economic problems is that the arguments are very weak. Attempts to evaluate the efficiency and equity implications of these spatial patterns exhibit a number of recurrent deficiencies.

The first problem is the definition of the spatial units on which all analyses are based. There is no single definition of 'region', 'urban', 'rural' or 'city'. This does not mean that analysis is impossible. Empirical research can proceed with the adoption of some or other working definition. However, it does mean that generalization is difficult, and there is a nagging suspicion, particularly when analysts are often forced to use data which apply to administratively- or legally-bounded spatial units, that the boundaries which define the region, or the city, or the urban–rural division, are neither socially nor economically meaningful, and that therefore any conclusions are just statistical artefacts.

Even if the spatial units are meaningful (whatever that may be), rather than merely convenient for data collection, the analyses rest upon assumptions about the way in which growth and differentiation occur. It is possible to avoid making these assumptions if the efficiency and equity of a spatial distribution is being evaluated in PURELY spatial terms. For example, the efficiency of the location of an industrial factory may be measured by calculating whether it minimizes the total *transport costs* of assembling raw materials and distributing the finished product to the market. Or the equity of the location of a network of health centres may be measured by calculating whether it ensures that the maximum population is *within a certain distance*, say one-hour travel-time, of any centre. However, as soon as efficiency and equity are defined in broader terms, it is only possible to evaluate the effects of spatial patterns by making assumptions about economic and social processes.

The problem with many of the analyses discussed in this chapter is that they have 'a tangled undergrowth of assumptions', to use Byres's phrase, which is rarely made explicit. In some cases, for example, Hirschman's argument that interregional economic inequality is a necessary condition for growth and Lipton's argument that the dispersal of resources to the rural sector is the best way to maximize growth, the assumptions about the optimal development strategy are in conflict. In general, the implicit assumption is that an economy behaves as it should in the neo-classical economists' perfect world in which prices respond to changing relative scarcities, and entrepreneurs and households to changing prices. To the extent that this assumption is wrong, the evaluations of the spatial patterns are wrong.

By keeping the assumptions implicit, it seems as if spatial distributions have *aggregate* social and economic effects for the country as a whole. It is, for example, possible to argue that: given x, y and z, which are propositions about the economic conditions under which national growth will be maximized, a particular spatial distribution of investments and economic activity will contribute towards or hinder the growth rate.

But if x, y and z are left unstated, it appears as if the spatial structure is a cause of (or hindrance to) national growth. It is true that some of the literature only writes in terms of a particular spatial distribution being a *necessary* condition for growth. But other analyses do not even recognize the distinction between necessary and sufficient conditions, and use loose language which slips from statements that a particular spatial pattern is necessary to achieve certain social effects, i.e. that without it the effects will not be achieved, to statements that such a pattern is sufficient, i.e. that with it the effects will be achieved.

The fact that assumptions are kept implicit is important for the formulation of regional policy for, as Lee (1977) writes, 'if spatial structure is considered cause, it is open to manipulation by planning to achieve desired goals' (p. 24). Whether or not these goals will be achieved through such spatial engineering depends on the validity of the assumptions. *But such efforts are likely to be confounded anyway as the analyses of the efficiency and equity implications of spatial patterns do not properly problematize the relations between society and space.* There is no analysis of the relationships between place prosperity and people prosperity. It is assumed that problems located in large cities are problems of large cities. The division between 'rural' and 'urban' is equated with the division between agriculture and non-agriculture. The way in which rural–urban inequality and intra-rural and intra-urban inequality are interrelated is inadequately examined.

However, the conclusion that one must draw, having identified the weakness of the analyses which evaluate spatial patterns in terms of efficiency and equity, is *not* that spatial patterns do not matter. But rather, that *the questions have been formulated in the wrong way.* They have been formulated in a way which tries to separate a spatial pattern from the social processes which are occurring within a country, and then evaluate its effects. All the problems noted in the previous paragraph would disappear, and the danger of making conclusions on implicit, untested assumptions would be avoided, if the focus of analysis was not spatial patterns, but processes of social and economic change, and questions were asked about *the spatiality of* those processes. Thus, for example, discussions of the inequity of rural–urban inequality should start with analysis of processes of differentiation and stratification in society and examine how rural–urban disparities may be mobilized in the social interactions which are an essential part of those processes. Similarly, discussion of the problems in large cities, for example the growth of shanty-towns, should start with analysis of the social and economic processes which explain this occurrence, and then examine how the 'largeness' of a city may affect the processes. Such a reformulation of the way in which the spatiality of economic and social life is examined rests on a conceptualization of space which interrelates rather than separates spatial patterns and social processes. But more on that later.

For there is a further conclusion which can be drawn from the analysis of the last two chapters. The weakness of the technical arguments which have been made to assess the efficiency and equity of spatial patterns, and the inadequacy of the argument that some patterns constitute a problem because they represent a condition of spatial disequilibrium, highlight the *paradox* of the proliferation of regional planning in developing countries. There may be an administrative rationale for co-ordinating decisions within a region to avoid duplication and to maximize the effects of complementary investments and in this sense there is a case for regional planning. But the technical justification for policies to rectify the three most commonly identified 'problems' is hollow. At the present state-of-the-art, regional disparities in development, the occurrence of very large cities and rural–urban inequality can only be said to be spatial patterns, and *not* social and economic problems. From this perspective, the impulse to adopt some form of regional policy cannot be seen as a *technical* necessity, but rather must be interpreted in *political* terms.

In asserting this, it is important to emphasize the *terms* within which the argument of the last two chapters has been framed. The three crucial spatial patterns have been evaluated from what is commonly called a 'national perspective'. They have been judged in relation to what the governments of countries like to describe as the 'national interest'. The discussion has focused upon the ways in which spatial distributions within a country can affect certain conditions of life *for the populace as a whole*, positing certain norms, such as efficiency, equity and equilibrium, as 'desirable'. In these terms, regional and rural–urban disparities and the size of metropoli do not appear to be problems. But this does not imply that they do not constitute a problem *for SOME social groups within a country*.

People living in a poor region in a country are, of course, likely to see that region's poverty as a problem, and people living in large metropoli are similarly likely to see the size of their city as a problem if rents soar and traffic is increasingly congested. Spatial distributions can thus be a source of local and regional grievances. Such grievances may be technically assessed from a national perspective, for example in terms of the extent to which they promote inequity. But the mere existence of grievances is not a *technical* justification for regional policy to meet them. Rather, such grievances are part of a political process in which resources are allocated between different groups in society. And crudely, the greater the threat which regional and local groups make to the stability of the state, the greater the *political* justification for regional policy.

This crude initial assertion can provide a starting-point for understanding why the governments of so many developing countries are adopting some form of regional policy and why particular policy objectives are selected. But the discussion is beginning to run ahead of itself. The final chapter of the book will put forward an interpretation of the politics of regional policy, and there, this initial assertion will be refined, and the rationale for the three common regional policy objectives reassessed. But before then, we must examine the nature of regional planning strategies which have been proposed as a means of achieving what are supposedly more desirable spatial distributions of population, activity and income within a country. For one cannot make any sense of regional policy objectives unless they are considered in relation to the strategies through which they are pursued. And by examining the structure of the theories which underlie the various regional planning strategies, and by inferring the practical implications which are built into them, we can gain much greater insight into the practical appeal of regional policies. To this task, therefore, we shall now turn.

Part Two

Rival Regional Planning Strategies

3

Urban-industrial growth pole strategies and the diffusion of modernization

State development policies are usually presented as technically rational plans of action which offer the best means to achieve defined objectives. The argument of the first part of this book suggests that common regional policy objectives can only be understood in political terms. But this does not imply that planning interventions designed to achieve political objectives can have no technical rationality. And the planner who is given the task of promoting more 'desirable' spatial distributions of economic activity, population and income – no matter what the justification for that task – can find within regional development theory the scientific bases for a number of courses of action. This second section of the book examines the theoretical underpinnings of some rival regional planning strategies which have been suggested within the literature as ways of achieving regional development objectives.

The term 'strategy' is one which is widely used within the regional development literature, though rarely defined. If one consults the Oxford English Dictionary, the following, somewhat disconcerting, definition is given:

> *Strategy:* generalship, the art of war; management of an army or armies in a campaign, art of so moving or disposing of troops or ships or aircraft as to impose upon the enemy the place and time and conditions for fighting preferred by oneself; instance of, or plan formed according to this.

Regional analysts use the term to refer to a broad qualitative approach which is designed to achieve defined planning objectives. The rival regional planning strategies ignore details of planning implementation and suggest how particular policy instruments may be used in concert to achieve desired goals.

The present chapter focuses upon a type of growth pole strategy, which may be termed the urban-industrial variant. Growth pole (or growth centre) strategies have been very widely applied by planners in developing countries, but, for reasons that will become apparent later in the text, they have assumed a variety of forms. There is not even any precise specification of the nature of an urban-industrial growth pole strategy, though in essence, as a regional policy, it aims to promote regional and rural growth through the establishment and promotion of industrial activity in a few large urban centres. Typically, the industries implanted in the urban centres have been large-scale, heavy or inter-mediate manufacturing operations such as iron and steel, aluminium, petrochemicals and heavy engineering; and the centres selected have been intermediate cities in the urban hierarchy whose populations were planned to reach a level of between one-quarter and one-half a million people within ten or fifteen years (Appalraju and Safier, 1976). The new industrial activities have been either set up directly through public sector investment, or promoted through a range of incentives to private investors or through the provision of basic infrastructure.

The simplest rationale for such a strategy, which channels develop-ment resources and development efforts to a few favoured places, is that it is impossible to develop everywhere at once. Given that resources are scarce, planners promoting development must select priorities, and spatial priorities are just as important as sectoral ones. In a planned industrialization programme, a few localities may offer particular advan-tages because of their under-utilized natural resources, and the selective concentration of development efforts may yield economies in the pro-vision of public infrastructure and create agglomeration economies for private investors. The deliberate acceleration of urban growth in inter-mediate cities may also ease the pressure on public facilities in the national metropoli and reduce the probable onset of agglomeration dis-economies in the biggest cities. An urban-industrial growth pole strategy may then be pursued with the aim of maximizing *national* growth.

But in practice, governments in developing countries have adopted this strategy with the stated aim of achieving *regional* development objec-tives. As part of India's Third Five Year Development Plan, large-scale public sector industries were established in the 'backward regions' of the country with the explicit aim of achieving more 'balanced' regional development (Misra, Sundaram and Rao, 1974). The strategy of the military government which took over in Peru in 1968 included the pro-motion of integrated propulsive industries located away from Lima, the capital city, with a view to utilizing more fully the country's natural resources and also reducing 'the disequilibrium of the distribution of the population over the national territory' (quoted in Hilhorst, 1981). And, as late as the mid 1970s, the Philippines, Indonesia, Malaysia and Thai-land were all pursuing a growth pole policy of industrial decentralization designed to achieve 'a better balance in urban growth among the regions, . . . to utilize the resource potential of peripheral regions where available, and through this expansion of their economic base, contribute to the reduction of regional disparities' (Salih *et al.*, 1978, p. 115). The purpose of this chapter is to set out arguments within regional development theory which appear to support such expectations.

THE ORIGINAL MEANING OF THE GROWTH POLE CONCEPT

We must begin with a curious fact. The growth pole concept, as originally defined, had nothing whatsoever to do with questions of regional development; it was not oriented to the particular economic problems facing the countries of Africa, Asia and Latin America; and it was not devised as a prescription for planning economic change. The concept was first conceived by a French economist, François Perroux, who, in the 1930s and 1940s, played an important role in introducing the ideas of both Keynes and Schumpeter to the French-speaking world, and who, in the 1950s, aspired, like these two great economists, to formulate a new vision of how economies function and grow. His intellectual project was no less than to reorientate our understanding of 'the economy of the twentieth century' (Perroux, 1961a), and the growth pole was a central element in his work. Once it was applied, Perroux believed that 'the history of national economies and the theory of their development must be considered again from scratch' (Perroux, 1955, p. 185).

The theoretical basis of all growth pole strategies stems from the transformation of the growth pole concept which occurred as Perroux's ideas were applied to the more mundane task of analysing and planning regional development. And the precise nature of this transformation may be understood by examining how the concept was originally defined in his overall vision of growth in the economy of the twentieth century.

Perroux's view of how growth occurs is very idiosyncratic and it may best be introduced in counterpoint to the growth models which mainstream economists of neo-Keynesian and neo-classical persuasion began to elaborate after the Second World War. These economists were concerned to construct mathematical models which related the growth of *national* economies to the behaviour of macro-economic *aggregates*, and there was a particular interest in the *equilibrium* path of growth. Neo-Keynesian analysis built upon the insights of Harrod and Domar, who took the *short-run* relationships which Keynes postulated to exist between investment and saving, saving and income, and income and investment, and interrelated them in a way which would predict the *long-run* dynamics of an economy. The basic growth equation in the Harrod-Domar formulation, $G = {}^S\!/_V$, relating the growth rate (G) to the propensity to save (S) and the capital-output ratio (V) was used to specify the conditions of 'steady growth', that is, the conditions under which an equilibrium path of growth with full employment and no inflation would be achieved. In the neo-classical models, assumptions were made within the model such that an equilibrium path of growth, in which both labour and capital are fully utilized, was defined. These models postulate an aggregate production function, which in its most basic form, $Y = f(K,L)$, relates the level of output in any economy to the level of inputs of capital (K), and labour (L), at a given level of technology, and which, through calculus, is converted into a growth equation.

One weakness of such models, from a Perrouxian perspective, was that they treated economies as if they were 'contained in a container', the national territory as defined by political frontiers. 'Recent analyses', he wrote, 'treat the nation as a local complex of factors of production, of which the contents are determined by the relative supplies of these factors contributed by various nations' (Perroux, 1950a, p. 33). There is also an accumulating literature which views the nation as a 'big individual, a collective entity which takes up a certain space' and has 'an aggregate of tastes, disposes of a stock of goods, indulges in productive plans and sometimes possesses bargaining power against other "big individuals"' (p. 33). Such analyses, according to Perroux, are likely to engender illusions, such as the 'naïveties of organicism' evident in discussions of the nation as a 'big individual'. Moreover, by treating economies as 'contained in a container', nationalist doctrines, which Perroux regarded as 'pathological', are reinforced;

> The men and objects contained in a containing national space appear in effect to be threatened if the nation is small, if it is surrounded, if it is not economically well-provided for, if it has not the outline which it believes it has a claim to by virtue of geographic configurations or historical traditions.   (p. 22)

Thus, such analyses, by binding their conclusions to 'a banal space bounded by political frontiers', accept fundamentally 'the very limits that ought to be devaluated' (p. 33). Economic analysis, in Perroux's view, needs to be 'delocalized', detached from *a priori* assumptions about where on the earth's surface the units which make up an economy are contained and about the territorial limits to the relationships which animate economic life.

Perrouxian growth analysis attempts such a task but also aims to put forward an explanation of economic growth which is more 'realistic' than that offered by models which tracked the equilibrium growth of economic aggregates. Perroux wanted to account for what he called the facts of *observable* economic growth, which, he argued, is neither smooth nor regular, as suggested in the equilibrium growth models, and is characterized by structural change – 'the appearance and disappearance of industries . . . the varying proportion of various industries in total output in the course of successive periods . . . the different rates of growth for different industries, during one period and in successive periods . . . the diffusion of the growth of an industry (or group of industries)' (Perroux, 1955, p. 182). Moreover he sought to explain these facts in a way which recognized that 'economic life is something different from a network of exchange' (Perroux, 1950b, p. 56). In the twentieth century, he argued, economies should be studied as 'a network of forces', in which the pursuit and exercise of *power* is as important a determinant of what happens as the pursuit of monetary gain and the allocation of resources through the price system. The network of exchange is, he wrote, 'simply the network of power relationships' (Perroux, 1961b, p. 276).

'Power' is one of the most difficult variables to specify in the social sciences, and Perroux attempted to systematize his conception of economic life with what he called 'the theory of economic domination'. 'Domination effects' were defined as occurring between two economic units, *A* and *B*, 'when, in a definite field, unit *A* exercises on unit *B* an irreversible or partially irreversible influence' (Perroux, 1950b, p. 56). Such 'effects' are recognized in conventional micro-economic theory in discussions of how, in monopolistic and oligopolistic market structures, a single firm may impose prices on consumers or try to eliminate its few competitors through price-cutting strategies. But to Perroux, they were also evident in 'dynamic competition', in situations where an entrepreneur making an innovation, such as introducing a new product, forces other entrepreneurs to change their production plans. And they could also occur between economic sectors, when one sector 'engenders a lowering or raising of costs and prices in another from which it does not receive influence comparable in breadth and intensity', and between nations, when 'one nation imposes on another goods and services or a general pattern of institutions of production and exchange' (Perroux, 1950b, p. 57). 'The domination effect', he wrote, 'far from being a rarity found only after long searching, can be discerned almost anywhere in the relations between individual units and unified groups of production and trade' (p. 72). Incorporating it into economic analysis threatens 'the harmonious and fragile, logical edifice' of equilibrium thinking. Yet it is the key to understanding the economy of the twentieth century.

In order to analyse how 'observable growth' occurs in a world economy characterized by domination effects, Perroux introduced the concepts of the 'propulsive unit' (*l'unité motrice*) and the 'growth pole' (*pôle de croissance*). The propulsive unit is a type of dominant economic unit which, when it grows or innovates, *induces growth* in other economic units. It may be a firm, a set of firms within the same sector (i.e. an industry), or a collection of firms which have some shared agreement (Perroux, 1961b, p. 302). During any given period, an economy which is growing will have some such propulsive units. Over time, a particular dominant unit, for example the textile industry, may lose its propulsive qualities, but if growth is to be sustained, then it will be replaced by others, say the steel or electronics industry.

Perrouxian growth analysis is concerned with identifying the characteristics of propulsive units and their growth inducement mechanisms. The study of these mechanisms requires that the *relationships* which propulsive units have with other economic units are examined, which is why the growth pole concept is so central in Perrouxian analysis. For if an economy in which domination effects occur is characterized as a 'field of forces', then propulsive units *located within this field* may be described as 'poles of growth'. As Perroux states clearly, the growth pole is 'a propulsive unit in a given environment' (Perroux, 1961b, p. 302); it is 'a propulsive unit *coupled with* the surrounding environment' (Perroux, 1968, p. 247).

Perroux identifies various growth inducement mechanisms associated with growth poles. His overall view of the growth process is in many ways similar to Schumpeter's. The latter, for example, suggests that:

> Progress – in industrial as well as any other sector of social and cultural life – not only proceeds by jerks and rushes but also by one-sided rushes productive of consequences other than those which ensue in the case of co-ordinated rushes. In every span of historic time it is easy to locate the ignition of the process and to associate it with certain industries and, within these industries, with certain firms from which the disturbances then spread over the whole system.
>
> (Schumpeter, 1939, p. 76)

But whereas Schumpeter focused on the way in which entrepreneurial behaviour and the act of innovation affected the dynamics of capitalist economies and elaborated a complex system of thought to explain cyclical change and secular growth, Perroux proposed, in his different publications, a range of mechanisms through which a propulsive unit could induce growth in other parts of an economy. It could occur because the expansion of an industry could, in certain circumstances, create what Scitovsky (1954) calls 'pecuniary external economies', that is, increase profits in other industries which supply it with inputs or purchase its outputs; because the setting of a new industry could stimulate imitations and innovations in other sectors, as Schumpeter argued; because the expansion of a sector could, through Leontieff input-output relationships, create multiplier effects in other sectors of an economy; because a dominant firm in an oligopolistic market structure could, through economic warfare, induce innovation and price cutting strategies in other firms; or even, because new investment in an industry could have multiplier and accelerator effects on an economy as analysed by Keynes (Perroux, 1961b).

Perroux's eclectic method of specifying the details of 'the process of polarization', as some French economists have called the process through which a propulsive unit induces growth in other parts of an economy (Hansen, 1967), has been a basic source of confusion within the literature elaborating his ideas. However, his overall view of the growth process, and the role of growth poles in that process, is clear. As he puts it, in a much quoted sentence:

> The fact rough but solid is this: growth does appear everywhere at the same time; it manifests itself in points or 'poles' of growth, with variable intensities; it spreads by different channels with variable terminal effects for the economy as a whole.   (Perroux, 1955, p. 182)

From the Perrouxian standpoint then:

> The national economy in growth no longer appears simply as a politically organized territory in which a population lives, nor as a supply of factors of production the mobility of which stops at the frontiers.
> (Perroux, 1955, p. 185)

Rather, it appears as a combination of propulsive and propelled economic activities. The former induce growth in the latter, but these growth forces may be felt both inside and outside a national territory. The national economy in growth can be seen, therefore, as 'a place of passage for forces' (Perroux, 1950a, p. 34). And the international economy, instead of being analysed as a set of trading nations, can be seen as a system of growth poles.

THE TRANSFORMATION OF THE GROWTH POLE CONCEPT IN REGIONAL THEORY

By the early 1970s, 'reliance on growth pole analysis' was 'a dominant characteristic of operational regional planning in both developed and developing countries' (Richardson and Richardson, 1974, p. 163). The history of how Perroux's vision came to be transformed for the purpose of regional planning would be interesting to recount, but cannot be pursued here. What is important is how the meaning of the growth pole concept changed as it was applied within regional theory, and the implications of that change for the theoretical basis of 'growth pole' policies.

In his paper 'Nôte sur la notion de pôle de croissance', published in 1955, Perroux discusses the characteristics of a set of related industries which can enhance the growth effects of a propulsive unit within that set. These characteristics include an oligopolistic market structure and *spatial agglomeration*. If that paper is read out of the context of Perroux's other work, it is easy to get the impression that a growth pole is a spatial agglomeration of related industries. And that is one basic way in which regional theorists began understanding the concept.

But from this basis, there have been further reinterpretations which may be illustrated by the following sequence of definitions taken from the many within the literature. A growth pole is:

1 a spatial agglomeration of related industries;
   e.g. McCrone (1969) 'A pole of growth consists of a sort of industrial complex of related industries which derive considerable economic advantage from locational proximity' (p. 72).

2 a spatial agglomeration of related industries which contains a growing propulsive industry;
   e.g. Lasuen (1974) 'A growth pole is a large group of industries strongly related through their input-output linkages around a leading industry and clustered geographically. The leading industry itself, and (through its inducement) the whole group, innovate and grow at a faster pace than industries external to the pole' (p. 26).

3 a spatial agglomeration of related industries, located in an urban centre, which, through *their* expansion, induce growth in *its* surrounding hinterland;
   e.g. Boudeville (1966) 'A regional growth pole is a set of expanding industries located in an urban area and inducing further development of economic activity throughout its zone of influence' (p. 11).

4 a growing urban centre inducing growth in its surrounding hinterland;
   e.g. Nichols (1969) 'A growth pole is an urban centre of economic activity which can achieve self-sustaining growth to the point that growth is diffused outward into the pole region and eventually into the less developed regions of the nation' (p. 193).

5 a growing urban centre;
e.g. Parr (1973) 'It will be assumed for the purposes of this paper that a growth pole represents an urban centre above some arbitrarily defined threshold size which over a given time displays one of the following growth characteristics: (a) growth of population (employment) at a rate greater than that for the regional benchmark economy; (b) an absolute growth of population (employment) which is greater by some given percentage of the total growth of the region' (p. 175).

In this sequence what began as a growing *economic* unit, a firm or industry, has become a growing *spatial* unit, a city. And the analysis of the way in which a propulsive industry may induce growth in other parts of an economy has become an analysis of how the growth of a *place* may induce growth in other *places*.

One consequence of the transformation of the growth pole concept within regional studies is that what is described as 'growth pole theory' is characterized by considerable definitional confusion. As Darwent (1969) points out, 'the semantic confusion of attributing to a location the growth characteristics of the pole (industry) that happen to be located there has been made repeatedly' (p. 541). In order to bring some order to the field, he suggested that purely spatial growth poles, such as those defined by Nichols and Parr, should be referred to as *growth centres*, and this convention has been adopted by many regional theorists since. But the terminological anarchy has continued with the proliferation of many subspecies of spatial growth pole – the growth point, growth foci, growth nuclei, growth area, core region –and with the adoption of a range of more or less arbitrary technical criteria to identify such growth centres in the real world (Figure 16).

This confusion is reproduced in planning practice where regional planners have used the growth pole concept to describe a variety of policy interventions which 'range from the relevant to the wildly inappropriate' (Richardson, 1978, p. 174). As Richardson illustrates, 'the designation of industrial estates has been described as growth-pole selection, as has the choice of small rural villages to serve as service centres for rural regions, to take one end of the size spectrum, or the promotion of million-plus metropolises as counter-magnets to the primate city to consider the other' (p. 174).

The semantic confusion makes it difficult to say precisely what a 'growth pole strategy' *really* is. But the muddle is merely symptomatic of a deeper problem. For in its metamorphosis within regional studies, the growth pole was divorced from its analytical basis in Perrouxian growth

Growth centres	Method of identification

1 Central place function

Size of circle indicates number of functions .

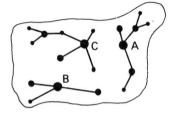

2 Nodal location

Lines indicate predominant flows.

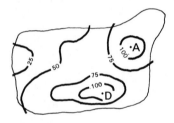

3 Location on the development surface

Isolines show the level of development in different locations.

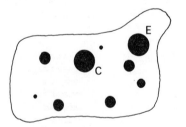

4 Population growth rate

Size of circle indicates population growth rate.

Figure 16 Some ways of identifying 'growth centres' in a hypothetical region.

Note: Towns A, B, C, D or E are 'growth centres'.

Source: adapted from Moseley, 1974, Figure 1.3.

Table 4 Facets of growth pole theory, according to Hermansen

Space \ Approach	STATIC and/or comparative static		
	Descriptive	Positive/explanatory	Planning/control
Industrial*	Inter-industry relations. Input-output tables.	Forward and backward linkage effects. Multiplier effects. Pecuniary external economies. Domination effects	Input-output models. Interrelated industrial complexes
Geographical	Urban hierarchy versus rank-size relations	Central place theory. General theories of spatial organization. Traditional theories of industrial location	Optimum city size and optimum spatial organization. Network theory. Service centre policy. New towns
Interplay between industrial and geographical space	Urban industrial patterns. Resource frontiers. Centre-periphery relations	Inertia due to inter-temporal relation and locational complementarities. Localized development poles based on industrial complexes	Optimum location of industrial complexes within the urban systems. Urban system planning

Space \ Approach	DYNAMIC		
	Descriptive	Positive/explanatory	Planning/control
Industrial*	Trends in industrial changes. Emergence of innovation sets in techniques and products	Sector theory. Leading industries. Propulsive and strategic industries. Functional development poles. Diffusion of innovations among industries	Dynamic industrial complex planning. Extension and diffusion policies. Establishment of propulsive or strategic industries
Geographical	Trends of urbanization. Identification of spatial growth centres. Mapping of polarized (nodal) regional systems	Role of the city. Hypothesis of urban growth patterns. Regional external economies. Localized development poles. Urbanization economies. Spatial diffusion of innovation	Planning of urban systems based on location of propulsive industries and localized poles of growth. Extension and diffusion service

continued

Table 4—continued

| Space \ Approach | DYNAMIC | | |
	Descriptive	Positive/explanatory	Planning/control
Interplay between industrial and geographical space	The urban realm and the shift to services. Development stages	Diffusion of innovations in industrial space conditioned by locational interrelations. Accumulation of advantages. The role of the city. Development stage theory	Comprehensive urban regional development planning based on central place, development poles and diffusion theory

* Delocalized economic analysis as Perroux originally envisaged.

Source: Hermansen, 1972.

theory. Once the growth pole is defined in purely spatial terms, it is possible to bring *any* body of theory, whether neo-classical, Schumpeterian, dualist, dependista, sociological or political, to bear on the understanding of the *spatial* relationships between growing centres and their linked hinterlands. And thus 'growth pole theory' has become an eclectic synthesis of ideas which relate to the behaviour of different types of 'growth pole' but which have no necessary coherence in terms of their underlying assumptions about how growth or development occurs (see Table 4). And as a consequence, the theoretical basis of *all* growth pole strategies, including what I have described as the urban-industrial variant, is ill-specified.

TWO FALSE STARTS

The 'pure' strategy of polarized development

The rationale for the urban-industrial growth pole strategy which is most directly derived from Perrouxian growth analysis is that presented by Boudeville (1966). As noted in the list of definitions above, Boudeville defines a regional growth pole as 'a set of expanding industries located in an urban area and inducing further development of economic activity throughout its zone of influence' (p. 11). Attempting to adapt Perroux's work for application in French regional planning he presents an 'operational planning model' which shows how growth may be promoted in 'polarized regions'. Such regions may be identified on the ground by examining patterns of spatial interaction between towns of different sizes (for example, traffic flows) and are defined in the abstract as 'the set of neighbouring towns exchanging more with the regional metropolis than with other cities of the same order in the nation' (p. 10). Growth may be promoted in such regions by policies which 'plan with the greatest possible efficiency the development of growth poles through the mechanism of their propulsive industries' (p. 112).

Propulsive industries are said to be able to induce two types of growth effect on the regional economy: first, 'Leontieff multiplier effects', which occur through the existing pattern of intersectoral relationships within the economy; and second, 'polarization effects' which occur when the establishment or increase in production of a propulsive industry induces 'the creation of other activities not yet localized in the region' (p. 114).* Referring to the arguments of Hirschman in his book *The Strategy of Economic Development* (1958), Boudeville suggests that the newly induced activities can be 'upstream' suppliers of inputs to the propulsive industry or 'downstream' users of its output. The setting-up of a cement factory, for example, may result in the establishment of a plant manufacturing bags for packing purposes and the establishment of a cement-block industry. And these backward and forward linkage effects, to use Hirschman's terminology, are likely to be supplemented by the general improvement in regional labour supply and social overhead capital which follows the industrial expansion and makes the region more attractive for investment.

Boudeville's analysis is the blueprint for what Coraggio (1974) has called 'the pure strategy of polarized development'. Once it is adopted, 'the problem of achieving the development of a region . . . can be subdivided into two parts: (a) how to ensure the localization of a propulsive activity in the region, and (b) how to prevent it from becoming an enclave' (Coraggio, 1974, p. 291). The latter situation occurs when the growth which a propulsive industry induces is not contained within the region, and will arise whenever multiplier effects of the growth of a regional industry are felt outside the region and the new activities induced by its growth do not locate within the region.

It all seems very logical. But unfortunately, Boudeville's analysis, which he describes as 'an operational planning model', is nothing more than a logical argument whose conclusions are derived from the definitions on

---

* The reader may note that this definition of polarization is not exactly the same as the one given earlier. As we shall see in the next section, Hirschman uses the term 'polarization effects' in yet another sense, and later in the text, still further meanings of this concept will become apparent.

which it is based. The possibility that new industry can have negative effects on the regional economy, for example, through the competition between factory and handicraft production, is excluded from consideration. A propulsive industry cannot have such an impact *by definition*, for if it did, it could not be described as 'propulsive'. The probability that the growth effects of the propulsive industry may 'leak out' of the regional economy, thus leaving the propulsive industry as an enclave, is similarly reduced *by definition*. If the polarized region is defined by 'the location of the network of maximum economic interconnections' (Boudeville, 1966, p. 38), then most of the growth effects of the propulsive industry will be contained within the region as long as the boundaries of the region have been drawn correctly. And finally, if the propulsive industry is located within the regional metropolis, growth effects will be felt in the surrounding hinterland, for a regional growth pole is *by definition* 'a set of expanding industries located in an urban area and *inducing further development throughout its zone of influence*'.

Boudeville's analysis does show how regional growth *can* occur. But all it suggests is that the regional economy will grow *if* the industries implanted in its nodal urban centre are propulsive and *if* the growth which they induce is contained within the regional hinterland. The factors determining these conditions cannot be derived from the analysis, for it is structured in a way which abstracts the behaviour of the regional economy from its national (and international) setting. There is thus every likelihood that a planner following this blueprint will merely create 'an industrial monument raised to the glory of future regional industrialization' to use Paelinck's graphic description (quoted in Hansen, 1967, p. 724).

Albert Hirschman: the interregional transmission of growth

The basic problem with Boudeville's analysis is that it contains no adequate *explanation* of how regional and rural growth *does* occur. This feature also characterizes some ideas of Hirschman on the interregional transmission of growth, which were not in themselves designed as an explanatory theory, but which, if taken out of context, can be seen as such and used to provide another misconceived justification for an urban-industrial growth pole strategy.

In his book *The Strategy of Economic Development*, as I noted in the last chapter, Hirschman advocates an 'unbalanced growth strategy' as the best way of planning development. The case for this strategy in fact rests on a sketch of the development process which is very similar to Perroux's analysis. Like Perroux, he maintains that development occurs through 'growth being communicated from the leading sectors of the economy to the followers, from one industry to another, from one firm to another' (p. 63). And like Perroux, he argues that 'the predictive and operational value' of neo-Keynesian steady growth models is 'low in developing countries', and that the process of development is better conceived as 'a chain of disequilibria', in which investment in particular industries raises profits and induces investment in other industries, which in turn promotes further rounds of investment and increased profits in other parts of the economy (pp. 65–6).

At the time he wrote, Hirschman believed that the key economic problems facing developing countries did not arise because of *scarcity* of resources, but rather from the fact that factors of production and abilities were 'hidden, scattered and badly utilized' (p. 5). Because of this, the best development strategy is one which sets up 'pressures' – 'tensions' which elicit and mobilize the largest amounts of resources, in effect *inducing* development decisions. The 'complementarity effect of investment', he argued, is 'the essential mechanism by which new energies are channelled toward the development process and through which the vicious circle that seems to confine it can be broken'. And 'a primary objective of development policy' must be 'to give maximum play to this effect' (p. 43).

Most of his book is concerned with how this may be done in macroeconomic planning, and in his discussion he argues that priority should be given to intermediate and basic industries, for they will induce the greatest backward and forward linkage effects (the idea picked up by Boudeville and, in a curious transfer of theory, applied to France); and that such industry should be located in large cities rather than small towns, because in that way pressure will be put on water, power, housing and other infrastructural facilities, and thus additional public capital formation compelled. But he completes his survey of the inducement mechanisms which a planner can utilize by considering how growth *can be* communicated from one region to another. And it is this account, which taken out of context, can suggest a false basis for the expectation that an urban-industrial growth pole strategy can achieve *regional* and *rural* growth objectives.

The account begins with the axiom 'that economic progress does not appear everywhere at the same time and that once it has appeared powerful forces make for the spatial concentration of economic growth around the initial starting-point' (p. 183). The momentum of growth in the 'regional centres of economic strength', which are termed 'growing points' or 'growth poles' (p. 183), is said to be fuelled by the ability of entrepreneurs to take advantage of agglomeration economies and the

dynamic growth atmosphere which develops within the 'poles'. However, in line with his general argument, Hirschman argues that the
cumulative concentration of growth does not proceed indefinitely, for
'once growth takes a firm hold in one part of the national territory, it
obviously sets in motion forces that act on the remaining parts' (p. 187).

To simplify analysis of these forces, Hirschman designates the region
which is experiencing growth as the 'North' and the lagging region as
the 'South' and argues that 'the growth of the North will have a number
of direct economic repercussions on the South, some favourable, others
adverse' (p. 187). The favourable effects are labelled 'trickling down
effects', while the unfavourable ones are labelled 'polarization effects'.
The 'trickling down of Northern progress', as it is called, occurs mainly
through the increase of Northern purchases and investments in the
South, but the marginal productivity of labour and *per capita* consumption levels in the South may also be raised by outmigration if there is
disguised unemployment in the poor region. 'Polarization effects' arise
partially because efficient producers in the North can, through competition, depress economic activities in the South, and partially through
selective migration, which 'denudes the South of its key technicians and
managers as well as of the more enterprising young men' (p. 188).

Within this framework of analysis, Hirschman recognizes that some of
the non-local effects of growth in the spatially defined 'poles' may be
negative, and that the cumulative concentration of growth in those poles
will at first increase regional economic disparities. But *within the terms of
his analysis* he is confident that in the long run, geographical trickledown
effects will be sufficient to reduce such disparities.

The inevitability of this trend partially stems from the expectation that
agglomeration *dis*economies will occur in the growing centres, thus
encouraging the dispersal of industry. But the optimistic conclusion ultimately rests on the theory of state intervention *which is an integral part of
Hirschman's unbalanced growth strategy*. Within this strategy, it is
assumed that state development policy is not only directed to establish
'tensions' and 'pressures', but also, if necessary, acts to resolve them.
The state is taken to be an equilibrating mechanism, a new kind of 'invisible hand'. And thus, 'if the market forces that express themselves
through the trickling down and polarization effects result in a temporary
victory of the latter, deliberate economic policy will come into play to
correct the situation' (p. 190).

Hirschman published his analysis of the interregional transmission of
growth one year after Myrdal's critique of the view that trade and factor
mobility would automatically reduce regional income disparities (see
chapter 1). Their work was independent and directed towards completely

different research questions. But there is an obvious *formal* similarity between Hirschman's 'trickledown' and 'polarization effects' and Myrdal's 'spread' and 'backwash effects', which has led many regional analysts to equate their work and try to explain geographical patterns of development in terms of their famous 'effects'.

If Hirschman's analysis of how growth *can* be communicated from one region to another within an unbalanced growth strategy is taken to be an explanation of how growth in a place *does* induce growth in other places, then it is possible to believe that a concentration of industrial investment within a large urban centre, increasing the local momentum of growth there, will eventually have positive trickledown effects in other parts of the country. But this cannot be properly inferred from Hirschman's argument. He does suggest that spatially concentrated growth *can* induce growth in other places. But ultimately, in Hirschman's analysis, it does so because the state authorities are induced to change the spatial distribution of public investment.

There is no doubt that Hirschman's general argument leads to the conclusion that an urban-industrial growth pole strategy offers the best way to achieve *national* growth objectives. And there is no doubt that it is possible to work out the way in which his unbalanced growth strategy may be applied to achieve *regional* and *rural* growth objectives. But if this were done, it is uncertain what the resulting planning interventions should be. As the earlier discussion of Boudeville's work shows, they would certainly be far more complex than the mere implantation, or expansion, of large-scale industries in a few major urban centres.

We do not seem to have got very far. But it is important to be aware of these two false starts, partially because the ideas of Boudeville and Hirschman have affected the way regional analysts conceive the nature of urban-industrial growth pole strategies, and partially because they illustrate the problems of applying general ideas about development in a spatial context. Moreover, we can now reach an important conclusion. *The idea that an urban-industrial growth pole strategy can achieve regional development objectives must be based on some explanatory theory of how cities, regions and rural localities 'develop'.*

It is possible to find within the literature theories about these processes which support the expectation that growing industries in growing urban centres do induce regional and rural growth. But these theories are not directly derived from Perrouxian growth analysis and, depending on one's definition, do not necessarily form part of 'growth pole theory'. The most compelling stem from empirical generalizations based on the regional growth experience of the USA and dualist analyses of rural–urban relationships, to which the discussion will now turn.

It may seem strange today to imagine that the regional growth experience of the USA has any relevance to understanding geographical patterns of development in the poorer countries of the world. But in the early 1960s, there had been little empirical research on regional development processes in developing countries. Moreover, Rostow's view of the process of national development was in good currency.

As every reader will recall Rostow, in his book *The Stages of Economic Growth: a Non-Communist Manifesto*, proposed a way of thinking about 'development' which rested on the idea that all countries pass through five broadly similar stages of growth: (i) the traditional society, (ii) the pre-conditions for take-off, (iii) the take-off stage, (iv) the drive to maturity, and (v) the age of high mass consumption. The critical stage in this sequence is 'the take-off stage', during which an economy makes the transition from a state in which it is locked in vicious circles of poverty to a state in which growth is 'self-sustaining'. One of the essential conditions for this to occur is the establishment of one or more new manufacturing sectors, which can act as 'leading sectors', in the sense that their growth has positive external effects on other parts of the economy. The 'leading sector' is exactly analogous to Perroux's 'propulsive unit', and Higgins (1959) even suggests that Rostow was influenced by Perrouxian thinking. But apart from this parallel, what is significant here is that once Rostow's idea that all countries pass through broadly similar stages of growth is accepted, then the development experience of the USA indicated the path which, in broad terms, poorer countries would follow as they broke out of the stagnation of 'traditional society' and moved, after the 'take-off' stage, towards 'an age of high mass consumption'.

A description of this path in regional terms, and its generalization to developing countries, was first made by Jeffrey Williamson (1965). In an important contribution, he hypothesizes that 'in the early stages of national development' regional income disparities will be accentuated, but that 'somewhere during the course of development' regional inequality will begin to diminish (p. 164). This hypothesis, which may be derived from Hirschman's exposition of 'North-South' interrelationships if that exposition is taken to be an *explanation* of how regional growth occurs, was tested using international data on regional income disparities in twenty-four countries in the 1950s.

The data set is far from ideal. *Average* regional *per capita* income is used as an indicator and Williamson notes that his results may be systematically biased as no account is taken of regional variations in the cost of living, which tends to be higher in the richer regions, and as regional income in poorer regions, with a large measure of subsistence production, may be underestimated. The regional units are given by existing administrative units which vary greatly in size, from the seventy-six *municipos* of Puerto Rico to the eighteen *states* of India. The sample of countries for the international comparison includes few countries at a low 'level of development' – none from Africa, only three, including Japan, from Asia; and four from Latin America. But nevertheless, using a weighted coefficient of variation* as a measure of dispersion in regional income levels, Williamson finds a striking pattern which confirms his hypothesis. When the countries are 'ranged' according to the level of development, the pattern of regional inequality is in the form of an inverted 'U' which reaches its peak in the 'middle income countries', that is Brazil, Colombia, Philippines and Puerto Rico (Table 5).

Williamson supplements his cross-sectional analysis with trend analyses of changes in regional income inequality in individual countries over time. Data for short periods, of up to twenty years, is available in sixteen of the twenty-four countries, and the existing trends offer further confirmation of the hypothesized pattern – the richer countries, in which one would expect regional convergence, are in fact either experiencing it or show no changes in regional income inequality, while the poorer countries are characterized by regional income divergence. But Brazil, somewhat embarrassingly, traces out the hypothesized inverted-U pattern 'through the later stages of her early development stages' (p. 183). And of the three countries for which data is available for a

---

* The weighted coefficient of variation, Vw, is calculated using the formula

$$Vw = \frac{\sqrt{\sum_i (y_i - \bar{y})^2 \frac{f_i}{n}}}{\bar{y}}$$

where f_i is the population of the i-th region
n is the national population
y_i is income *per capita* in the i-th region
$\bar{y}$ is national income *per capita*.

This formula measures relative dispersion of regional *per capita* incomes around the national average, weighting each regional contribution to the overall dispersion measure by the size of the regional population. It is important to note that this is a measure of *relative*, rather than *absolute*, regional disparities. Williamson notes that 'to expect the regional convergence typical of national maturity will also produce reductions in *absolute* differentials is to expect a great deal indeed' (p. 191).

Table 5 Regional income inequality and national development: the results of Williamson

Level of development*	Average weighted coefficient of variation
High *Group 1* Australia, New Zealand, Canada, UK, USA, Sweden	0.139
Group 2 Finland, France, West Germany, Netherlands, Norway	0.252
Group 3 Ireland, Chile, Austria, Puerto Rico	0.335
Group 4 Brazil, Italy, Spain, Colombia, Greece	0.464
Group 5 Yugoslavia, Japan	0.292
Low *Group 6* India	0.275

* The countries are grouped according to a classification proposed by Kuznets and refer to the level of development at the time to which the regional incomes data refer. Japan, for example, is said to be in Group 5, during the period 1951–9.

Source: adapted from Williamson, 1951.

sufficiently long period to cover the three phases of increasing, stable and declining regional inequality, Germany follows a pattern which is inconsistent with the hypothesis; France follows the expected pattern, though the data is described as 'very thin'; and only the USA conforms well with the hypothesis. Williamson notes that the USA has undergone a 'growth experience somewhat unique among nations' (p. 178). But nevertheless he suggests that, in terms of regional growth, its history traces out 'the "classic pattern" of regional inequality' (p. 179).

THE USA AS AN IDEAL TYPE: (2) JOHN FRIEDMANN (1966)

Williamson's findings have been an important source of controversy among regional development theorists (see Gilbert and Goodman 1976;

Lo and Salih, 1981). But what is significant here is that his conclusion, which is based on Rostovian assumptions, that:

> Rising income inequalities and increasing North-South dualism is typical of early development stages, while regional convergence and the disappearance of severe North-South problems is typical of more mature stages of national growth and development.   (p. 179)

was accepted by many regional development theorists in the late 1960s and early 1970s as either the pattern which *would* occur in developing countries,* or the pattern which *should, through policy intervention, be made to occur.* And the urban-industrial growth pole strategy was seen as a way in which the reversal in the trend towards increasing regional disparities could be effected.

The most influential contribution to this view was made by John Friedmann. In his book *Regional Development Policy*, published in 1966, he put together a series of propositions about the process of regional development in developing countries which were the major statement on the subject in the 1960s. And on the basis of these propositions he advocated a regional development policy, the cornerstone of which was a type of urban-industrial growth pole strategy.

As we saw in chapter 1, the 'stages of spatial organization', which a country ideally passes through as its economy grows, conform to the 'classic pattern' delineated by Williamson and clearly identifiable in the USA. But Friedmann not only posited this as a *general pattern* which it was the purpose of policy to achieve, but also, argued implicitly that *the process* of regional development in the poor countries, if and when it occurred, *would occur as it did in the USA.* For his propositions on that process are based on the research findings of a number of studies which analysed regional and rural change in the USA as its economy became more industrialized. The antecedents of Friedmann's synthesis are found in the work of North (1955), Perloff *et al.* (1960) and Schultz (1950, 1951).

Douglass North: regional exports and economic growth

The most important of these contributions is that of Perloff and his associates. But they build on the earlier work of Douglass North, an economic historian, who proposed that in North America, 'the success of the export-base has been the determining factor in the rate of growth of regions' (p. 346).

---

* The reader may note the similarity with El-Shakhs' findings on the relationship between primacy and development (see above, p. 64).

The idea of the export-base was first used by city planners who were concerned to predict the *short-run* dynamics of local *urban* economies. To do this they constructed a quantitative model of the urban economy which divided it into two sectors: an *export-base sector* (which includes all those activities for which demand is external to the city) and a *residentiary sector* (which includes all activities for which the demand is internal). Within the model it is assumed that the residentiary sector has no autonomous capacity for growth but can only expand when extra income is brought into the local economy through increases in external demand for locally produced goods which lead to the expansion of the export-base sector. In the short-run, changes in the level of total urban income (or employment) could be predicted by changes in 'export' demand, with the relationship between the expansion of the export-base sector and the expansion of the total economy defining the size of the local multiplier.

North applied this idea to understand the *long-term* changes in *regional* economies. Using the Pacific Northwest as an empirical base he argued that external demand for a region's exports, in that case lumber, furs, flour and wheat, affects not just the level of absolute and *per capita* income there, but also influences 'the character of subsidiary industry, the distribution of population and pattern of urbanization, the character of the labour force, the social and political attitudes of the region and its sensitivity to fluctuations of income and employment' (p. 346). 'A given increase in demand for the region's exports', he suggests, 'has resulted in a multiple effect on the region, inducing increased investment not only in the export industry, but in all other kinds of economic activity as well'. And: 'As a region's income grows, indigenous savings will tend to spill over into new kinds of activities. At first, these activities satisfy local demand, but ultimately some of them will become export industries' (p. 347).

Whether or not a region can successfully develop an export-base depends, according to North, on its comparative advantage with respect to other regions in terms of production and distribution costs. But 'the concerted efforts of the region's residents', in reducing costs and attracting outside suppliers of capital, can be particularly important in reinforcing regional growth (p. 347).

Harvey Perloff: industrial location, natural resources and regional growth

The export-base multiplier mechanism which North identifies is an important element in the theoretical rationale for urban-industrial growth pole policies. But North himself argued that 'there is no reason why all regions must industrialize in order to continue to grow' (p. 343). However, as his ideas were extended by Perloff and his associates, manufacturing industry was identified as central to the explanation of regional economic growth. Indeed their analysis is based on the '*assumption*' that 'the critical elements in the changing patterns of regional economic development are the locational and production requirements of the major industries' (Perloff *et al.*, 1960, p. vi; emphasis added).

Perloff and his research team argue that in examining regional economic development it is necessary to distinguish volume aspects of the process, that is, changes in the level and composition of economic activity, from welfare aspects, that is, changes in *per capita* income. The volume of economic growth in any region, they stress, is ultimately determined by 'national parameters', such as technological change, population growth and shifts in demand. But while these factors influence the overall rate of growth, *regional deviations* from the national average depend on the share which a region claims of the nation's rapid-growth or slow-growth industries, and the individual characteristics of different regions which can result in particular industrial sectors growing faster or slower than the national average. Both these patterns are explained by Perloff *et al.* in terms of the principles that govern the location of economic activity.

Businessmen are said to 'select production sites which enable them to maximize profits'. In doing so they compare production costs and revenues at different sites. These vary from site to site because of variations in access to the basic inputs and markets which are required by a particular industry. The maximization of profits requires 'the maximization of total access' to inputs and markets. The relative growth in a given area's volume of economic activity may then be said to be 'directly related to two factors: its access at competitive costs to the inputs of production and its access at competitive costs to markets for the outputs of this production' (p. 75).

But regional economic growth (or decline) 'is not simply a consequence of a discrete set of locational decisions' (p. 93). Any location decision, or injection of investment in a region, sets off a train of economic effects which are encompassed within the concept of *regional multipliers*. In a short-term perspective these multiplier effects depend on the inter-sectoral pattern of monetary payments, which may be described by an input-output matrix. But in a long-term perspective, the multiplier effects define a sequence of structural change and growth within a region, with the location of new industry changing the input-output access advantages of that area, and those changes attracting further new industry in subsequent rounds of investment. The spatial agglomeration of productive activities promotes this process and is, in turn, an effect of it.

Applying these principles to understanding the details of regional growth in the USA is a complex task. But Perloff and Wingo (1961) identify some broad general trends which have occurred as the US economy moved 'from early agricultural beginnings to status as an advanced, industrial-and-service oriented economy' (p. 307). Over that period, different natural resources have assumed more or less significance as the economy matured, and different regions have prospered to a greater or lesser extent because of their endowment with 'natural resources that count' (p. 308). But in general:

> Regional growth has typically been promoted by the ability of a region to produce goods and services demanded by the national economy and to export them at a competitive advantage with respect to other regions.   (p. 316)

'This ability to export', Perloff and Wingo continue, 'induces a flow of income into the region which through the familiar multiplier effect, tends to expand the internal market of the region for both national and regional-serving goods and services' (p. 316). 'The extent of multiplier effects' depends on 'certain "internal" features that characterize the social and economic structure of the region', especially: the nature of the export industry; the scope of localized industrial linkages; the quality and quantity of labour and the level of wages; and the local income distribution (p. 316). But:

> As the regional market expands and region-serving activities proliferate conditions may develop for self-reinforcing and self-sustaining regional growth, and new internal factors may become important in determining the rates of regional growth, such as external economies associated with social overhead capital and the agglomeration of industries, and internal economies of scale.   (p. 317)

The accumulation of such 'cumulative advantages' is most evident in the USA in the north-eastern part of the country, which Perloff and Wingo describe as the industrial 'heartland'. That area has been the major centre of manufacturing activity since the beginning of the century when the iron and steel industry was the leading sector of the economy (Figure 17). But:

> The emergence of industrial heartland set the basic conditions for regional growth throughout the nation – it was the lever for the successive development of the newer peripheral regions: as its input

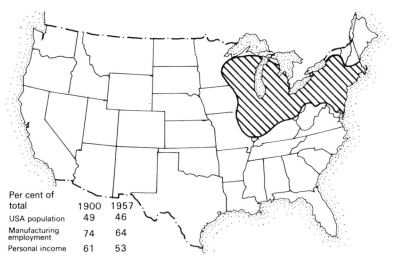

Per cent of total	1900	1957
USA population	49	46
Manufacturing employment	74	64
Personal income	61	53

Figure 17   The US manufacturing belt, 1900 and 1957.

Source: Perloff *et al.*, 1960, p. 49.

requirements expanded, it reached out into the outlying areas for its resources stimulating their growth differentially in accordance with its resource demands and the endowments of the regions.

(Perloff and Wingo, 1961, p. 322)

Thus, first-stage resource processing industries have been established in 'hinterland' regions, and these areas have then grown mainly by a 'filling-in process . . . a threshold-by-threshold upward movement as resources expand and as the regional markets grow in size' (p. 329).

Perloff and his associates stress that welfare aspects of regional growth are subject to 'a different constellation of forces' to volume aspects. But this 'filling-in process' is one basic element in a major trend in regional *per capita* income differentials which has occurred in the USA since 1920 – that is, a pattern of convergence in the average incomes in different states. In the USA the main component of income which contributes to the regional differentials is wages and salaries, and if the major industries in a state tend to be high-paying, then that state will have an income *per capita* which is above the national average. Agricultural incomes tend to be lower, and thus 'the states with the largest proportion of persons working in farming generally have lower average *per capita* incomes than states in which manufacturing and service activities predominate' (Perloff *et al.*, p. 101). Inter-state income differentials have declined in the present century as industrial capital investment occurred in the poorer 'hinterland' regions of the south-west and south-east.

But migration from low-income to high-income regions has also been important. It may well be selective and thus have contrary effects. And it is certainly sluggish. But in regions which do not possess any great comparative advantage in the production of goods demanded by the national market, 'it is only through outmigration that upward pressure on wage levels can be exerted and *per capita* incomes raised' (p. 606). Thus regional convergence has been promoted by a process of 'emptying-out' – occurring in areas where opportunities and wages decline below the national average – working alongside the process of 'filling-in' – occurring in areas where opportunities for capital and labour are unusually good.

Theodore Schultz: urban-industrial growth and agricultural incomes

Theodore Schultz was particularly concerned with variations in agricultural income in the USA and he poses the question: why, when the USA was experiencing unprecedented growth, did the standard of living fall below the national average in *some* agricultural communities? His initial answer is that such relative poverty was not determined by the physical characteristics of land but rather by the proximity of agricultural communities to 'centres of economic progress' (Schultz, 1950). And in 1951 he formalized this idea into what he called 'the retardation hypothesis', which he said offered 'a comprehensive approach which relates location to economic development'. The hypothesis consists of three parts:

(1) Economic development occurs in a specific locational matrix. There can be one or more such matrices in an economy. . . . (2) These locational matrices are primarily industrial-urban in composition; the centres of these matrices in which economic development occurs are not mainly in rural or farming areas, although some farming areas are situated more favourably than are others in relation to such centres. (3) The existing economic organization works best at or near the centre of a particular matrix of economic development, and it also works best in those parts of agriculture which are situated favourably in relation to such a centre; it works less satisfactorily in those parts of agriculture which are situated at the periphery of the matrix.

(Schultz, 1951, pp. 205–6)

This hypothesis was tested by Nicholls and Tang in South Carolina, Georgia and Tennessee (see Nicholls, 1961). The correlation between various indicators of the efficiency of local labour and capital markets and the degree of urban-industrial development in different counties within the study area was examined over the period 1860 to 1950. And the results confirmed the hypothesis. Both labour and capital markets on that statistical evidence were found to be more efficient in urban-industrial counties, and the indicators suggested that agriculture was more productive and rural incomes higher in areas near to urban-industrial development. This was ascribed to the effects of such development on agricultural factor markets.

Friedmann's synthesis

If one can believe that these research findings on regional and rural growth in the USA apply equally in the poorer countries of the world, then they provide a strong theoretical basis for urban-industrial growth pole policies. The implantation of industrial activity in the large urban centres of peripheral regions may induce a 'filling-in process' such as that described by Perloff and Wingo, and proximity to the centres of urban-industrial expansion will increase agricultural incomes.

Such a transfer of theory requires a major leap of faith. North cautions that his account of the relationship between the export base and regional growth would only apply equally well in: '(1) regions that have grown up within a framework of capitalist institutions and have therefore responded to profit-maximizing opportunities, in which factors of production have been relatively mobile, and (2) regions that have grown up without the strictures imposed by population pressure' (North, 1955, pp. 332–3). Perloff and his associates' account is similarly based on the assumption of profit-maximization and free capital mobility. And though Nicholls suggests that his findings on the relationship between industrialization and local agricultural incomes may have wider policy relevance in 'underdeveloped countries', Schultz's stricture that his 'retardation hypothesis' only applies 'in a period covering decades, during which the economy as a whole grows and develops in the sense that the real output of workers rises, not by some small percentage, but one, two or more-fold as has been the case in the USA' (Schultz, 1951, p. 205), certainly gives grounds for caution in expecting quick results.

Nevertheless, Friedmann took these research findings and synthesized them into eight propositions about 'the spatial incidence of economic growth' which were explicitly designed to provide planners with 'a way of thinking about the process of regional development' (Friedmann, 1966, p. 20). Baldly stated, his propositions are:

1 Regional economies are open to the outside world and subject to external influence.

2 Regional economic growth is externally induced.
3 Successful translation of export sector growth into growth of the residentiary sector depends on the socio-political structure of the region and the local distribution of income and patterns of expenditure.
4 Local leadership is decisive for successful adaptation to external change. Yet the quality of leadership depends on the region's past development experience.
5 Regional economic growth may be regarded, in part, as a problem in the location of firms.
6 Economic growth tends to occur in the matrix of urban regions. It is through this matrix that the evolving space economy is organized.
7 Flows of labour tend to exert an equilibrating force on the welfare effects of economic growth. But contradictory results may be obtained.
8 Where economic growth is sustained over long periods, its incidence works toward a progressive integration of the space economy.

(p. 38)

Each of these propositions, except the last one, can be traced back to the work of North, Perloff and his associates, and Schultz.

The eighth proposition describes the sequence of 'stages of spatial organization' through which an economy passes as it grows. The sequence, outlined in chapter 1, in fact describes what supposedly has occurred in the USA. The 'centre-periphery structure', which is imposed on the space economy as it starts to industrialize is, in descriptive terms, the equivalent of Perloff and Wingo's 'heartland-hinterland structure' and the final stage of a fully integrated space economy is the pattern which Friedmann himself, in an earlier publication, suggests is occurring in the USA as it becomes a 'post-industrial society' (Friedmann and Miller, 1965). But as we saw in chapter 1, Friedmann is quite sanguine about the prospects of the periphery developing spontaneously through market forces. Policy intervention is necessary to break down the centre-periphery structure. And the strategy which Friedmann advocates, though complex in its details, essentially entails the *replication* of what occurred in the USA.

On the one hand this involves 'the activation of new core regions' in the periphery. 'Core regions' (said to be similar to Perroux's concept of '*pôles de croissance*') are defined as 'metropolitan areas with a high propensity for economic growth and for filtering this growth to other parts of the economy' (Friedmann, 1966, p. 217). They can be classified into a hierarchy as follows:

Rank order of core region	Descriptive name
First	National metropolis
Second	Regional capital
Third	Sub-regional centre
Fourth	Local service centre

and in activating them, regional planners should proceed from the largest to the smallest. In each case this may be done through public investment policies which create 'environmental conditions so favourable that they will induce individual firms to choose, on purely economic grounds, a location within them' (p. 214). Priority should switch from larger to smaller urban centres whenever 'self-sustaining growth' is achieved at any given level of the urban hierarchy.

But the growth of 'core regions' may be threatened if the rate of urbanization is too fast. Thus alongside the strategy of planned urban-industrial growth, the government should undertake 'the resettlement of rural population and land reclamation on an extensive scale to relieve the poverty in depressed agricultural areas and to ease the costs (and social strains) of new urbanization'. Outward migration should be particularly encouraged from 'downward transitional areas' whose resources 'suggest as optimal a less intensive development than in the past' (p. 43). Through such an 'emptying-out process', undertaken in conjunction with the core-region development strategy, the pernicious centre-periphery structure can be transformed into a space economy which conforms to the final stage of perfect integration.

THE USA AS AN IDEAL TYPE: (3) BRIAN BERRY

In setting out his eight propositions about the process of regional development, Friedmann hypothesized that 'impulses of economic change are transmitted in order from higher to lower order centres in the urban hierarchy' (p. 31). At the time he wrote there was little evidence to support this hypothesis. But subsequent research by Berry, again in the USA, confirmed it and was used to provide a further, though slightly different, justification for a 'growth centre' strategy in which industrial development is encouraged in large 'intermediate' cities, away from the metropoli (Berry, 1969a; 1969b; 1971a; 1971b).

Berry's argument is based on the assertion that:

growth centres' developmental role involves the simultaneous *filtering* of innovations that bring growth down the urban hierarchy and the *spreading* of the benefits occurring from the resulting growth, both nationally from core to hinterland regions and within these regions from their metropolitan centres outwards to the inter-metropolitan periphery.   (Berry, 1971b, p. 108)

Growth, in his view, occurs as a consequence of the adoption of innovations by firms and households. Regional inequities arise 'because the income effect of a given innovation is a declining function of time [i.e. the later an innovation is adopted in a region, the less the consequent increase in income], and is also subject to a threshold limitation – a minimum size of region – beyond which diffusion will not proceed' (p. 109). And urban centres can themselves play a 'developmental role' because they strongly influence the timing of innovation adoption in different places.

Berry demonstrates this proposition by examining the spatial diffusion of TV stations (an entrepreneurial innovation) and of the ownership of TV sets (a household innovation) in the USA during the period 1940–68. Three cities, New York, Philadelphia and Chicago, all within the heartland of the USA, opened TV stations before the Second World War, and thereafter there is a clear tendency for larger cities to open stations earlier (Figure 18a). By 1958, almost complete national coverage was achieved. Mapping the pattern of market penetration in terms of household TV ownership, Berry finds that in the early phases of the diffusion process, market penetration declined with distance from the urban centres where TV stations had been opened but that over time there was what he describes as a 'wavelike sequence' of household innovation with market saturation increasing to higher and higher levels in the places distant from TV stations (Figure 18b). Berry also finds that cities which opened TV stations earlier than one would expect in view of their size tended to be near-neighbours of cities where stations had already opened and that market saturation was achieved first in the heartland.

The relevance of these findings to the understanding of regional growth patterns is debatable (see Pred, 1976). But Berry is confident enough to generalize his empirical work and suggest that 'hierarchical diffusion and the attendant spread effects characterize the *entire range* of innovations that bring growth and incomes to cities and regions' (p. 135, emphasis added), and that 'growth occurs as a consequence of the filtering of innovations downwards through the urban hierarchy, and the spread of use of the innovations among the consumers residing within the urban fields of the adopting centres' (p. 136).

Various policy implications may be derived from this conclusion. In broad terms, policies to promote regional growth should be directed towards accelerating the diffusion of innovations and facilitating their

A   Hierarchical diffusion of TV stations

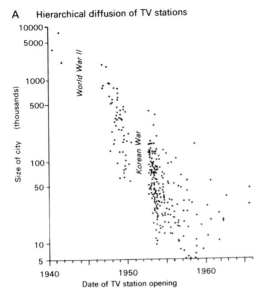

B   Wavelike diffusion of TV ownership(schematic)

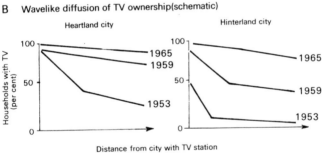

Figure 18 The spatial diffusion of TV stations and TV sets in the USA.

Source: adapted from Berry, 1971b.

penetration into poorer regions and smaller towns. And if, as Berry suggests, the 'innovation potential' of an urban centre is a function of its size and its accessibility to centres which have already adopted the innovation, measures should be undertaken to promote population growth in urban centres in peripheral regions and improve their accessibility to the largest, and earliest adopting, centres. But in applying these views on the hierarchical diffusion of innovation to developing countries, Berry adds a further twist to the analysis. For he argues that 'the filtering mechanism that produces hierarchical diffusion ... works poorly, if at all, in many parts of the world' (Berry, 1971a, p. 139). What is expected to occur, as the USA provides an ideal typical account of the regional development process, does *not* occur in developing countries. As he puts it:

> Instead of development trickling down the urban size-ratchet and spreading its effects outwards within urban fields, growth is concentrated in a few urban centers, and [there is] a wide gulf between metropolis and small city. Rather than articulation there is polarization.   (p. 139)

Planning efforts should therefore be directed *to make hierarchical diffusion occur*, and what these efforts should consist of depends on the diagnosis of why it is *not* occurring.

Explaining why a process does not occur is obviously a somewhat tendentious task. But Berry suggests that it is due to the poorly developed urban hierarchies in developing countries which have colonial administrative origins and to the high rates of migration to the metropoli which, supposedly, have kept wage rates low and thus reduced the attractiveness of alternative locations to industrial entrepreneurs. The governments of developing countries need to pursue policies which sustain the national growth rate. Otherwise, there would be no growth to trickledown! But at the same time, 'programs of decentralization into new growth centres' should be pursued (p. 142). This will 'bring new or under-utilized resources into the development process' and create 'alternative magnets for migrants' and in the end will enable 'the "natural" filtering process to reassert itself' (p. 143).

THE DUALIST PERSPECTIVE AND THE GEOGRAPHY OF MODERNIZATION

I have focused upon the arguments of Friedmann and Berry as they were important opinion leaders in Anglo-American regional development theory and their work was influential in forming the conventional wisdom on the process of regional development which was held in the late 1960s and early 1970s. But to complete the account of ideas which support the expectation that an urban-industrial growth pole strategy may promote regional and rural growth, it is necessary to consider general arguments made within a dualist perspective, which are particularly important in suggesting that urban-industrial growth could promote positive economic and social changes in the surrounding hinterland.

Various dualist models of development have been proposed but one general feature which they have is that the 'modern' ('capitalist', 'industrial', 'urban') sector is said to be dynamic, while the 'traditional' ('noncapitalist', 'agricultural', 'rural') sector is said to be stagnant. From this perspective, the growth and development of the 'traditional sector' is induced through contact with the 'modern sector', and the rate of change in the 'traditional sector' is critically determined by 'barriers' to interaction. Transposed into a spatial context, such analyses imply that the promotion of 'modern' urban-industrial growth within a region could have major positive 'spread effects' on the 'traditional' rural areas.

This could occur through various mechanisms, the most important of which is the interaction between agriculture and industry. The classic paper on this subject is by Lewis (1954) and, though other economists have developed Lewis's argument (see Fei and Ranis, 1964; Jorgenson, 1969), one basic conclusion reached in all the dualist analyses is the same. It is that the transfer of labour from agriculture to industry is a major mechanism through which agricultural growth occurs.

The conclusion follows from particular assumptions about the nature of a dual economy. It is assumed firstly that agricultural production is primarily for subsistence, and output is a function of labour and land. Accumulation of capital does not occur in the agricultural sector and production is assumed to be stagnant. Furthermore, and this is the critical assumption, it is assumed that there is a labour surplus in the agricultural sector. This manifests itself in the phenomenon of 'disguised unemployment', which implies that the supply of labour in the agricultural sector may be reduced without reducing agricultural output.

The dualist analyses show what will happen as growth occurs in the industrial sector. As the industrial sector grows, which it is likely to do as entrepreneurs in that sector are assumed to be interested in capital accumulation and to follow profit-maximizing behaviour, more labour is demanded in that sector and it is supplied by the 'surplus' existing in the agricultural sector. Labour may be transferred from agriculture to industry without any loss in output in the former sector until all the disguised unemployment is eliminated. Once labour becomes scarce in the agricultural sector, farmers are *forced* to change their methods of production and the capitalization of agriculture begins. The transfer of labour to the industrial sector also necessitates the commercialization of agriculture and if the producers, who at the outset are assumed to be 'subsistence-oriented', begin to respond to price incentives, a further inducement for change may be set up by the rising prices of foodstuffs and a shift in the terms of trade in favour of the agricultural sector.

The dualist analysis of the positive effects of the transfer of labour from agriculture to industry implies that the migration of people from the rural hinterlands to urban-industrial centres could engender positive effects in those rural areas. But it is not the only way in which interaction between the 'modern' and 'traditional' sector has been seen to induce economic change in the latter.

Hoselitz (1953) suggests another which is based on the assumption that 'one of the chief barriers to rapid economic advancement in many parts of the world . . . is the traditionalism of the social values of the bulk of the population' (p. 187). He poses the question:

> To what extent is the growth of an urban culture in underdeveloped countries the vehicle for changing the values and the beliefs of the society so as to make it more inclined to accept economic growth?
>
> (p. 196–7)

And his answer is clear:

> The cities, even in underdeveloped countries, are modelled, at least in some significant aspects, after the urban centres of the west. They exhibit a spirit different from that of the countryside. They are the main force and the chief locus for introduction of new ideas and new ways of doing things. One may look, therefore, to the cities as the crucial places in underdeveloped countries in which the adaptation of new ways, new technologies, new consumption and production patterns and new social institutions is achieved. The main problem remaining is the nature of this adaptation in the various underdeveloped countries and the degree to which the changing culture of the urban centres affects the surrounding 'sea' of traditional folk-like ways of life.
>
> (p. 197)

Following this paper, Hoselitz organized a conference which addressed this research problem and, in his summing up, he refined this viewpoint, suggesting that cities may be either 'generative', that is, have a positive impact on economic growth in the regions, or countries within which they were situated, or 'parasitic', that is, have a negative impact (Hoselitz, 1955). Following Redfield and Singer (1954), he identifies particular circumstances in which urbanization may be parasitic, but in general he finds that 'it is not easy to discover actual instances in which the city has exerted a *long-run* parasitic influence on the economic development of the region which it dominated' (Hoselitz, 1955, p. 282; emphasis added).

Within much of the literature which sees the process of development as a transition from 'traditional' to 'modern' society, it is taken as axiomatic that the city is a major agent of change. But a series of studies by geographers in the late 1960s and early 1970s provided empirical evidence which substantiates this view. These studies, directed by Peter Gould, mapped the spatial distribution of indicators of modernity in a number of former British colonies during the period 1900 to 1970 (see, for example, Soja, 1968, on Kenya; Riddell, 1970, on Sierra Leone; Gould, 1970, on Tanzania; and Leinbach, 1972, on Malaysia). The studies, constrained by data availability, use information collected by colonial authorities, and thus map the distribution of primary and secondary schools, health facilities, roads and railways, postal and telephone facilities, district headquarters, courts and police officers as 'indicators of modernity'. But clear and recurrent patterns emerge in all the studies.

Using what Gould calls 'a modernization surface' to describe the spatial pattern of modernity at any given point in time, it is clear that cities stand out as 'islands of modernity'. The modernization surface is constructed through the multivariate statistical technique, factor analysis, which provides a method of combining individual indicators into a composite measure of the 'modernity' of different places within a country. This is then mapped by ranging all places on a scale from 0–100 with the most modern places scoring 100 and the least modern 0. When this statistical manipulation is completed, a map such as those shown in Figure 19 may be constructed. The towns, as Gould emphasizes, stand out far ahead of rural areas in terms of their degree of modernity, and there is also quite a sharp distance decay in the modernization surface as one moves away from the urban peaks.

Comparing the modernization surfaces for the early colonial period with those of the late period, it is evident that places which initially were more 'modern' tend to remain more 'modern'. But over time, as the studies repeatedly assert, 'modernization' diffuses outward from the initial centres of colonial contact. And just as TV stations filter down the urban hierarchy in the USA, so do many of the key economic and social institutions, such as banks, schools and hospitals, which are taken to indicate modernity. As Riddell (1970, p. 129) in the conclusion to his study of Sierra Leone, puts it, 'the spread of political, social, economic and institutional change funnelled through the transportation network and cascaded down the urban hierarchy'.

What precisely may be inferred from the patterns portayed in the geography of modernization studies is debatable (see Brookfield, 1971), and Gould in particular is careful to stress that the maps are not in themselves an explanation of the process of modernization. But nevertheless, both Soja and Riddell, whose studies are the most comprehensive, emphasize the key role which large cities play in promoting change. In Kenya, Nairobi, the capital, and the three towns which are found to be the 'most highly modernized' are said to contain 'the prime generators, transformers, interpreters and distributors of the forces of change'

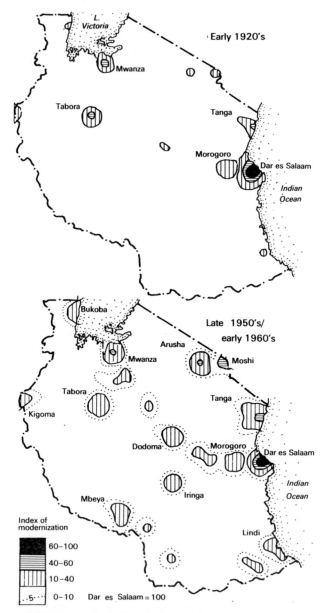

Figure 19 Tanzania: the modernization surface for the early 1920s and late 1950s/early 1960s.

Source: adapted from Gould, 1970, pp. 256, 262.

(Soja, 1968, p. 109). And in Sierra Leone, Freetown, the capital, is said to have played a 'catalytical role', indeed to have 'dominated the process of modernization' (Riddell, 1970, p. 129).

CONCLUSION

This chapter has summarized a diverse set of ideas drawn from many different sources. They may seem to fit uncomfortably together, but that, I believe, correctly reflects the nature of the theoretical rationale for urban-industrial growth pole policies. The material presented has been selected on the general principle which Friedmann himself uses to intro-duce his eight propositions on the spatial incidence of economic growth. It is that: 'Planners who would interfere in regional development must understand the process by which it is generated' (Friedmann, 1966, p. 20). Following that principle, attempts to apply Perrouxian growth analysis in a spatial context have been largely ignored. For they have led on the one hand to inadequate explanations of how regional and rural growth actually occurs (see Hansen, 1967, and Thomas, 1972), and on the other hand to the conclusion that regional development objectives are best achieved through policies which manipulate general economic relationships rather than through policies designed to change the spatial distribution of industry and urban population directly (see Lasuen, 1969, 1973; and Holland, 1976a, 1976b).*

The ideas may be drawn from different sources. But they have a sig-nificant feature in common. They are based on a Rostovian stages-of-growth conception of the development process and a dualist analysis of conditions within developing countries. They indicate relationships between urban-industrial growth and regional and rural development which support the expectation that an urban-industrial growth pole strategy can achieve various regional planning objectives. These relation-ships have all, in some way, been 'empirically verified'. But whether or not the strategy can be successful ultimately depends on the assumptions about how 'development' occurs which underlie the regional theories.

* Holland's work specifically applies to advanced capitalist countries, but includes useful general arguments which suggest that many orthodox regional planning concepts have limited utility, and that their weakness stems from the fact that 'Too much regional theory abstracts from the system in which regional problems occur, failing to see the underlying causes of regional imbalance in capitalism itself' (1976, p. v). In rectifying this failure, Holland states that he is concerned to build upon the insights of Marx, Myrdal and Perroux, but in this unlikely trio the last is most important. Indeed, although Holland is not usually identified as a 'growth pole theorist' by regional analysts, his discussion of the effects of unequal competition between big and small firms on patterns of regional change is the most rigorous and elaborate extension of Perrouxian thinking in the literature.

4

Some anti-theses: polarization and the development of underdevelopment

Urban-industrial growth pole policies were most widely advocated and adopted in the 1960s, 'in the heyday of national development policies aimed at accelerated industrialization' (Appalraju and Safier, 1976, p. 156). In the 1970s, the approach was rejected in many Latin American countries (Conroy, 1974) and in India (Misra, Sundaram and Rao, 1974). As Appalraju and Safier show in their survey of the evolution of growth centre strategies in Commonwealth countries, policies to develop small market towns as 'rural growth centres' and policies which aimed to create a 'national system of growth centres', including the metropoli, intermediate cities and small towns, became more popular at that time. Moreover, in some countries, administrative decentralization and the devolution of power to regional and local levels were promoted as a means of achieving regional and rural development (Cheema and Rondinelli, 1983).

The reasons for these policy shifts are complex, and must be interpreted in the light of local historical circumstances. But some regional theorists began to argue that where growth pole strategies had been pursued, they had failed. The main evidence to support this assertion came from studies which examined the intensity and extent of local spread effects in the vicinity of urban centres treated by planners as 'growth poles' or 'growth centres'. The evidence is summarized by Stöhr and Tödtling (1977) and it supposedly shows that such planned 'growth poles' had not induced growth or development in their hinterlands. They may have been successful in reducing *inter*regional disparities in development, but as local spread effects were weak, they had at the same time exacerbated *intra*-regional, and in particular rural–urban, disparities.

This *alleged* policy failure is the base from which the various alternative policy proposals within the regional development literature begin. But I stress the word 'alleged', as the empirical evaluation of growth pole strategies is far from convincing.

The first problem with it is related to the difficulty of measuring the impact of the policy. A basic method which has been suggested is to map the spatial pattern of a set of development indicators in the vicinity of an urban centre which is taken to be a 'growth pole' or 'growth centre' (Robinson and Salih, 1971; Gilbert, 1975). If the development surface declines with distance from the centre (as illustrated in Figure 20), it is concluded that the centre has, in some unspecified way, induced 'development' in the surrounding areas. As Gilbert (1975) puts it, a curvilinear surface 'reflects a situation where the benefits from the centre diffuse to a restricted geographical area and not beyond' (p. 327).

But how valid is such a conclusion? The inference upon which it rests is that if 'development' is related to accessibility to an urban centre, then it has been caused, at least partially, by something that has happened in that centre. But this inference denies the possibility that 'development', however it is measured, may be promoted by other factors which also are related to distance to the urban centre, but which have nothing to do with economic changes within it. For example, if the urban centre is located in a valley, the natural quality of farm land may decline with distance from the centre and as a result of this there may be a 'curvilinear development surface'.

Strictly speaking, the impact of a growth pole policy may only be assessed using this method if the actual development surface is compared with one which would be *expected* in the absence of the policy being pursued. But the expected surface is very difficult to construct. A second best solution would be to examine the development surface before and after the policy, trying to isolate the influence of general changes which occurred over the period. But no empirical studies of this nature have been conducted.

Even if a better method of measuring the impact of policy is devised, there is a second problem which undermines empirical evaluation. Given the confusing transformation of the growth pole concept as it was applied by regional theorists in a spatial context, and also the lack of perseverance in pursuing growth pole strategies, it can be argued that any failures of policy which may be observed are due to faulty implementation or too hasty abandonment. Richardson and Richardson (1974, p. 169), reviewing the Latin American experience, write, for example:

> The disenchantment with growth centre policies in many countries is not evidence that the principle of polarization is wrong. On the contrary, it reflects the over-optimism and short-run time horizon of regional policy-makers, the failure of sustained political will, the use

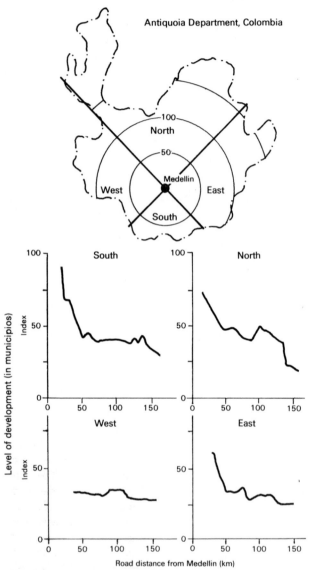

Figure 20 The incidence of development in the vicinity of a growth centre: the case of Medellin, Colombia.

Source: adapted from Gilbert, 1976, Figures 2 and 3.

of deficient investment criteria, bad locational choices and lack of imagination in devising appropriate policy instruments.

This conclusion is irrefutable. On theoretical grounds, an urban-industrial growth pole strategy cannot be expected to achieve any of the desired results *in the short run*. And thus, as Richardson (1976) argues at length, the observation that local spread effects have not set in within the first years in which the policy has been applied does not necessarily mean that it has failed. In some cases, therefore, the rejection of the policy has *prevented* empirical evaluation. But even if there were cases which illustrate the policy's impact over a long period, the confusion within growth pole theory effectively stymies evaluation. For this confusion has the corollary that what constitutes a 'proper' urban-industrial growth pole strategy is not clearly specified. And this means that in any given example of policy, it can always be argued that the growth pole concept has not been applied in the 'appropriate' way or has not been applied for 'sufficient' time.

I stress these points because the empirical critique of policy experience is widely accepted within the regional development literature. But this critique did not occur in a vacuum, for at the same time a number of new theories of urban and regional development were proposed. These theories offer different explanations of the geographical pattern of development to those summarized in the last chapter and, if accepted as valid, they imply that the strategy will not work because the assumptions about the regional development process on which it is based are wrong.

JOHN FRIEDMANN, 1972: A 'GENERAL THEORY' OF POLARIZED DEVELOPMENT

John Friedmann, as always, was in the thick of developments within the field. Soon after publishing *Regional Development Policy*, he revised his views on the regional development process in a paper ambitiously entitled 'A general theory of polarized development'. The paper, originally written in 1967 but first published in 1972, begins with a brief review of the theories upon which the regional planners could base their decisions at the end of the 1960s. Friedmann's conclusion is clear: 'None of them can be accepted as an adequate framework for regional development planning in its more general connotation' (p. 41). Even the eight propositions upon which he bases his proposal for activating core regions in Venezuela (which he describes as 'the substance of contemporary regional growth theory', p. 56) are deficient. Contemporary regional growth theory, he writes, is only applicable in 'the reasonably advanced and integrated spatial systems of the United States, West Germany and/or Sweden' (p. 57). It is *not* applicable to industrializ*ing* countries.

The aim of his paper is to construct a *general* theory of 'the development process in its spatial dimension', and this task, he suggests, requires that a link is established between 'the separate but correlative theories of social change and spatial organization' (p. 41). The problem, then, is to select a 'relevant' theory of social change. Friedmann asserts that there are 'two main contenders' – Everett Hagen's ideas on the psychological bases of individual motivation, and Ralf Dahrendorf's model of social conflict – and he adopts the latter as 'a promising beginning for formulating a general theory of polarized development' (p. 43).

Friedmann's choice is very curious. To someone with even the barest knowledge of sociology, Marx and Weber would stand out as the most important theorists of social change. Furthermore, Dahrendorf elaborates his model in a book entitled *Class and Class Conflict in Industrial Society* (1959) and it is specifically based on the concept of 'industrial society', that is, society in which there is mechanized commodity production in factories. Dahrendorf was concerned to criticize Marxist notions of class conflict under capitalism, and one of the key points in his analysis is that not all industrial societies are capitalist and that the richest parts of the world are industrial societies, but post-capitalist. His ideas are, by definition, not specifically oriented towards the poor countries of the world.

The choice is even more curious given the way in which Friedmann applies Dahrendorf's ideas. Dahrendorf argues that there are two separate ways of viewing society – either as a functionally integrated social system, or as a social structure held together by force and constraint – and that in any explanation of a particular social phenomenon it is necessary to choose between them. His account of the formation of conflict groups within society is explicitly a coercion theory of society, and within it the basic unit of analysis is what he calls an 'imperatively coordinated association', that is an organization, such as a firm or university or state, which has some determinate distribution of authority. In this schema, conflicts arise because some groups possess authority, that is the legitimate right to issue commands to others, and some groups are excluded from it. Friedmann takes Dahrendorf's idea that social conflict stems from authority relations and applies some of Dahrendorf's arguments about the possible outcomes of such conflict. But he ignores the fact that Dahrendorf's model only applies within 'imperatively coordinated associations' and attempts to show how *spatial systems* are *integrated* through authority-dependency relations. To Friedmann, then, Dahrendorf's work truly represents a promising *beginning* for formulating a general theory of polarized development. In *elaborating* that work and applying it within a spatial context, he jettisons the basic assumptions which make Dahrendorf's analysis, in any sense, meaningful.

In the 'general theory' Friedmann welds the notion that development occurs through innovation to Perroux's idea that when an entrepreneur makes an innovation, he or she can 'dominate' an economic environment, adds Dahrendorf's idea that social conflicts stem from authority relations, and projects them into a spatial context. The result is difficult to summarize briefly, and the reader is advised to consult the original text. But its basic axioms, and some of its flavour, may be gathered from the following quotations:

1 Development may be studied as a discontinuous, cumulative process that occurs as a series of innovations which become organized into innovative clusters and finally into large-scale systems of innovation. (p. 45)

2 Innovation is the successful introduction of ideas or artefacts perceived as new into a given social system. . . . Every innovation requires a measure of organization and adaptation to the conditions and functional requirements of the medium into which it is introduced or alternatively, a change in certain aspects of the medium itself. Innovation and medium must be structurally compatible. (pp. 45–6)

3 To have power is to exercise a measure of autonomy in decisions over a given environment and to have the ability to carry out these decisions. Successful innovation gives to both innovators and adopters a relative advantage over possible competitors in controlling a given environment. Successful innovation tends to increase the potential power of innovators. (p. 48)

4 Socially legitimate power will be called authority. Innovators generally seek to translate a prospective gain in power into some form of (legitimate) authority. Where the innovation is socially compatible, this process is relatively automatic. Society will reward the innovator with esteem and invest him with a measure of authority. Where the innovation is incompatible with the social medium, however, efforts to render a prospective gain in power legitimate will put innovators in conflict with the holders of established authority. (p. 49)

5 Individuals or groups seeking to legitimize prospective gains in power frequently establish alliances among themselves in order to confront established authorities from a position of collective and, consequently, greater strength. Such alliances lead to the formation of counter-elites to established authority. (p. 49)

6 The conflict between innovating counter-elites and already-estab-
lished authorities is often posed as a wider conflict over the legitimacy of some or all authority-dependency relations within a given
spatial system. It is consequently a conflict that may bear directly on
the social bases for integration of that system. This conflict can have
four possible outcomes:

Suppression: counter-elites are prevented from gaining access to positions of authority (their attempt to legitimize prospective gains in
power is frustrated).

Neutralization: established authorities oscillate between acceptance
and rejection of the proposed innovations, frequently adopting their
external forms but managing them so as to neutralize their effects.
Counter-elites fail in gaining full access to authority.

Co-optation: counter-elites are drawn into the established structure
of authority. Their innovations may be adopted, but in a highly
restricted form. Counter-elites are pacified by being allowed to
share to a limited extent in the exercise of established authority.

Replacement: counter-elites are successful in replacing the established authorities and substituting their own authority for them.

(pp. 49–50)

Friedmann applies these axioms in a spatial context by asserting that
'development', viewed as a process of innovation, 'will tend to have its
origins in a relatively small number of *centres of change* located at the
points of highest potential interaction within a communication field',
and that 'innovations will tend to spread downward and outward from
these centres to areas where the probability of potential interaction is
lower' (p. 51). Adopting, and changing the meaning of terminology used
in his earlier work, he defines the major centres of innovative change as
core regions and defines *peripheral regions* as 'territorially organized syb-
systems of society whose development path is determined chiefly by core
region institutions with respect to which they stand in a relation of substantial dependency' (p. 51). Core and periphery are then said to 'constitute a complete spatial system . . . integrated through a pattern of
authority-dependency relations that is focused on the dominant core
regions' (p. 51).

It is possible to identify such spatial systems at various scales – the
world, the multinational region, the nation, the sub-national region, the
province – and thus, according to Friedmann, 'core regions are located
within a nested hierarchy of spatial systems' (p. 54). As he puts it, 'a
second-order core region for a higher spatial system may also appear as a
first-order core for a lower-ranking system' (p. 55). This complicates

what Friedmann calls 'the actual working out of core-periphery relations' (p. 56). But he suggests some general principles which relate the pattern of core-periphery relations both to the spatial pattern of development within any given spatial system and to the development of that spatial system as a whole. Theoretically, these principles apply at any spatial scale.

The crux of the argument is that 'core regions systematically transmit impulses of innovation to the peripheries they dominate' (p. 55) and that these innovations lead to conflict between core region 'élites' and peripheral region 'élites'. This process occurs in three phases. *First*, 'core regions impose a condition of organized dependency on their peripheries' through establishing institutions in the peripheral regions that are controlled by core region authorities (p. 51). Many of these institutions may be regarded as innovations within the periphery. But they can threaten the authority positions of peripheral élites as they imply that 'decisions vitally affecting local populations will henceforth be made by core region authorities' (p. 52). *Second*, once a core region has imposed this condition of 'organized dependency', a 'self-reinforcing process' consolidates its dominance over the periphery. This is ascribed to 'six major feedback effects of core region growth':

1 *Dominance effect:* a steady weakening of the peripheral economy by a net transfer of natural, human and capital resources to the core.

2 *Information effect:* an increase in potential interaction within the core region (owing to growth of population, production and income) which tends to induce a higher rate of innovation.

3 *Psychological effect:* creation of conditions more favourable to innovation at the core, e.g. rendering opportunities for innovation more visible, creating expectations of innovation.

4 *Modernization effect:* the transformation of existing social values, behaviour and institutions in the direction of greater acceptance of, and conformity with, rapid cumulative change through innovation.

5 *Linkage effects:* the tendency of innovations to breed other innovations.

6 *Production effects:* creation of an attractive reward structure for innovative activity, operating through the exploitation by innovators of their temporary monopoly position, the appearance of linked systems of innovations and growing specialization. (p. 53)

But *third*, 'introducing core region innovations into the periphery will augment the flow of information to the dependent region from the core' and this trend will result in what Friedmann calls 'an unanticipated side-effect of core region dominance' (p. 53). This is conflict between core region and peripheral region élites. As he puts it:

> Sustained contact with the core region will tend to arouse portions of the peripheral population not only to possible new ways of life, but also to their comparative disadvantage in gaining access to them. New desires and frustrations will encourage demands for greater regional autonomy in areas of vital decision and may lead to prolonged conflict with the core.

It is this conflict, and the way in which it is resolved, which will determine both the development of any given spatial system as a whole and also the spatial patterns of development within it. Reformulating his earlier analysis of the way in which centre-periphery relations and the continuing concentration of economic activity in the 'centre' can threaten national growth, he writes:

> Up to a certain point in time, the self-reinforcing character of core region growth will tend to have positive results for the development process of the relevant spatial system; eventually, however, it will become dysfunctional, unless the spread effects of core region development to the periphery can be accelerated, and the periphery's dependence on the core region reduced. The approach of this critical turning point will be registered in the growing political and social tensions between core and periphery that are likely to drain core region strength and reduce its capacity for further development.
>
> (pp. 55–6)

The outcome of the conflict between core region and peripheral region élites is indeterminate, and depends upon whether peripheral élites are repressed, neutralized or co-opted, or succeed in replacing central élites. However, if there is 'a successful challenge of core region autonomy by their peripheries', the probability of information exchange and the probability of innovation will increase 'over the surface of a given spatial system' (p. 56). This tendency 'will induce the physical spread of existing core regions, a weakening of their hierarchical order, the emergence of new core regions on the periphery and the gradual incorporation of large parts of the periphery into one or more system cores' (p. 56). In such circumstances, development will become less polarized, in a spatial sense, and 'enclaves of economic backwardness will appear in the areas lying between expanding core regions and/or limited urban sectors of the cores themselves' (p. 56).

The 'general theory' is important within the evolution of regional development theory as it illustrates how regional theorists attempted to introduce a political dimension into their analysis in the early 1970s. At that time, various regional theorists began to argue that urban and regional development could not be analysed in purely economic terms, and that there was a need to examine power relations in spatial systems (see, for example, Hilhorst's 'domination theory of regional development', 1971). Such ideas led to the conclusion that 'attempts to change the spatial pattern of resource allocation are usually limited by the *spatial distribution* of decision-making power' (Stöhr, 1975, p. 78; emphasis added), and stimulated policy proposals such as Stöhr's 'double-forked strategy of regional development', in which regional development is stimulated not just through a re-location of economic activities within the national territory, but also through decentralization of decision-making functions and devolution of power to regional and local levels.

However, this current within mainstream regional development theory did not form the basis for the theories of urban and regional development which most directly attacked the technical rationale for the urban-industrial growth pole policies. Those theories were linked more closely to general arguments within development studies which questioned the conventional wisdom about the nature of economic and social change in poor countries by examining the position of those countries within the international economic system.

André Gunder Frank's spatial image of the 'world capitalist system'

The main protagonist in this general reappraisal of what earlier theorists regarded as the 'development' process was André Gunder Frank. In his early work, Frank totally rejected analyses of development which assumed that developing countries could be described in dualist terms and which conceptualized economic and social change as occurring through a universally applicable series of stages or through a diffusion process. Underdevelopment, he argued, is not an original condition, characterized by 'backwardness' and 'traditionalism', as in Rostow's model. 'Underdeveloped countries', as he called them, have a history and the key fact in that history is that since the beginning of the mercantile age in the sixteenth century all countries have been integrated in a world-wide system of exchange, the 'world capitalist system'. The dualist assumption, that particular areas have 'remained underdeveloped' because of their isolation from the modern centres of the world and national economy, is therefore fallacious. The evident conditions of poverty in such areas are not a consequence of the failure of western technology, capital and values to diffuse into such areas. Rather, they stem from the nature of relationships within the 'world capitalist system'.

This system is described by Frank in a model which bears a remarkable similarity to Friedmann's 'general theory'. 'As a photograph of the world taken at a point in time', he writes:

> this model consists of a world metropolis (today the United States) and its governing class, and its national and international satellites and their leaders – national satellites like the southern states of the United States, and international satellites like Sao Paulo. Since Sao Paulo is a national metropolis in its own right, the model consists further of its satellites: the provincial metropolises, like Recife or Belo Horizonte, and their regional and local satellites in turn. That is, taking a photograph of a slice of the world we get a whole chain of metropolises and satellites, which runs from the world metropolis down to the hacienda or rural merchant who are satellites of the local commercial metropolitan centre but who in their turn have peasants as their satellites. If we take a photograph of the world as a whole, we get a whole series of such constellations of metropolises and satellites.
>
> (Frank, 1967, pp. 146–7)

Within this chain of metropolitan-satellite relationships 'each metropolis holds monopoly power over its satellites' (p. 147). The source and form of monopoly has changed over time, for example, as the countries of Latin America, Africa and Asia gained political independence, or as mercantile trading firms switched to industrial investment within the underdeveloped countries. And it may also vary from place to place. But Frank takes it as axiomatic that the whole system has a monopolistic structure which leads first, to the 'misuse and misdirection of available resources throughout the whole system and metropolis–satellite chain', and second, 'as part of this misuse', to 'the expropriation and appropriation of a large part or even all of and more than the economic surplus or surplus value of the satellite by its local, regional, national or international metropolis' (p. 147).

The fact that the metropoli expropriate the *economic surplus* of their satellites and appropriate it for their own use is central to Frank's understanding of the process of development and underdevelopment. Implicit within his analysis is the argument of Baran (1957) that the size and use of the surplus is the key determinant of economic growth. Diverging from the classical Marxist concept of surplus value, which cannot be separated from the social relations of production, Baran defines the *actual surplus* within a country as the difference between current net output and current consumption, and the *potential surplus* as the difference between what could be produced and what is the minimum essential consumption. The rate of economic growth within any country may be less than that which is possible because of a gap between actual and potential surplus. If the country is totally isolated, this may occur if potential surplus is diverted into 'luxury' consumption, or 'wasteful' investment in weapon systems, or expenditure on advertising campaigns to boost demand. But if a country is integrated into the world economic system, it may occur through *the transfer of surplus* for use elsewhere.

The transfer of surplus from satellite to metropolis has a double effect. It not only stymies growth in the satellite, but also fuels growth in the metropolis. Thus, as Frank puts it, 'economic development and under-development are opposite faces of the same coin' (p. 9). The metropolis grows at the expense of its satellites, and 'polarizing tendencies' mani-fested in increasing disparities in income are evident at all levels in the metropolis—satellite chain.

Frank uses the terms 'metropolis' and 'satellite' to refer to both social groups and spatial units. In his description of the world capitalist system, the hacienda owner who hires labour or the large city merchant who lends capital to a small peasant farmer is just as much a 'metropolis' as Sao Paulo and Santiago. The trend towards metropolitan-satellite polarization which Frank identifies thus refers as much to increasing social inequality as increasing spatial inequality. But the spatial image of a chain of relations extending from the centres of the world capitalist system to the farthest outpost and peasant suggests an immediate explanation of regional and rural—urban disparities within underdeveloped countries.

Poor regions and rural localities are poor not because of their isolation or lack of integration into the world system. Rather, they have been 'under-developed' through their close ties with that system. The benefits of urban-industrial growth do not 'trickledown' into surrounding 'traditional' hinterlands. Quite the reverse – the national and regional metropoli within underdeveloped countries appropriate the economic surplus from these areas. Yet their own development is itself 'limited' and 'misdirected', for their surplus is in turn appropriated for use higher up the chain.

David Slater: colonialism and the spatial structure of underdevelopment

Within Anglo-American regional development theory, one of the first thinkers to take up Frank's idea of the world capitalist system and to apply it to understanding spatial patterns within 'underdeveloped' countries was David Slater. In an important paper (Slater, 1974), he exposes the Rostovian and dualist assumptions which underpin many of the analyses

of regional development undertaken in the 1960s and in a longer monograph, entitled 'Underdevelopment and spatial inequality: approaches
to the problem of regional planning in the Third World' (1975) he
describes the spatial structure of underdevelopment which has evolved
within African countries under colonialism.

Slater defines 'colonialism' as 'a formal device by which large parts of
Latin America, Africa and Asia became incorporated into the international capitalist economy' (Slater, 1975, p. 137). His view of the world
economy under colonialism is very similar to that portrayed in Frank's
early work. Each colony, he suggests, trades largely or exclusively with
its respective metropolitan country (Figure 21). The key positions within

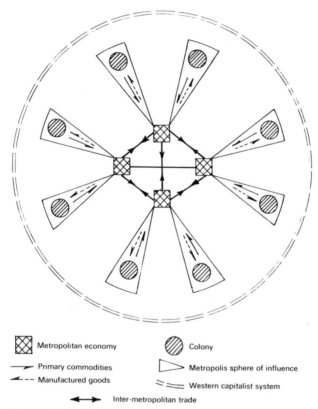

Metropolitan economy   Colony

Primary commodities   Metropolis sphere of influence

Manufactured goods   Western capitalist system

Inter-metropolitan trade

Figure 21 European metropoles and African colonies: a centre-periphery presentation of their trading links.

Source: Slater, 1975, Figure 3.1.

the various colonial economies are controlled by foreign metropolitan capital, and mining and commercial companies usually had monopolistic power. The colonial monetary system, with no exchange controls, allowed the 'siphoning of funds' from the colony, and the drain of 'surplus' was further promoted by the 'unequal exchange' (in Emmanuel's sense) of agricultural commodities produced in the colonies for industrial goods produced in the metropoles. Local capital accumulation was thus severely restricted.

Slater summarizes the impact of colonialism in Africa with the blunt statement that 'it was integration that produced underdevelopment' (p. 137). But his main concern is to examine the spatial structure *of* underdevelopment and to do so he constructs an historical schema which portays the evolving spatial patterns in four phases:

1 Pre-colonial spatial structure (before the 1880s);
2 Colonial penetration, initial concentration and the beginnings of internal expansion (1880s to 1914);
3 Colonial organization and continued extension (1919–1950/60);
4 Neo-colonial concentration and limited attempts at restructuring (1950/60 and onwards). (Figure 22)

The schema contrasts sharply with Friedmann's evolutionary model of the 'stages of spatial organization' which any country passes through as its economy grows. Slater's first phase is not characterized by a patchwork of isolated, autarchic local economies, as in Friedmann's model, but rather by developing interregional trading networks. The volume of both interregional and intra-regional trade was low, Slater notes, but the pre-colonial and pre-capitalist spatial structure 'had some degree of internal cohesion and interdependence' (p. 141). And after the first phase, what happened was not a process in which the space economy became increasingly integrated. Capitalist penetration, on the contrary, resulted in external integration and internal *disintegration*. Indeed, the key feature of the space economy after the colonial impact was that it was 'internally atomized and externally tied' (p. 168).

Slater distinguishes two phases in this process of change. In the initial phase of colonial penetration, the drawing of the political boundaries which defined the colonial territories itself led to 'the atomization of space', for the boundaries bore 'little or no relation to indigenous social organizations and trading networks' (p. 140). The 'capitalist mode of production', in the form of plantations, settler estates and mining concerns, was introduced into 'predominantly pre-capitalist' territories during this phase, and railways were constructed to serve these limited capitalist enclaves. Some urban centres began to grow during this period.

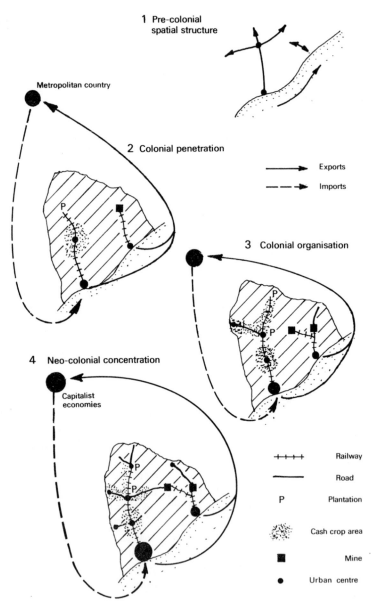

1 Pre-colonial spatial structure

Metropolitan country

2 Colonial penetration

Exports

Imports

3 Colonial organisation

4 Neo-colonial concentration

Capitalist economies

++++ Railway

Road

P Plantation

Cash crop area

Mine

Urban centre

Figure 22 The evolution of spatial structure under colonialism.

Source: adapted from Slater, 1975.

But they were not necessarily the same places as the centres based on the indigenous economy, some of which declined, and they mainly functioned as 'ports fulfilling the role of receiving and exporting centres for the colonial empires', 'intermediary points in the distribution and marketing of agricultural produce', 'towns which had a very close connection with the exploitation of minerals', 'outlying strategic centres which were formed for the purpose of colonial security', or 'as a policing agent for the countryside being responsible for the collection of taxes and the extraction of surplus from the rural areas' (p. 144). The focal points for administrative and military control were, of course, the colonial capitals, which were often also ports.

The spatial extent of capitalist penetration was limited in the initial phase. But the second phase saw 'the development of capitalism in depth' in the areas of initial concentration and 'the development of capitalism in breadth', that is, the extension of capitalist domination to new areas. The spatial extension of export crop production was a notable feature of this period, and by the 1930s, in a colony like Tanganyika, it was possible to identify three distinct types of socio-economic region:

1 those areas that specialized in production for export, and the towns;
2 'surrounding zones' which supplied the export-producing regions with food and other services; and
3 'extending out beyond the export and food-producing regions, peripheral zones which either supplied migrant labour or involuted in near-isolation from the dominant export-oriented areas'.   (p. 154)

The expansion of the transportation system was an integral part of the consolidation and extension of colonial control. Road transport assumed more significance in the later part of the second phase and opened up more areas of the colonial territory. But the colonial capitals and the ports remained the focal points of the transport network, and the alignment of routes transformed some parts of the continent into 'one-line economies'. In French West Africa, for example:

Each economic region corresponds to a 'one-line economy', an axis based externally on a port where imports and exports were brought, and comprising a series of adjacent branches which subdivide in turn until they peter out in the bush. The axis and branches were followed by an ascending current, that of produce imported and by a descending current, that of exportable products. Each region resembled a kind of lung with its system of veins and arteries running parallel, receiving its oxygen at the level of agricultural production. But the heart was placed outside, far beyond the seas; the impulses that regulated the nature and the intensity of the flow were external ones.

(Suret-Canale, quoted in Slater, 1975, p. 145)

In the creation of such one-line economies, contiguous zones were 'in a combined and contradictory fashion ... internally disintegrated' (p. 145).

In the final phase of Slater's historical schema, the former colonies have gained political independence but they remain as 'neo-colonies' which are still economically dependent on a series of metropoles. During this period, some attempts at restructuring have been made, and these include growth pole planning. But such efforts have met with little success. 'The spatial structure bequeathed from the colonial period remains noticeably rigid' (p. 146) and import-substitution industrialization policies have even reinforced the concentration of industrial and commercial activities in the capital cities and major ports. This reflects their *continuing* integration into the international capitalist economy. In countries which have disengaged from that economy, such as Cuba, North Korea, Vietnam and China, 'their previous spatial disintegration has been replaced by a system of spatial organization which utilizes to the full the resources of all of the various territories so as to satisfy internal needs'. In those countries, 'interregional interdependencies and exchanges have evolved and matured as an important solidifying agent of national economic integration'. *But*, 'so long as the space economy is internally atomized and externally tied, such development is not possible' (p. 158).

MILTON SANTOS: THE SHARED SPACE

The analyses of Frank and Slater fall within a branch of development studies which is sometimes called 'dependency theory'. This body of ideas is so varied that dependency 'theory' should best be regarded as a paradigm, or framework, for analysing change in the poor countries of the world. All theorists who adopt this framework take it as axiomatic that:

(i) processes of change can only be understood through examining a country's history;

(ii) what has happened, and what is occurring now, *within* the poorer countries reflects their *external* relationships, in particular the manner of their integration into the world economic system; and

(iii) poor countries occupy a dependent position within that system, dependency being most generally defined as 'a conditioning situation in which the economies of one group of countries are conditioned by the development and expansion of others'.

(dos Santos, 1969, p. 76)

The part of the work of Frank and Slater which I have summarized exemplifies an extreme position within the dependency approach. With his arresting phrase 'the development of underdevelopment', Frank adopts a 'stagnationist thesis' which suggests that the conditioning situation of dependency leads to a constant worsening of economic conditions within the underdeveloped countries. The 'contradictory combination' of external capitalist penetration and internal spatial disintegration which Slater describes is the spatial counterpart of the thesis of increasing social immiseration.

Other dependency theorists, most notably Cardoso and Falletto (1979), have adopted a more flexible position and argued that some form of development is possible within a dependency situation. However, such 'dependent' development is regarded as 'distorted' or 'limited' development for it is not 'self-centred', but 'associated' with development occurring elsewhere. In analyses made from that position (which Frank himself adopts in his later work), more emphasis is placed on the nature of the social and political structures created by the external relationships of dependent countries, and on how the internal dynamic of these structures, in conjunction with the external relationships, constrain 'authentic' development. This leads to a much more sophisticated view of the process of change in dependent countries as the work of Milton Santos shows.

Santos elaborates his ideas in a book with the intriguing title, *The Shared Space* (1979). In that book, he is concerned to present a new theory of urbanization in underdeveloped countries. Existing urban and regional policy, he argues, is based on 'immature theories' which assume that patterns of change in the industrial west also apply in less developed countries. He rejects this assumption emphatically, asserting that in order to understand urbanization it is necessary to adopt a historical methodology and that 'a particularly fruitful approach to evaluating the historical processes that have operated in a given country is to think in terms of *modernizations*' (p. 12).

'A modernization', he writes, 'is the diffusion of an innovation from a "polar" region to peripheral subordinate regions, and/or from an anterior historical period to a subsequent one' (pp. 12–13). The 'polar' regions on a world scale are the developed countries and the historical evolution of any 'peripheral' Third World countries may be understood by examining 'when it first felt the impact of external forces of modernization' and 'the sequence of successive modernizations' (p. 13). Broadly, Santos suggests, it is possible to identify three distinct phases of modernization in peripheral countries: a *commercial* phase, which lasted from the end of the sixteenth century to the industrial revolution in western Europe, a phase which corresponds to the transport revolution in world shipping; an *industrial* phase, from the mid eighteenth to the mid twentieth century, which corresponds to the industrial revolution and its consolidation; and a *technological* phase which began after the Second World War and is associated with the application of new technology in industrial processes, and the spread of rich-country consumption norms in the periphery. The forces of economic and social change are said to be different in each of these phases and Santos concentrates upon the nature of urbanization in peripheral countries during the latest phase.

The use of the term 'modernization' within this context may be somewhat confusing, for the word usually connotes something 'good'. However, Santos's argument falls squarely within the dependency viewpoint that externally conditioned development is 'distorted' development. 'Contemporary modernization', he writes, 'is controlled by large-scale industry, which basically consists of multinational firms and their supporting systems' (p. 15). These firms invest selectively in the most profitable sectors of the economy. They transfer capital for reinvestment back to the rich countries of the world. And they tend to occupy a monopolistic position within the local markets, allowing them to fix prices and maintain excess capacity in local plants. Their activities are encouraged by state policy, either through the complicity or weakness of the local ruling class, which subsidizes foreign investment under the ideology of promoting growth. Under these circumstances the economy as a whole may grow. But as investment tends to be capital-intensive, as the local process of capital accumulation is short-circuited by the transfer of profits, as local demand is depressed by monopolistic pricing, and as the state has little revenue to support indigenous ventures, few employment opportunities are generated and thus the mass of the population in urban centres is forced to subsist by engaging in such 'informal' activities as petty trading or petty commodity production.

The urban economy in underdeveloped countries during the present era of 'modernization' thus consists of two circuits: *an upper circuit*, comprising such activities as banking, export trade and industry, 'modern' urban industry, trade and services, and wholesaling and trucking; and a *lower circuit*, comprising 'non-capital-intensive forms of manufacturing, non-modern services generally provided at the "retail" level and non-modern and small-scale trade' (p. 18). Each of these circuits has different characteristics (Table 6). But more significantly, for the analysis of the

Table 6 Characteristics of the two circuits of the urban economy in under-developed countries

	Upper circuit	*Lower circuit*
Technology	capital-intensive	labour-intensive
Organization	bureaucratic	primitive
Capital	abundant	limited
Labour	limited	abundant
Regular wages	prevalent	exceptionally
Inventories	large quantities and/or high quality	small quantities, poor quality
Prices	generally fixed	negotiable between buyer and seller (haggling)
Credit	from banks, institutional	personal, non-institutional
Profit margin	small per unit; but with large turnover, considerable in aggregate (exception – luxuries)	large per unit; but small turnover
Relations with customers	impersonal and/or on paper	direct, personalized
Fixed costs	substantial	negligible
Advertisement	necessary	none
Re-use of goods	none (waste)	frequent
Overhead capital	essential	not essential
Government aid	extensive	none or almost none
Direct dependence on foreign countries	great; externally orientated	small or none

Source: Santos, 1979, Table 2.2.

urbanization process, there is a specific pattern of relationship between them which occurs within any specific urban economy and also in terms of city–hinterland relations (Figure 23).

To Santos, the failure to recognize that the city consists of a 'shared space' has stymied analyses of urbanization in underdeveloped countries. 'For too long', he writes, 'both economists and geographers have identified the modern component of the urban economy with the whole city. . . . Most research thus examines only one sector of the city rather than all of it, thereby precluding the emergence of an authentic theory of urbanization' (p. 9). His aim is to construct such an 'authentic' theory, and to do so he considers that it is necessary to analyse the interplay of

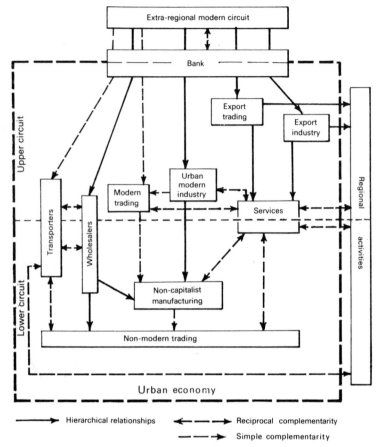

Figure 23 Relationships between the two circuits of the urban economy.
Source: Santos, 1979, Figure 1.

the two circuits – or the 'formal' and 'informal' sectors, to use the jargon which is more common within development studies – *in a spatial context*.

The wealth of detail within Santos's book precludes a complete summary of the many points which he raises. But he asserts that 'the recognition of the two circuits necessitates a reappraisal of concepts such as urban exports, central places and growth poles, which have until now furnished the theoretical basis of regional planning' (p. 9). And I shall focus, in the rest of this section, upon arguments which directly undermine the technical rationale for urban-industrial growth pole policies.

First, it is necessary to emphasize that upper circuit industries tend to be controlled by multinational corporations and to be monopolistic.

Both these facets of contemporary industrialization in 'underdeveloped' countries have general consequences which are ignored in regional analyses which consider industrialization as an abstract process, and merely focus upon the growth performance of particular sectors. Foreign capital investments are made selectively in totally unconnected industries and this means that there are few local linkages. According to Santos, 'the harmonious growth of the upper circuit [which is envisaged by Boudeville and Friedmann] can only take place when policy is formulated in the context of national and urban space'. But, 'in reality, there exists a world system of relations, dominated by private interests which intrinsically oppose, by all possible means, any effort at local integration, consequently blocking all initiatives in *authentic* national development' (pp. 56–7). The idea that it is possible to plan 'a spatially unified and interlinked industrial structure' in such circumstances is fanciful. The monopolistic position of upper circuit industries, which is often created by state policy, similarly implies that the mere establishment of industries within a country is unlikely to have the desired 'propulsive' effects. On the contrary, 'the classical conditions of development are blocked by the development of monopolies . . . [and] the economy is soon condemned to stagnation' (p. 66).

Going further, Santos suggests that it is possible to identify two different types of industry in underdeveloped countries: those oriented to supply the domestic market (which have often developed through a process of import-substitution industrialization); and those supplying an external market, either through the preliminary processing of local resources, or (as has become more common in certain countries such as South Korea and Taiwan since the 1960s) through the manufacture of consumer goods. And each has a distinct locational pattern with respect to different types of urban centres. These are classified in a rough hierarchy as: (i) *local towns* (or cities) which 'develop in response to new (usually consumption) demands' and which 'constitute the first urban tier able to satisfy the minimum basic demands of a given population'; (ii) *intermediate cities*, which 'are a response to more sophisticated demands and are characterized by increased production and/or distribution capacity'; and (iii) the *metropoli*, which are 'responsible for macro-spatial organization', and are said to be '*complete*', if they are 'capable of responding autonomously to most of its social and economic needs, such as the production of capital goods and/or the adaptation of foreign technology to the requirements of the national economy', and '*partial*', if they are not (pp. 152–3).

According to Santos, the probability of industry setting up outside the metropoli is greater for export-oriented production than domestically oriented production. This is because the former type of industry does not need a local market of any particular size, and because 'external economies' may be created within the large-scale corporations setting up factories to produce for export. This makes export-oriented industries more locationally flexible and thus it is particularly easy for a government to attract such activities to poor regions through the provision of subsidies and the establishment of local infrastructure in the form of an industrial estate. But the urban-industrial concentration that develops as a result of such investment almost always has 'the characteristics of an enclave' (p. 185), for it is 'externally oriented *both* in terms of its supply of factor inputs *and* the demand for its output' (p. 184, emphasis added). 'Little local dynamic is exerted by these industries', and although they contribute to aggregate economic growth, the infrastructural investments modify 'the organization of national space' in favour of foreign interests, and the subsidies absorb scarce public revenue.

Domestically oriented industries tend to be concentrated in the metropoli which have 'the locational advantages of city size, degree of cosmopolitanism, externalities and the existence of a national and regional infrastructure serving the city . . . and greater accessibility to general and specialized information' (p. 178). Intermediate cities and local towns have a low potential for supporting such upper circuit industry because local and regional markets are small. And improvements in transport, rather than increasing the attractiveness of these centres to such activity, have actually had contrary effects, because with these improvements, the entire national market may be served from a few production points for some products. A vicious circle of stagnation may thus be started: 'If a city does not produce a certain product, the product will be sold there at a higher price; consequently the residents buy less and prices increase even more. As for mobile, well-off consumers, the intermediate city can be bypassed by purchasing in the more important cities' (p. 172). In such circumstances, 'the lack of dynamism of the urban economy recoils on the region and vice versa' (p. 172). Regional disparities are accentuated; the locational advantages of the metropoli are increased; and there is little likelihood of industry 'filtering down the urban hierarchy', as Berry suggests.

While upper circuit industries are established for the purpose of making profit, lower circuit activities proliferate because of the need of the urban populations of underdeveloped countries simply to survive. The high technology, capital-intensive character of the industries which are set up 'inhibit the growth of upper circuit employment' and thus 'as the host country industrializes, urbanization becomes more and more tertiary in character' (pp. 82–3). Within the cities, most of the population are forced to eke out a living in petty production and petty distributional activities in which employment 'is seldom permanent and its remuneration is often at or below the subsistence level' (p. 21).

Entry into the lower circuit is said to be relatively easy and has a 'self-inflationary' character in that it caters for the consumption demands of the poorer sections of the population, often by providing short-term credit. But the fractionalization of activities between more and more people means that profit margins are usually low, and turnover small. Capital circulates, but is not accumulated. Thus, Santos writes, 'poverty and the lower circuit are locked together in an indisputable relationship of cause and effect' (p. 85). Within the cities, therefore, *within* the so-called 'growth centres', there are gross income disparities, with the conditions of absolute poverty being manifested in the formation of shanty-towns.

Santos argues that just as it is possible to relate the distribution of upper circuit industry to different types of city, so the significance of the lower circuit varies within the urban hierarchy (Figure 24). The pattern reflects the fact that 'the lower circuit is *created* by demand' (p. 24). Competition between the upper and lower circuit for the control of the same market may mean that some lower circuit activities exist in smaller urban centres as 'they fulfil the functions of an often non-existent modern service-sector' and they are protected by distance from the upper circuit production points. But usually the upper and lower circuit do not compete for the same market; they cater instead for different income groups. The absolute size of the lower circuit is then greatest in the metropoli as the demand of the mass of the urban population is greatest there. Though it

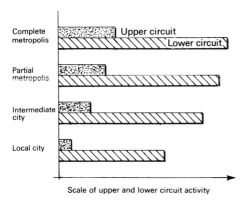

Figure 24 The relative significance of the two circuits in different types of city.

Source: adapted from Santos, 1979, Figure 12.

should be noted that the *relative* significance of lower circuit activities, *vis-à-vis* the upper circuit, increases in local towns.

Although both upper and lower circuit activities have distinctive locational patterns within the urban hierarchy, Santos stresses, throughout his book, that they cannot be understood in isolation from each other. The relationships between the two circuits are said to be both complementary and competitive. Complementarity is found when 'the activities of one circuit require the inputs from the other circuit' and when 'certain activities of one circuit constitute external economies for the other' (p. 139); and competitive relations occur when activities in both circuits compete for the same market. But in either case, 'upper circuit activity tends to dominate the entire economy', and the lower circuit 'tends to be controlled, subordinated and dependent' (p. 24). When the two circuits are in competition, the establishment of new upper circuit activities tends to eliminate lower circuit activities, or to stymie the evolution towards more complex organizational forms. When the two circuits are complementary, the upper circuit tends to siphon off profits made in the lower circuit.

Santos does not specify exactly how this 'upward flow of capital' occurs. One could hypothesize various mechanisms (see Bromley and Gerry, 1979). But its significance lies in the fact that it limits capital accumulation within the lower circuit and perpetuates the poverty of the mass of the population. As Santos himself puts it, 'through the multiple contacts it establishes with the mass of the population, the lower circuit is in a position to collect daily savings and earnings and transfer them to the capitalist sector' (p. 204). The relationships between the two circuits thus both promote capital accumulation within the upper circuit and at the same time help to sustain the market upon which the existence of the lower circuit depends.

Santos argues that the 'upward flow of capital' has 'no real counterpart in the opposite direction' (p. 204). And, therefore, the linkages between the upper and lower circuit are not of the propulsive kind envisaged by growth pole theorists. On the contrary: they are part of the process through which the poor finance the technological modernization from which they gain so little.

In terms of spatial relationships, Santos suggests that 'the lower circuit finds the elements of its integration in the city and its regions, while the upper circuit usually seeks this integration outside the city and its region' (p. 24). Within a country, the sphere of influence of upper circuit activities is discontinuous and characterized by '*vertical*' relations *within* the urban hierarchy (Figure 25). These relations are 'asymmetrical' in the sense that there is a downward flow of goods – 'all agglomerations

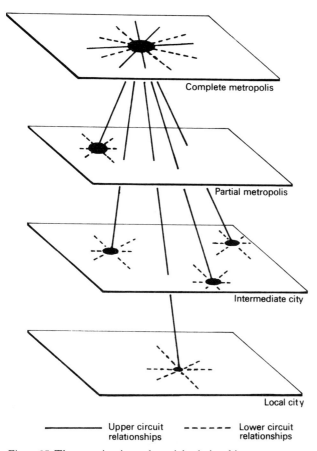

Complete metropolis

Partial metropolis

Intermediate city

Local city

—————— Upper circuit relationships   – – – – – Lower circuit relationships

Figure 25 The two circuits and spatial relationships.

rely on higher level cities for the commodities they are unable to produce themselves' (p. 157); and with industrialization and transport improvement, 'a short-circuiting within the urban system takes place: lower level agglomerations no longer need to interact with cities immediately above them in the urban hierarchy, but can deal directly with the most important cities' (p. 157). 'The task of maintaining continuous relations with the rural areas' is generally left to the lower circuit, and it is through its activities that the *horizontal* rural–urban relations are articulated.

But the mere presence of these linkages does not mean that rural producers benefit from the growth of the cities. Producers are generally in a weak bargaining position both as sellers of foodstuffs and buyers of urban goods. There may be a long chain of middlemen between the farmer and consumer, and wholesaler and transporters often occupy a strategic position in the chain that allows them to depress farm gate prices. The reduction of rural purchasing power further limits the 'development potential' of small towns and intermediate cities. Yet at the same time it increases the upward flow of rural migrants to the larger cities which in turn inflates the numbers of people trying to survive through lower circuit employment, thus further limiting the possibility of capital accumulation within the lower circuit. The rural-urban linkages do not therefore act as channels through which growth trickles down into rural areas. Rather, they are linkages of shared poverty.

Santos's prognosis for the future is bleak. 'If present trends continue', he writes:

> There will be an accelerated circulation of the means of production, commodities, capital and labour engaged in technologically modern activities, thereby accelerating the outflow of surplus value, since those enterprises capable of mobilizing these productive factors would be most able to control the economy.
>
> It is clear that this situation will only benefit the upper circuit: the lower circuit will become progressively 'lower'. In absolute terms the upper and lower circuit will develop [i.e. expand] but the relative gap between them will become pronounced.   (p. 199)

In general, then, 'the spatial diffusion and penetration of the upper circuit also means the diffusion of impoverishment' (p. 205).

CONCLUSION

The theories of urban and regional development considered in this chapter are based on very different development assumptions to those which provide the explanatory basis for urban-industrial growth pole strategies. Friedmann, rejecting his earlier synthesis, argues that regional development should be understood as a political process. And Slater and Santos suggest that spatial patterns in 'developing' countries must be analysed historically and take account of the dependent position of those countries in the international economic system.

All these theories may be said to be 'anti-theses' in the sense that they were put forward in opposition to existing conventional wisdom. But, in addition, those elaborated from a dependency perspective are antithetical in a stronger sense. They *invert* the explanatory propositions which support the urban-industrial growth pole strategy. An oligopolistic market structure, according to Perroux, enhanced the growth effects of a propulsive unit. Now, a non-competitive market structure is said to lead to stagnation. Friedmann, in his earlier (1966) formulation, suggested that growth is externally induced. Now, external demand and external capital are said to promote the 'development of underdevelopment'. Before, improved transport and communications systems were seen as part of a process of spatial integration. Now, such improvements are said to engender spatial *dis*integration. Berry argued that the diffusion of innovations 'brings' growth and income to cities and regions. Now, it supposedly leads to the 'diffusion of impoverishment'.

The validity of the alternative theories ultimately depends on the validity of the development perspective upon which they are based. But the reader has probably noticed a structural similarity in the logic of explanation adopted in theories based on different development perspectives. This similarity reflects the way in which 'space' is related to 'development' in the different theories. New conceptions of the development process have been introduced. But the conception of space remains the same.

This theme will be taken up in the third section of the book. But first it is necessary to complete the survey of ideas within the field by examining some regional planning strategies which have been suggested as alternatives to the urban-industrial growth pole strategy. Some of these alternatives take account of political dimensions of the regional development process and the influence of the condition of dependency, and some do not. But they are all based on a re-evaluation of what planning 'development' means and what the general goals of a national development strategy should be.

5

Neo-populist regional development strategies

THE QUESTION OF NATIONAL DEVELOPMENT STRATEGY

In the early 1950s when economists first began studying the particular conditions of 'underdeveloped countries', as they were then called, it was often suggested that those countries were locked within self-perpetuating vicious circles of poverty. The key question was to determine how growth could be *started* and then *sustained*. There were invariably disagreements on this issue within the literature, but many economists agreed that because of the existence of dynamic production complementarities, such as those identified by Perroux, the price mechanism could not allocate resources effectively and therefore there was some need for central planning of the 'development' of national economies. A country was generally said to be 'developing' when its national economy was growing, and growth was accompanied by structural change. And in addition it was usually assumed that such 'development' required industrialization, and that the planning strategy which was most likely to promote 'development' was one which gave priority to the establishment and expansion of manufacturing activities.

The urban-industrial growth pole strategy is, in a loose way, the spatial corollary of this growth orthodoxy. The connection is only loose for, within the orthodoxy, there are some disagreements about the best development strategy and the spatial implications of the different viewpoints have never been fully worked out.

Three different theses about the best development strategy may be related to the growth pole approach. The first is that proposed by Rosenstein-Rodan who, as early as 1943, argued that, because individual investors could not be expected to take account of the external effects of their actions, it was desirable in situations of development that 'the whole of industry to be created is treated and planned like one huge firm or trust' (Rosenstein-Rodan, 1943, p. 204). This idea was later elaborated into 'the theory of the big push', which postulated that a critical minimum level of co-ordinated investment was a pre-condition for a successful development strategy (Rosenstein-Rodan, 1961). The second is the 'unbalanced growth strategy' proposed by Hirschman (1958). This approach, discussed in chapter 3, was deliberately formulated as an anti-thesis to 'balanced growth' strategies such as Rosenstein-Rodan's. And the third is a strategy designed to secure a Rostovian 'take-off', in which the propulsive industries are treated as leading sectors.

The idea that industrial investment concentrated in a few large urban centres can induce further regional and rural growth is most closely related to Hirschman's unbalanced growth strategy. Indeed, in development studies in general, Perroux's concept of '*le pôle de croissance*' has been incorporated in the debates on the merits of such a strategy. But within regional studies, the spatial transformation of the growth pole concept has obscured the general strategic assumptions of different growth pole strategies.

As indicated in chapter 3, Boudeville uses Hirschman's concept of backward and forward linkage effects to indicate how the growth of a polarized region may be promoted. But at the same time he notes that the *joint creation* of interrelated industries as a 'development block' can enhance the regional propulsive effects of the planners' interventions. Such 'industrial complex planning', as it is called by North American regional scientists (see Isard and Vietorisz, 1955), is the spatial corollary of Rosenstein-Rodan's 'theory of the big push', *against* which Hirschman was arguing.

Friedmann's strategy of 'activating core regions' seems designed to secure a *regional* take-off in the Rostovian sense. He even suggests that 'core regions may be thought of as equivalent, in spatial terms, to the leading production sectors of an economy' (Friedmann, 1973a, p. 141). But if one wishes to promote a Rostovian take-off, it is certainly necessary to work out how all the essential conditions for a national take-off apply in a regional context. According to Rostow, these conditions are:

1 a rise in the rate of productive investment from say, 5 per cent or less to over 10 per cent of national income;
2 the development of one or more substantial manufacturing sectors, with a high rate of growth;
3 the existence or quick emergence of a political, social and institutional framework which exploits the impulses to expansion in the modern sector and the potential external economy effects of the take-off and gives to growth an on-going character.

(Rostow, 1971, p. 39)

But in Friedmann's proposals of 1966, the implications of *all* of these are never elaborated.

The lack of clarity in the strategic assumptions which underlie urban-industrial growth pole policies has been a basic source of confusion within the regional development literature. But as such policies are loosely related to the growth orthodoxy of the late 1950s and 1960s, they may be challenged not just by questioning the *explanations* which suggest that regional and rural growth depends on urbanization and industrialization, but also by questioning the basic strategic assumptions which were broadly part of that orthodoxy.

Throughout the period in which the growth orthodoxy was widely accepted by development experts, some argued that it was necessary for planners to allocate resources to agriculture as well as industry. And in the early 1970s, the importance of giving priority to rural development was more firmly asserted by the suggestion that planning 'development' was not solely a matter of increasing the national growth rate and engendering structural change in the economy. In an important paper entitled 'The meaning of development', Seers argued that development strategies needed to take account of poverty and employment, and should foster self-reliance. The World Bank advocated a strategy of *Redistribution with growth*, which entailed the identification of poor 'target groups' within a country and the formulation of policies to raise both their productivity and incomes. And the ILO launched its World Employment Programme, in which employment-oriented development strategies were devised for a number of countries.

Kitching (1982) describes these policies, and the theories which underlie them, as 'neo-populist'. He identifies 'populism' with a current in European and Russian thinking which arose at the beginning of the nineteenth century as a reaction to the dehumanizing effects of industrialization and urbanization. Defined in these terms – and some would disagree with the particular use of the label – 'populist' thought is evident in romantic literature, art and poetry which celebrates the virtues of the rural good life and in economic and social theory which argues that it is possible for progress in social well-being to occur within a society based on small-scale agricultural production and artisanal industries. 'Neo-populist' theory, according to Kitching's definition, emerged in Soviet Russia and eastern Europe after the First World War and is characterized by much more sophisticated economic arguments which were designed to show that there was an alternative way of achieving higher material living standards than the path of state socialist industrialization which was eventually adopted by Stalin. Kitching shows that the major arguments of the development theorists of the 1970s who challenged the 'growth orthodoxy' of the 1960s reiterate the arguments earlier in the century, and that the underlying aim – that is, to detail 'an alternative pattern of trajectory of economic development which can be just as effective or more effective than large-scale industrialization in eliminating mass poverty, and can also be less costly in social and human terms' (Kitching, 1982, p. 21) – is exactly the same.

Once 'neo-populist' thinking is adopted, the theoretical rationale for an urban-industrial growth pole strategy loses its force. It does not matter whether it can achieve its *growth* objectives or not. The policy may be deemed to be inadequate because the objectives are wrong from the start. The problem of planning regional development has been re-defined. And the task of the regional analyst is to formulate regional development strategies which take account of the new concerns with preserving equality and community, fostering the evolution of small-scale enterprise, promoting peasant agriculture, engaging 'the people' in the development process, and removing the bias towards big cities, large-scale industries, and centralized forms of organization. The present chapter outlines some of the strategies suggested.

URBANIZATION POLICIES FOR RURAL DEVELOPMENT

E. A. J. Johnson: market towns as rural growth centres

One of the first alternatives to the urban-industrial growth pole strategy was put forward by a North American economic historian, E. A. J. Johnson. As I indicated in chapter 2, Johnson argues that a primate city size distribution hinders a country's development. He sees the increasing volume of migration from villages and small towns to the large metropoli as entailing high social *and* economic costs: it is 'a cruel process of disordering social change that has led to the waste of vast amounts of productive energy and creativity, which could have been utilized for constructive development tasks' (Johnson, 1970, pp. 161–2). The process has been encouraged by development planners who 'have ascribed to large-scale industrial establishments puissant and mysterious developmental powers' (p. 379) and who have accepted 'the euphoric, though false, myth of urban magnetic fields that automatically diffuse development' (p. 378).

These myths Johnson debunks. But he is careful to avoid the counter-myth which idealizes village life. 'In a world as now economically organized', he writes, 'the village of four or five hundred people is an archaic extravagance that a developing country cannot afford. It wastes land, limits capital formation and above all misuses manpower' (p. 375). Urbanization is not *in itself* bad. The problem is the spatial and hier-archical distribution of the urban population. In the end, developing countries need to bridge 'the void between the ubiquitous villages and parasitic great cities' (p. 212) by building a 'proper' Löschian hierarchy of urban centres which ranges from small towns to intermediate cities and national metropoli. But this task cannot be done from the top of the urban hierarchy downwards, as Berry and Friedmann suggest. What is required is a development policy which creates a network of small market towns and which integrates the villages into larger 'functional economic areas' which are focalized upon these towns.

As a first step in this policy, a well-dispersed network of promising 'growth points' should be selected in different regions of a country. Johnson does not specify the criteria that may be used to select these 'growth points'. They are merely described as 'rural sites which have better than average prospects for becoming future agro-urban communities' (p. 219). He is also ambivalent towards the question of which regions should receive priority. On the one hand, the future prospects of the new market towns are likely to be most assured in regions with the greatest agricultural output and with the highest potential productive capacity. But on the other hand, he notes that concentrating investment in such regions will increase regional disparities in productivity, farm incomes and the commercialization of agriculture and perhaps, in the long run, act as a constraint on development. However, he argues strongly that, within the selected regions, it is necessary to adopt a 'saturation' approach so that 'something similar to the classical landscape of market hexagons might result' (p. 218). And he is clear about the major elements of any town-building programme.

It requires, first, the creation of institutions, such as properly supervised markets, vocational and general schools, banks and credit unions, clinics and health centres. It requires the co-ordination of public capital investment in projects such as rice mills or grain storage facilities, and their concentration within the selected centres. It requires infrastructural investments, in electricity, but most important of all in road construction, which will strengthen the locational advantages of the small towns to private entrepreneurs. And it requires the creation of industrial estates and the provision of incentives to encourage small-scale 'modern' manufacturing activity. The most appropriate industries, according to Johnson, are those which are labour-intensive and which either serve the local market with consumer goods such as soap, matches and hand tools or process local agricultural produce. But with careful planning, it is possible to implant large-scale 'key' industries into some of the centres and, à la Hirschman and Perroux, realize beneficial linkage effects.

All this may seem prohibitively costly, given the resource constraints within which the governments of most developing countries work. But

Johnson believes that the present government capital budget would be used much more effectively if allocations took account of *spatial* priorities as well as sectoral priorities. It would be necessary to establish some form of planning authority at a local and regional level. But then, existing capital allocations could be co-ordinated within the framework of the town-building programme. Moreover, scarce resources currently absorbed in large-scale metropolitan industry could be diverted towards promoting small industry in market towns and the smaller cities. Such a commitment to industrial dispersal would certainly entail the loss of some economies of scale and the agglomeration economies which accrue to industrialists in the metropoli. But, Johnson notes, it is a more economically viable way of bringing 'the benefits of modern industrialization to the villages' than a policy of direct rural industrialization. And in the dispersion of industry to small towns, 'hidden resources of innovation and creativity might be released' (p. 250).

Moreover, the town-building programme, which Johnson envisages, is not designed merely to benefit town-dwellers. Indeed, the basis of his proposal is the observation, which he supports with historical evidence from England, Belgium, Japan and the USA, that development requires 'agrarian commercialization' and that agrarian commercialization in turn requires the creation of a network of small market towns. The process of agrarian commercialization occurs when farmers become more closely integrated into the market economy both in terms of the purchase of inputs to the production process and in terms of the scale of output. It is possible to achieve this through establishing peasant plantations or state farms, or through collective farms. But Johnson rejects the former as uneconomic and the latter as 'congenitally unacceptable to most peasant communities' (p. 207). This leaves the small-scale farmer improvement approach as the only viable alternative.

The problem, then, is how to promote the commercialization of small-scale peasant agriculture. In arguing that it can only be achieved through the creation of small market towns, Johnson makes three major assumptions about the nature of the agrarian economy in developing countries. First, most farmers are mainly only producing to meet their own subsistence needs. Second, the stagnation of agricultural output does not reflect the inefficiency of small-scale farmers, or their commitment to 'traditional' methods of production and aversion to change. 'He [the subsistence farmer] does not need education and psychological reorientation', Johnson writes; 'what he lacks is a wider marketing system in which his uncanny skill in combining productive factors can be profitably exercised' (p. 376). And this is his third assumption. The major constraint on the improvement of peasant agriculture is the absence of competitive markets through which the farmer can buy cheap inputs and cheap consumer goods, and sell his or her produce at a fair price. Social relations of production, such as land tenure patterns and share-cropping arrangements, are ignored in Johnson's argument. At the level of production, the problem of achieving an increase in agricultural output and productivity is merely a technical one. The key constraints on agricultural change lie in the sphere of distribution.

Johnson argues that the economic organization of the market system reflects the physical inaccessibility of farmers to small towns. 'Without access to truly competitive markets', he writes, 'farmers can be victimized by monopsonistic village traders while their urgent need for cash income usually compels them to sell their produce immediately after harvest when prices are lowest' (p. 178). And:

> Because the countryside is inadequately provided with accessible market centres where farm produce can readily be sold and where shops filled with consumer and producer goods can exert their tempting 'demonstration effects', the incentives to produce more for the market and the inducement to invest in better tools, fertilizer, or better livestock in order to generate a larger marketable surplus are weak.
>
> (p. 171)

The town-building should thus be designed to tackle these problems. Indeed, it should be organized in such a way that it creates 'a punctiform grouping of business enterprises that can, by the communicative power of its proffered goods and services, stimulate greater agricultural production, improve the quality of farm produce, and induce farmers to augment the market surpluses' (p. 223).

In order to achieve this end, in which the market towns act as 'rural growth centres', Johnson advocates that investment should be planned within the 'functional economic areas' which consist of the towns plus their immediate geographical hinterlands. These areas can become 'truly functional', as Johnson puts it, by promoting rural-urban linkages through infrastructural investment and also by fostering a variety of interrelated economic activities. Ideally there should be an 'occupational pyramid', which consists of a base of primary production activities, processing industries and industries supplying the local market, some 'export' industries, and a tertiary sector of specialized merchants, brokers and traders. It may take time to build up such a pyramid. But if such a unit is created, it 'should "involve all classes" and thereby elicit the vital forces and latent creativity that reside in an area's human resources' (p. 247).

USAID: the strategy of integrated regional development

Johnson's work illustrates what Kitching calls 'neo-populist' thinking in a number of ways. His argument rests on the notion that it is possible to release the latent creativity of the people through the proper spatial manipulation of investment and that increasing material progress can, and must, be achieved through improving the productivity and incomes of the mass of the population in developing countries, the small-scale peasant farmers. Village life is not romanticized; and urbanization and industrialization are not rejected as inherently 'bad'. But there is a need for more small-scale industries and a less concentrated spatial and hierarchical pattern of urban growth. In planning change, central government has a role to play. But its resources should be directed towards providing incentives for private enterprise and establishing the infrastructure which facilitates the 'spontaneous' developmental forces of the market economy.

Yet in one respect Johnson diverges from the tenets which characterize the neo-populist current within development theory of the 1970s. He ignores questions of equality and distributional justice. 'The beaconlight of developmental policy in a nation, a region, or a "functional economic area"', he writes, 'should be to increase the total areal volume of economic activity' (p. 184). Economic growth is still the major objective.

This is perhaps not surprising as he formulated his policy proposals in the 1960s before the international development agencies and development experts began to focus upon the relationship between growth and income distribution.* However, in the 1970s a group of consultants to USAID, the most notable of whom was Dennis Rondinelli, picked up his ideas and, in a way which should now be familiar to the reader, adopted their spatial form and transformed their developmental content.

The USAID strategy, which has been called a strategy of 'integrated regional development', is said to be a spatial policy for *equitable* growth. The strategy is outlined most fully by Rondinelli and Ruddle (1978). In essence, it is the same as Johnson's proposal, but in the 'new strategy', planning efforts should be directed towards establishing a three-tier hierarchy of urban settlements in predominantly rural regions – rural service centres, small market towns and a regional centre – and more emphasis is placed on the importance of establishing both rural–urban linkages and inter-urban linkages within the hierarchy. An 'operational methodology' which relies on the principles of central place theory,

---

* Johnson's proposals can be seen as a *particular* application of the strategic viewpoint, espoused by some development theorists in the late 1950s and 1960s, that agricultural and industrial growth must proceed together and in step if planners wish to maximize national growth.

to decide which urban functions should be located in which centres, has been evolved to analyse socio-economic conditions within a region and to show how particular projects may be combined into investment packages which will foster the desired spatial structure (see Rondinelli, 1980). And, it is suggested that, to make the strategy work, development efforts should be guided by what Rondinelli and Ruddle call a 'transformational approach'. This involves the following eight principles:

1 building on existing culturally embedded resources, institutions and practices;
2 involving local people, who will be affected by transformation and change, in the processes of development planning and implementation;
3 adapting modern technologies, services and facilities to local conditions;
4 promoting specialization in production and exchange activities based on existing spatial comparative advantages;
5 using appropriate, low-cost, culturally acceptable methods of change to generate 'demonstration effects' that can lead to widespread adoption of those methods that prove successful;
6 planning for displacement of unproductive and unadaptable traditional institutions and practices as change occurs;
7 establishing, through planning based on 'strategic intervention', the pre-conditions for transformation and change in social, technical, political, economic and administrative structures and processes and in elements of the spatial structure; and
8 creating a planning process that is flexible, incremental, and adaptive and that provides for experimentation and adjustment as transformation takes place. (1978, p. 181)

The major objective of the strategy is to create an 'integrated' system of production and exchange and this, it is believed, can be achieved through promoting a variety of spatial linkages (Table 7). As Rondinelli and Ruddle put it:

Transformation of communities and productive activities – the evolution of subsistence into commercial farming, of simple handicrafts into more specialized processing and manufacturing, of scattered and isolated economic activities into concentrated nodes of production integrated into a national system of exchange – requires a well-articulated spatial structure. Settlements of various sizes, specializing in different economic and social functions, must be linked to each other through a network of physical, economic, technological, social

Table 7 Major linkages in spatial development

Type	Elements
Physical linkages	Road networks River and water transport networks Railroad networks Ecological interdependences
Economic linkages	Market patterns Raw materials and intermediate goods flows Capital flows Production linkages – backward, forward, and lateral Consumption and shopping patterns Income flows Sectoral and interregional commodity flows 'Cross linkages'
Population movement linkages	Migration – temporary and permanent Journey to work
Technological linkages	Technology interdependences Irrigation systems Telecommunications systems
Social interaction linkages	Visiting patterns Kinship patterns Rites, rituals, and religious activities Social group interaction
Service delivery linkages	Energy flows and networks Credit and financial networks Education, training and extension linkages Health service delivery systems Professional, commercial and technical service patterns Transport service systems
Political, administrative and organizational linkages	Structural relationships Government budgetary flows Organizational interdependences Authority-approval-supervision patterns Interjurisdictional transaction patterns Informal political decision chains

Source: Rondinelli and Ruddle, 1978, Table 3.

and administrative interaction. The linkages – patterns of transaction among groups and organizations located in spatially dispersed communities with sufficient threshold sizes of population to support their own specialized activities – are the primary means of expanding the system of exchange and transforming underdeveloped societies.

(1978, p. 160)

How this will all lead to more *equitable* growth is unclear. But, as I noted in chapter 2, Rondinelli and Ruddle assert that 'the failure of developing countries to achieve growth with equity can be attributed largely to their poorly articulated spatial systems' (p. 175). The underlying assumption is that the growing gap between the rich and the poor in developing countries is rooted in 'inequitable access to productive activities and social services' (p. 21), and that by increasing the accessibility of the rural population to the regional hierarchy of urban centres, greater social equity will ensue. Though quite aside from this assumption, it should be noted that, within the countries which are experimenting with the USAID methodology, the Philippines, Bolivia and Peru, the approach has invariably been applied within the poorer, or poorest, rural regions.

SELECTIVE SPATIAL CLOSURE AS A REGIONAL DEVELOPMENT STRATEGY

From a dependency perspective, neither Johnson's town-building programme nor the USAID strategy of integrated regional development are likely to achieve their objectives. Johnson's argument is rooted in a dualist conception of developing countries in which the process of agricultural change is viewed as a transition from subsistence to commercial cultivation. This conception is reproduced in the USAID strategy. A dependency theorist would argue that the failure to achieve growth with equity cannot be attributed to 'poorly articulated spatial systems', but rather to the nature of the relationships within those systems. Johnson considers those relationships, and indeed argues, with a spatial image similar to Suret-Canale's 'one-line economies', that peasant farmers in many former colonies live at the end of 'dendritic marketing systems', which are focused upon a port city and monopolistically controlled by city-based merchants. But he does not examine how the present structure of the international economy may render his proposals ineffective.

From a dependency perspective, such as that elaborated by Santos, any strategy which tries to promote the closer integration of villages into the national economy is liable to increase rural inequalities and this trend makes the creation of an 'organic' functional economic area, in which the town and its hinterland mutually support each other's growth, impossible. The beneficiaries from the town-building programme will increase their consumption in the metropolitan centres, promoting further economic growth there; and those who lose from the policy will continue to migrate to the largest centres, which offer the greatest hope. Moreover, any growth which occurs within the putative 'functional economic areas' will depend either directly or indirectly on conditions within the international economy.

One may conclude from the most pessimistic dependency perspective that *no* regional policy can achieve its 'development' objectives until the dependent countries disengage from the world economy. This is precisely the position adopted by Slater in 1975. But it is not a common one within mainstream regional development thinking. In the late 1970s a new strategy was suggested that could accommodate the dependency theories of regional and rural development. That strategy does not advocate the closer integration of localities and regions into the national and world economy. Nor does it seek local, regional and national autarchy. Rather, it is based on the idea that local and regional development may be promoted through *selective* spatial closure. That is: the devolution of power to local and regional 'communities' so that they can not only plan the development of their own resources according to their own needs, but also control any external relationships that have any negative effects upon them.

The term 'selective spatial closure' was first coined by Stöhr and Tödtling in a paper entitled 'Spatial equity: some antitheses to current regional development doctrine' (1979). It is worth noting their case for the adoption of such a strategy because, although the idea can easily be fitted to the dependency theorists' diagnosis of the problem of regional development and is the logical policy corollary of the inversion of growth centre analysis, their argument is *not* based on the dependent position of poor countries within the world economy. Their case is in fact rooted in an evaluation of regional policies in both developing and developed countries (see Stöhr and Tödtling, 1977; 1979). And, significantly in the present context, that case is based on 'neo-populist' notions of development and incorporates the neo-populists' concern for the ill-effects of centralization and large-scale organization.

In their evaluation, Stöhr and Tödtling (1979) adopt 'spatial equity', or the reduction of spatial disparities in the level of living, as the yardstick to assess the success of regional policies. The 'level of living' may be measured in terms of material progress, but Stöhr and Tödtling argue that 'non-material aspects of the quality of life', such as 'family, local and regional solidarity, individual and small-group self-realization, individual and local access to relevant decision-making powers' (p. 152) are just as important indicators of success as the material ones.

The evidence they present is necessarily patchy, referring mostly to advanced industrial countries and inferring changes in the non-material intangibles. But the conclusions are clear: first, 'spatial disparities in material living levels in most market and mixed economies have not decreased, or if they have decreased at one level (e.g. the interregional) they have usually increased at other spatial levels (e.g. the intra-regional or urban level)'; and second, that 'the subjective perception of conditions of living by concrete regional communities seems to show growing discontent on the part of sub-national groups (including local and regional ones) about the increasing impact upon them of exogenous economic and social determinants . . . and their ability to resist them and to shape their own destiny within large and still expanding economic and political systems' (p. 134).

Stöhr and Tödtling go on to analyse the failings of existing regional development practice. They argue that its limitations stem from its conceptual basis: the theoretical reliance on neo-classical economics, the obsession with material living conditions and the practical reliance on large-scale, vertically integrated institutions. They suggest that regional policies are being pursued during a time in which there is 'increasing functional and spatial integration of interacting systems of growing size, complexity and lack of controllability' (p. 135) and argue that the world-wide trend towards centralization has intensified the economic, social and cultural and political backwash effects on 'specific regional communities'.

Three possible strategies are identified for 'resolving emerging conflicts': first, giving priority to functional change, that is, continuing conventional policies; second, giving priority to what is called 'territorial integrity'; and third, complex systems management of functional change and territorial integrity. The last option is rejected as being overly technocratic and beyond the capability of systems analysis, given the state of that art. The first option places policy-makers in a double-bind. If they pursue functional integration, they can only reduce spatial disparities in material living conditions by adopting a powerful central redistributive mechanism which will inevitably *increase* spatial disparities in *non-material* living conditions. The only option, therefore, is giving priority to 'territorial integrity'. That entails the devolution of power to so-called 'territorial communities' so that they can regulate backwash effects. As Stöhr and Tödtling put it:

It is maintained that satisfactory solutions to existing problems at intermediate and small social scales will only be possible if, along with the presently dominating strategies for system-wide spatial integration (and regional openness) explicit instruments of selective spatial closure at various levels are applied. Essentially this would imply devolving some of the decision-making powers which have become vested in functionally organized (vertical) units back to territorially organized (horizontal) units at various spatial scales.   (p. 136)

Overall:

> The guiding objective would be to design consistent policies of regional development which apply spatial closure at different levels in such a way that the less-developed areas are put into a position to fully utilize their own development potential and to lock in, to the maximum possible, the development impulses received from higher developed areas.   (p. 158)

TERRITORIAL REGIONAL PLANNING AND DEVELOPMENT FROM BELOW

Interestingly, the seeds of the idea of selective spatial closure may be traced back to the work of Hirschman. In *The Strategy of Economic Development*, he speculates that:

> if only we could in some respects treat a region as though it were a country and in some others treat a country as though it were a region, we should be able to create situations particularly favourable for development.   (p. 199)

Selective spatial closure is designed to filter out the negative 'backwash' effects which growth in the dynamic centres of an economy has on peripheral localities, while retaining the positive 'trickledown' effects. But the emphasis placed on the need to harness 'internal' forces of change and meet local 'territorial' interests is new. And in the late 1970s these new elements formed the basis for a proposed *paradigm shift* in regional planning.

John Friedmann, with yet another radical switch in thinking, was one of those who advocated change. In a book written with Weaver, he suggests that there are two basic approaches to regional planning: the *functional* approach and the *territorial* approach (Friedmann and Weaver, 1979). Functional regional planning is, according to Friedmann and Weaver, concerned with the location of economic activities and the spatial organization of an urban system of nodes and networks. It is conceived as a purely technical exercise which relies heavily on mathematical models, such as input-output analysis or the gravity model of spatial interaction, and which is rooted in theories which claim universal validity. It emphasizes efficiency and policy decisions are usually made outside the regions which are affected by them, in a few centres of power. The urban-industrial growth pole policy, and the urbanization policies discussed in the present chapter, are examples of the functional approach, and in general, they have failed. As Friedmann and Weaver boldly put it, 'growth centre doctrine is quite useless as a tool of regional development' (p. 175).

Territorial regional planning, Friedmann and Weaver argue, offers a better alternative approach to the task of promoting regional development. In contrast to the functional approach, territorial regional planning is concerned with the integrated mobilization of the human and natural resources of specific historically defined regions. Territorial planning is an 'endogenous activity' conducted within the regions where its decisions take effect. It engages the people of that region within the planning process, which necessarily becomes a political process, and it emphasizes equity through seeking a general improvement of the quality of living for all the people in the area.

Friedmann and Weaver strongly advocate a paradigm shift from 'functional' to 'territorial' regional planning. But they are not the only regional theorists who have suggested an alternative paradigm for regional planning. Stöhr and Taylor (1981), addressing the particular problem of how regional planning in developing countries may reduce spatial inequalities, have similarly identified two basic approaches. These are defined as 'development from above' and 'development from below'.

The first approach, 'development from above', conforms to 'functional regional planning' and follows what is described as a *top-down centre-outward* development paradigm. The paradigm equates development with economic growth; emphasizes urban and industrial capital-intensive investment, maximum use of internal and external economies of scale, large-scale projects and the newest technology; and is concerned to reduce any economic, social, political, cultural or institutional barriers to trickledown effects. The approach has been implemented through growth pole and growth centre strategies, on the assumption that 'development is driven by external demand and innovation impulses and that from a few dynamic sectoral or geographical clusters, development would either in a spontaneous or induced way, "trickledown" to the rest of the system' (p. 1).

'Development from below', in contrast, rests upon another paradigm, the *bottom-up periphery-inward* development paradigm. In this paradigm, development is defined as 'an integral process of widening opportunities for individuals, social groups and territorially organized communities at small and intermediate scale, and mobilizing the full range of their capabilities and resources for the common benefit in social, economic and political terms' (Stöhr, 1981, pp. 39–40). The criterion of economic efficiency is not totally dismissed, but 'instead of maximizing the return of selected production factors on an international scale, the objective would be to increase the overall efficiency of all production factors of the economically less-developed region in an integrated manner' (p. 45) and, it may be added, to do so in a way in which the population of the region as a whole broadly benefited. Within the paradigm, it is envisaged that regions will have a greater degree of self-determination and may then be free to decide their own development path and, if necessary, to institute selective spatial closure as a means of enhancing the possibility of self-reliant development.

Both the 'alternative' paradigms, territorial regional planning and development from below, bring the region back to the centre of Anglo-American regional development theory. As Weaver (1979, p. 406) puts it, 'with a territorial doctrine of planning, regional development is a regional project'. But this seemingly different conceptualization of *space* is deceptive. The origins of the idea of selective spatial closure in Hirschman's work suggest that the way in which 'space' is related to 'development' may have remained unchanged in what appears to be a radical shift in thinking. I shall argue this point in detail in chapter 7. For the moment, what is important is that the alternative paradigms are definitely based on reconceptualization of the best *development* strategy.

As usual within regional development theory, identifying the strategic assumptions with precision is difficult. Stöhr (1981, p. 40) admits that 'unlike development "from above", which was nurtured by the economic theories of the past three decades (particularly the neo-classical one), there seems to be no well-structured theory available as yet for an alternative paradigm of development "from below"'. But broadly, both 'territorial regional planning' and 'development from below' are *neo-populist*.

They both arise from the perceived failure of the strategy of accelerated industrialization. And they both attempt to apply ideas from the neo-populist current within modern development theory within a regional context, striving to reverse the 'urban bias' in current planning practice, to promote greater equality and the satisfaction of the 'basic needs' of the majority of the population, to re-establish local and regional 'communities', and to avoid the centralization of economic and political decision-making. 'Development "from below" strategies', write Stöhr and Taylor, 'are basic-needs oriented, labour-intensive, small-scale, regional-resource-based, often rural-centred, and argue for the use of "appropriate", rather than "highest" technology' (p. 1). Territorial regional planning, argue Friedmann and Weaver, represents an attempt to accommodate 'regional development doctrine' to the new 'policy response space' which emerged in the 1970s, their view of which is summarized in Figure 26.

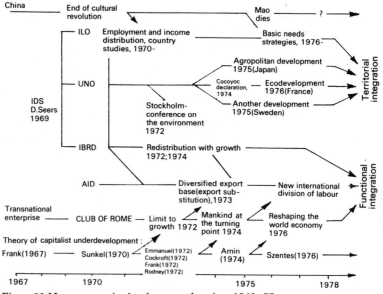

Figure 26 New streams in development doctrine, 1969–77.

Source: Friedmann and Weaver, 1979, p. 165.

The case for shifting to the new paradigms is then basically rooted in dissatisfaction with the growth orthodoxy of the 1960s and the appeal of neo-populist development thinking. But the justification for the adoption of territorial regional planning is reinforced by further arguments. The contrast between territorial and functional forms of social organization was originally made by a political scientist, Ashford, who was differentiating two principles of political representation in western democracies (see Tarrow *et al.*, 1978). Ashford was concerned that the functional principle was dominating the territorial, and the problem he perceived was the dilution of democratic control associated with the emergence of functionally specified interest groups which were detached from the territorial units which were the main means of representation.

In Friedmann's hands, 'territory' and 'function' are transformed into two all-pervasive bases of social integration which constitute a 'cosmic contradiction' in the organization of social affairs (Friedmann, 1979). A 'contradiction' is defined as 'a standing in mutual opposition of two social forces which, though interpenetrating and clashing, are complementary to one another, comprising a unity, a whole' (p. 25). And a 'cosmic' contradiction, in contrast to an 'historical' contradiction which arises at a particular moment in human history, is 'constitutive of the human condition' (p. 25). The cosmic contradiction between territory and function is between 'linkages among entities organized into hierarchical networks on a basis of self-interest' (functional forms of social integration) and 'those ties of history and sentiment that bind members of a geographically bounded community to one another' (territorial forms of social integration) (p. 29). Typical functionally organized social entities are an 'interest group', or a 'social class', or a 'corporation'; while a 'folk', a 'tribe', a 'nation' and a 'people' are representative examples of territorially organized social entities (p. 31).

Friedmann and Weaver assert that 'Territory and function are both needed for development' and that the key question is which principle of social organization is to be master: 'shall function prevail over territory, or territory over function'? (1979, p. 171). In advocating a shift from functional regional planning to territorial regional planning they support the latter option. 'The time is ripe', they write, 'for the containment of functional power and its subordination to a *territorial will*' (p. 227, emphasis added). This, they argue, is necessary at the present moment because transnational corporations, which are functionally organized, have increased their power relative to nation states, which are 'territorial' forms of organization. This in itself is undesirable because:

> The managers of transnational power are ultimately responsible to no one but themselves. Unchecked by territorial and, indeed, by any other power, they wish to totalize their grasp upon the world. The exclusive interest they have is to retain and to enlarge the bases of their power. Those who are integrated into their system will be materially rewarded; those who are not – a majority of the world's population – must be controlled by force.   (p. 187)

But if one values 'egalitarian development' more than 'polarized development', the territorial principle will invariably have a major role to play in development, for:

> Functional ties are based on mutual self-interest. Given inequalities at the start, a functional order is always hierarchical, accumulating power

at the top. Territorial relationships, on the other hand, though they will also be characterized by inequalities of power, are tempered by the mutual rights and obligations which members of a territorial group claim from each other. (p. 7)

Moreover, according to Friedmann and Weaver, there is a precedent for 'territorial regional planning' within the Anglo-American tradition of regional planning. Reviewing the evolution of thinking within the field, they argue that 'functional regional planning' only became predominant in the period from 1950 to 1975. Before the Second World War, theorists like Howard Odum, the man who was the driving-force behind regional sociology in the US south during the 1930s, advocated regional policies which followed 'territorial' rather than 'functional' principles (see Odum, 1934; Odum and Moore, 1938). What Friedmann and Weaver are suggesting is a return to these intellectual roots.

The rationale for a shift to 'territorial regional planning' is thus very complex. But nevertheless, its basis can still be described as 'neo-populist'. The only sensible meaning that can be given to the phrases 'territorial power' and 'territorial will' is the power and the will of *the people* in a territory. Territorial regional planning is thus a populist charter in the simplest sense that it advocates the empowerment of 'the people' and the promotion of development in service of 'the people's will'. Furthermore, it draws inspiration from the populist intellectual tradition of the 1930s in the United States, which grew in response to the threat which metropolitanization and industrialization posed to 'the American way of life'. Thus, for example, Odum's major concern is summarized by Friedmann and Weaver as follows:

Odum advocated a cultural regionalism that would withstand the onslaught of industrialism with its ruthless tendencies towards cultural levelling. He understood the threat which industrialism posed for territorially integrated regional societies, and he hoped to contain and move this force through what he called 'regional-national social planning'. (p. 5)

The new 'territorial regional planning' is a revival of this concern to combat the adverse consequences of industrialization, transferred to the poorer countries of the world. But in that transfer, the paradigm has been 'stiffened' by the neo-populist currents within the development studies of the 1970s.

THE EXAMPLE OF AGROPOLITAN DEVELOPMENT

It would be easy to disparage the new 'neo-populist' paradigms for regional development policy as utopian. Friedmann's distinction between territory and function, which is reminiscent of Durkheim's dichotomy between organic and mechanical solidarity, appears to romanticize the quality of life in territorially organized 'communities'. And the call for 'the recovery of territorial life', as Friedmann and Weaver put it, seems to be a wish to return to a lost pre-industrial world. 'Traditional regional planning', they write:

> will no doubt continue for many years. But the cutting edge of professional thinking and practice already lies elsewhere – wherever the interests of territory are being asserted over those of function in the Herculean task *to reverse more than two centuries of attrition of territory integrity* throughout the world.   (p. 207, emphasis added)

However, my purpose in identifying the strategic bases of the alternative paradigms as 'neo-populist' is certainly not to engage in critique through labelling. One reason why I have been attempting to relate particular regional policy proposals to theories of development and theories of development strategy over the last three chapters is that this *then* allows a much deeper appreciation of the regional policies. I have aimed to be even-handed in the treatment of the different developmental perspectives which inform regional policy, and I do not intend to abandon that course now. However, to complete the account it is necessary to take a closer look at a regional development strategy associated with these alternative paradigms. A paradigm is merely a framework of thinking and it is possible to envisage various strategies which may conform to it. The one which has been elaborated most fully is the strategy of agro-politan development.

Interestingly, the strategy was first constructed *outside* the all-embracing frameworks of 'territorial regional planning' and 'development from below'. It was suggested by Friedmann and Douglass (1978) in a paper which begins with a wealth of statistics portraying the failure of the strategy of accelerated industrialization to raise the living standards of the majority of the population in Asian countries, and with an argument which suggests that, given the current crisis in the world economy, it is unlikely that even the high rates of growth observed in some of the Asian countries following industrial development policies can be sustained. Friedmann and Douglass advocate an alternative development strategy for Asian countries which would include the following elements:

1   limited and specific human needs should replace unlimited generalized wants as the fundamental criterion of successful national development . . .

2 agriculture should be regarded as a leading or 'propulsive' sector of the economy . . .

3 attaining self-sufficiency in domestic food production should be regarded as a high priority objective . . .

4 existing inequalities in income and living conditions betweeen social classes and between urban and rural classes should be reduced . . .

5 facilitative measures to increase production of wage goods for domestic consumption should be given high priority . . .

6 a policy of planned industrial dualism should be adopted whereby small-scale production for the domestic market is protected against competition from large-scale capital-intensive enterprise.

(pp. 181–2)

The strategy is described as 'a strategy of accelerated rural development', and agropolitan development is said to be its 'spatial correlate' (p. 189). It is, as they put it, 'a *spatial policy* for the emerging paradigm' (p. 164, emphasis added), the 'emerging paradigm' in this case referring to the new ideas of development experts who were challenging the growth orthodoxy of the 1960s.

In brief, what the agropolitan approach involved in its first version was (i) the creation of a network of local government units within a country, the agropolitan districts; (ii) a devolution of power and change in centre-local taxation arrangements such that 'each unit has sufficient autonomy and economic resources to plan and carry out its own development' (p. 185); (iii) land reform to ensure that 'wealth is returned to the control of members of each agropolitan district' (p. 186); and (iv) the commitment of central government 'to support locally initiated developments with financial, material and technical resources, to undertake projects of national significance, to ensure interregional equity in the allocation of development funds, and to maintain system-wide balances in the major macro-economic parameters' (p. 186).

The agropolitan districts would normally be centred upon a town of 10,000–25,000 inhabitants, and district boundaries, though taking account of local particularities such as religious and linguistic divisions and ecological complementarities, would normally be defined by 'a commuting radius of between five and ten kilometres (or approximately one hour's travel time by bicycle)' (p. 185). Though smaller than Johnson's 'functional economic areas', they are in principle the same. And just as Johnson advocates a diversity of economic activities in his 'functional economic areas', Friedmann and Douglass argue that the development efforts of agropolitan districts would involve social facilities, infrastructure, agricultural improvements *and* light labour-intensive industry.

Indeed the presence of industries within the districts along with the devolution of political decision-making to local level is what gives the approach its name. It aims 'to transform the countryside by introducing and adapting elements of urbanism to specific rural settings . . . [to] transmute existing settlements into a hybrid form we call *agropolis* or city-in-the-fields' (p. 183).

In its original version, the strategy of agropolitan development was specifically designed for contexts where there are low levels of urbanization (less than 20 per cent), high and rising rural population density patterns (in excess of two hundred people per square kilometre), a settlement pattern of clustered villages and towns, and conditions of extreme poverty (p. 182); it is thus said to be particularly suitable in Asia. In a second version (Friedmann and Weaver, 1979), it is said to be suitable for Asia *and* parts of Africa and it is transformed from 'the spatial correlate of a strategy of accelerated rural development' to 'a basic-needs strategy of territorial development' (p. 193). The changes involved in this transformation highlight the shift in thinking from 'functional' to 'territorial' regional planning.

First, although the agropolitan district is still defined as a unit of local government within which development programmes will be formulated and implemented, it is now stressed that the district boundaries should be coterminous with a *local community of interest*, or a 'primordial unit of territorial integration', as Friedmann and Weaver put it (p. 197). These territorial 'communities' may be identified at various spatial scales – from the locality to the region to the nation. Agropolitan districts are 'the smallest of these territorial units that are still capable of providing for the basic needs of their inhabitants with only marginally important resource transfers from outside' (p. 197).

Second, three basic conditions are said to be 'essential' for successful agropolitan development: 'selective territorial closure, the communalization of productive wealth, and the equalization of access to the bases for the accumulation of social power' (p. 195). Selective territorial closure, or 'spatial' closure in Stöhr's terminology, should be applied at the 'relevant levels of territorial integration: district, region and nation', in order 'to prevent the outward transfer of resources' (p. 201), and is essential because it is then possible to ensure that the benefits of local development accrue to *local* people. And the last two conditions are necessary to ensure that the *whole* local community benefits from development efforts. 'Where benefits are appropriated primarily for private use, so that the gains accrue unequally', Friedmann and Weaver note, 'even the initial effort is not likely to be made, and the productive potential of the community will be realized only in part' (p. 195).

Third, the expansion of production within the agropolitan districts, as well as being oriented towards meeting basic needs, should follow the principles of 'self-reliant development'. The aim should be to create a diversified local economy, so that local needs are met as much as possible from local production, and developments should as far as possible be self-financed by the local territorial communities. Furthermore, development efforts should attempt to mobilize local natural resources, within the constraints set by the need for conservation of ecosystems, and should rely heavily on local knowledge. Agropolitan district institutions should promote what Friedmann and Weaver call 'social learning' to enhance the capacity of the local community to solve its own problems and 'to teach the general principle that development is not "imported" but produced through one's own efforts' (p. 203).

The fact that 'the strategy of agropolitan development' has at least two connotations is unfortunate. With Douglass elaborating the strategy in a slightly different way (see Douglass, 1979), and with Friedmann, in an even later version, presenting the agropolitan district as a territorial framework for a participatory style of rural development planning (Friedmann, 1981), there is a danger that the term 'agropolitan development' will become as nebulous as the terms 'growth pole strategy' and 'growth centre strategy'. But a more telling criticism of the new strategy may be made by enquiring how sound it is as an application of neo-populist social and economic theory. The key question which neo-populist development theorists must address is how to achieve their social objectives given the economic constraints which limit all development efforts within the poorer countries of the world. The problem has been sharply focused in development studies in the 1970s, and some of the 'neo-populist' contributions to the field, such as Lipton's thesis of urban bias, elaborate complex arguments to show that the pursuit of equity objectives is not merely going to result in a more equal sharing of poverty and drudgery. However, it is precisely at this point that the formulation of the agropolitan development strategy is weakest.

It is recognized that it is unrealistic to plan to eradicate the existing metropoli in developing countries (as the Pol Pot régime did in Cambodia), and it is also recognized that it is necessary to have 'projects of national significance' as well as the small-scale, basic-needs oriented projects within the agropolitan districts. In particular, in both the versions of agropolitan development which I have summarized, it is envisaged that there will be national investment in industrries which can complement the development programmes formulated and implemented within the agropolitan districts. Thus Friedmann and Weaver argue that *alongside* the cellular economy of the districts there will be an 'urban-based corporate economy'. The industries within this 'parallel economy', as they put it, should not compete with the agropolitan industries, but can develop 'backward and forward linkages with the thousands of small industries in agropolitan localities' (pp. 204–5). Friedmann and Douglass are even more explicit. Their strategy is intended to achieve accelerated rural development, but the agropolitan development programme 'would be complemented with a policy of selective industrialization primarily for export and for supportive basic materials' (p. 183). In effect, as they state, there will be 'a policy of planned industrial dualism' (p. 182). Alongside the small-scale, technologically appropriate, labour-intensive agropolitan industries, there would be capital-intensive large-scale industries using the latest technology. These industries, Friedmann and Douglass note, can achieve agglomeration economies and are thus best located in close proximity to one another, forming industrial complexes or 'growth poles'. But the agropolitan industries should be protected from the competition with them, and therefore 'these "poles" would constitute regional enclave economies at major ports or in other suitable locations and would not necessarily be spatially integrated with agro-politan development' (p. 183).

In recognizing the necessity of a 'parallel economy', the advocates of an agropolitan development strategy avoid presenting a utopian vision of a network of poor small communities, each somehow achieving the de-velopment they each want through the resources they each possess. But at the same time, the existence of the 'parallel economy' in an agro-politan development strategy raises difficult theoretical questions which neither Friedmann and Douglass nor Friedmann and Weaver address. The main problem is to explain how basic and intermediate industries and 'projects of national significance' will be financed when one of the objectives of the strategy is to avoid increasing dependence on the out-side world. It may be that this problem can be resolved. However, at the present, the formulation of the agropolitan development strategy is weakest at precisely the point where 'neo-populist' development theory requires the most careful argument.

CONCLUSION: DEVELOPMENT THEORY AND REGIONAL THEORY

Enough précis. It has been a tortuous path to get from '*le pôle de croissance*' to 'agropolitan development', and in the end we seem to have returned to the beginning. But it should be evident that there are sharp disagreements within Anglo-American regional development theory about how the geo-graphical pattern of development in the poorer countries of the world may be explained and about how a more desirable pattern may be engineered through planning intervention.

The ideas outlined do not summarize the whole of the field and, in particular, explanations of spatial change based on the regional disaggregation of neo-classical and neo-Keynesian growth models (see Richardson, 1969) and on the application of classical Marxist political economy (see Harvey, 1982) have been ignored. But within the spectrum of regional development theory, both these approaches lie outside mainstream thinking: the former because of the arguments of Perroux, Myrdal and Hirschman against equilibrium analyses and the latter because classical Marxist theory, in contrast to the so-called neo-Marxian analyses of dependency relations and surplus transfer, presumably has too radical implications.

Within mainstream thinking, the account has only focused on a few important contributions in the literature. This approach has been adopted because it allows a more faithful summary of the ideas of different theorists, but it may lead some readers to question why the work of some authorities has been excluded. It is important that readers test the argument of the book by widening the sample of 'important' contributions. But a more comprehensive review will, I would argue, lead to the same two conclusions:

1 the basic disagreements within Anglo-American regional development theory are rooted in different conceptions of what 'development' is, how it occurs, and how it may best be planned; and
2 Anglo-American regional development theory has evolved as a *derivative* subject in which new explanations of regional change and new regional planning strategies have been proposed through the application of different development theories in a spatial context.

To the general development theorist some of the applications may seem curious. Some of the ideas about social and economic change, such as Perroux's domination theory and Dahrendorf's conflict model of authority-dependency, are marginal to the major debates in development theory. And other ideas are distorted in their translation into regional theory, either because some essential elements are omitted (as in implicit applications of Schumpeterian analysis of innovation adoption and economic change), or because ideas drawn from incompatible development theories are wrenched from their initial analytical framework and improperly synthesized for the purposes of regional analysis. For the sake of clarity this latter feature has not been emphasized in the foregoing account, though Friedmann's 'general theory' offers a good illustration, and the reader may usefully refer to Hilhorst (1971) and Soja and Tobin (1972) for other examples of synthetic explanatory theory.

The identification of the development perspectives which underpin the rival regional planning strategies is a first necessary step in elaborating a critique of them. Once this logical exercise is completed, it is possible to see inconsistencies in the developmental assumptions of particular policy proposals and also to bring the powerful arguments within development theory, about how development occurs and on how it may best be planned, to bear on the derivative suggestions within regional development theory. For *ultimately* the validity of any regional development theory and the success of any regional planning strategy depends on the assumptions about the development process which inform it. *If the developmental assumptions are weak, the regional theory will be weak.*

In the foregoing account, some examples of inconsistencies have already been given. But I shall leave the reader to judge the literature in terms of its developmental assumptions. For although, in the end, those who seek to understand and plan the 'development' of cities, regions and rural localities must have a clear understanding of the process of development, this, *in itself*, is not sufficient. Anglo-American regional development theory has 'progressed' through the introduction of new, and supposedly more valid, development perspectives. Yet despite this, there is a deep problem within all mainstream thinking, *no matter what development perspective is adopted.*

This problem stems from the way in which 'space' is related to 'development' within the literature. The conception of space weakens the explanations of urban and regional development on which the rival regional planning strategies are based and sets strict limits to what may be achieved through them. The nature of the weaknesses and the precise limits are the subject of the final part of the book.

Part Three

The Poverty of the Spatial Separatist Theme

6

Space and explanation in regional development theory

The spatial separatist theme has been defined by Robert Sack as the notion that 'it is possible to identify, separate and evaluate the *spatial* either as an independent phenomenon or property of events examined through spatial analysis' (Sack, 1974b, p. 1). The argument of this book is that the basic weaknesses within Anglo-American regional development theory stem from adherence to this theme. One side of this argument was completed at the end of Part One when it was concluded that normative statements about the socio-economic implications of spatial distributions are weak and that their weakness is a consequence of the attempt to isolate the effects of spatial distributions from the development processes of which they are an integral part. This final part of the book completes the argument by showing how the spatial separatist theme is at work in the explanatory theories of urban and regional development discussed earlier in the book, and by examining the logical limitations and practical implications which stem from the way in which these theories relate 'space' to 'development'.

CONCEPTIONS OF SPACE

While it is fairly simple to identify the developmental assumptions which regional theorists use, defining the conception of space within the field presents major problems. The most basic assertion that may be made is that there is confusion over what 'space' is and how it may be incorporated in explanations of regional development. The confusion may be illustrated, and its source identified, by taking a closer look at discussions about 'space' which relate to the concept of the growth pole.

The example of economic space

As noted in chapter 3, regional theorists redefined Perroux's idea of the growth pole as they applied it to the problem of explaining and planning regional development. Part of the transformation which occurred was founded on sheer ignorance of Perroux's original intentions. But it also reflected difficulties of interpreting a concept which Perroux introduced as a means of 'delocalizing' economic analysis. That concept is *economic space*, and precisely what it means greatly illuminates how space is treated within the field.

Perroux introduces the concept in a paper in which he passionately argues that economists should stop analysing economies as if they were 'contained' in a 'container', the national territory. And in that same paper, ironically, in view of the subsequent history of the growth pole concept, he castigates any attempts to explain the geographic location of economic activity on the earth's surface as 'banal'. Analyses of the firm in geographic space, he suggests, are at best only possible with great simplification and may, in the worst case, lead to serious illusion. It may be possible to determine where the buildings, machines and workmen of a small single-plant firm are situated when it is functioning, but the large firm 'is often composed of establishments geographically dispersed, among which are formed bonds of varying strength . . . [and] the means of production comprise machines and materials and also electric current and money in the bank' (p. 26). The economic zone of influence of a large firm such as Michelin, he writes, 'defies cartography' (p. 28). Thus, as he grandly puts it:

> The time has come to provoke consciously *a change of visual angle*, to run systematically, knowing full well what we do, counter to economic analysis which tries to determine the *place* and the *causes of the place* of an economic unit in everyday space. (p. 28)

He proposes that economists, instead of thinking of 'space' in the everyday sense of geographic location on the earth's surface, should view 'space' as 'a structure of abstract relations' (p. 23). He asserts that 'there are as many spaces as structures of abstract relations', and that 'these abstract spaces are sets of relations which respond to questions without involving directly the location of a point by two or three co-ordinates'. The relevant 'spaces' for the economist are 'economic spaces' which may be broadly classified into three types: '(i) space as defined by a plan; (ii) space as a field of forces; and (iii) space as a homogeneous aggregate' (p. 29).

Illustrating again with the case of the firm, he writes:

> The firm has, in the first place, a space defined by a plan. This plan is the set of relations which exist between the firm and, on the one hand, the suppliers of *input* (raw materials, labour, power, capital) and, on the other hand, the buyers of the *output* (both intermediary and final).

The economic distance measured in monetary terms, that is to say in terms of prices and costs, is determined by factors outside the plan; it depends on the structure and arrangement of the plan of the firm, as well as on the structure and arrangement of the plans of groups in relation to the firm. . . .

In a second aspect, the firm has a space defined as a field *of forces*. As a field of forces, economic space consists of centres (or poles or foci) from which centrifugal forces emanate and to which centripetal forces are attracted. Each centre being a centre of attraction and repulsion, has its proper field, which is set in the fields of other centres. Any banal space whatever, in this respect, is a collection of centres and a place of passage for forces. . . .

The firm, in a third aspect, has a space defined as a *homogeneous aggregate*. The relations of homogeneity which define economic space in this respect are relative to the units and to their structure, or relative to the relations between these units.

The firm has, or has not, a structure more or less homogeneous with those of other firms which are its neighbours topographically or econ-omically − it belongs to a space where, roughly speaking, one price reigns. To speak more exactly, each firm has its price. Even in a régime approximating to competition, each firm does not have exactly the same conditions of production, or sale, or cost, as the next firm. But it happens that various firms are placed in approximately the same conditions and set approximately the same price, for a clientèle situ-ated at the same physical distance. Alternatively, firms placed in very unequal conditions regarding cost, can offer the same price for clients situated at very different physical distances. These firms are in the same economic space, whatever their co-ordinates in everyday space.

(Perroux, 1950a, pp. 27−8)

I quote extensively here as it is difficult to summarize in words what exactly is meant by 'abstract economic space'. It is perhaps easiest to regard the phrase as just another way of saying 'economic relationships', which have nothing whatsoever to do with geographic space. This image is evident in the earlier work of Schumpeter (1939), who refers to the effect of innovations in opening up new investment opportunities as 'the creation of new economic space' (p. 135), and it is probable that Perroux derived the term from that source.

But that is not how all regional theorists have interpreted it. Boude-ville (1966), for example, suggests the following definition:

If space were formed solely of economic variables, it could be a math-ematical one; it could be anywhere. But economic space, on the contrary, is an application of economic variables on or in geographic space, through a mathematical transformation which describes an economic process. (p. 2)

This notion is 'clarified' with a diagram:

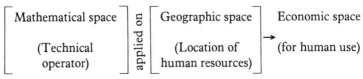

$$\begin{bmatrix} \text{Mathematical space} \\ \\ \text{(Technical} \\ \text{operator)} \end{bmatrix} \text{applied on} \begin{bmatrix} \text{Geographic space} \\ \\ \text{(Location of} \\ \text{human resources)} \end{bmatrix} \rightarrow \begin{matrix} \text{Economic space} \\ \\ \text{(for human use)} \end{matrix}$$

which is said to describe 'what happens when industrialists set up and operate a factory, or when administrators decide to build a bridge or a road' (p. 2). Essentially, for Boudeville, economic space seems to refer to the *location* of economic characteristics, economic relationships and economic plans *in* geographic space. The set of French *départements* with high *per capita* income are thus said to be in the same homogeneous economic space. And: 'A polarized space could be defined as the set of spatial units [for example, towns] conveying with one of them (called the dominant pole) larger flows than with other poles of the same order' (p. 10). A programming space is somewhat opaquely defined as a set of locations in which there is 'coherence or unity of economic decisions' (p. 16).

A second interpretation of abstract space is offered by Friedmann and Alonso (1964). They write:

> The traditional concept of space (which Perroux calls *banal*) is defined by studying the extent, density and sequence of physical phenomena on the earth's surface. . . . In a rather simplified form it is the space we mean when we say that Iceland has 38,900 square miles, or that Karachi lies approximately 700 miles south-west of New Delhi. But this concept of space is rudimentary and allows one to make only a small number of inferences. As a scientific concept, it is not very productive, and as a concept in planning it is practically worthless. A more useful reading is obtained if the physical distance between New Delhi and Karachi is modified according to the mode of travel used, the degree of social and political compatibility between India and Pakistan, Hindus and Moslems, and the cost of shipping commodities across an international frontier. (p. 18)

With this view, the Perrouxian notion of abstract space is a transformation of distance relations. Physical distances are evaluated differently by different people according to the tasks they undertake and thus, as Friedmann and Alonso put it, 'space is shaped by the functional interrelationships being considered and there will be as many varieties of space as fundamental relations' (p. 19).

The existence of such various interpretations of Perroux's way of conceptualizing space has been a fundamental source of confusion within growth pole theory. But they have a wider significance, which becomes apparent when 'the change in visual angle' which Perroux proposed is compared with conceptions of space used by *physicists*.

Within physics, there are two basic conceptions of space: an absolute view and a relative view. The absolute view formed the working basis of that science from Newton's day until the theories of Einstein. With this conception, space is seen to exist independently of the objects in it and its properties may be measured using the Euclidean geometric system. It is a kind of framework for things and events: 'something like a system of pigeon-holes or a filing system, for observation' (Popper, 1963, p. 179). If things are put into this framework, its properties do not change and as it exists absolutely, it can exert effects in a predictable way. Thus, for example, in Newton's law of gravity, the gravitational attraction of two masses decreases as the square of the *distance* between them.

The concept of absolute space was challenged by philosophers both during and after Newton's lifetime and the question whether 'space' could exist absolutely and independently of substances had puzzled them even earlier. The philosophical problem is to explain the entity 'empty space' which remains when the objects in it are removed. As Melissus, a Greek philosopher put it: 'What is empty is nothing. What is nothing cannot be' (quoted in Blaut, 1961). Nevertheless, the absolute conception of space provided the working basis for physics until the late nineteenth century, when mathematicians began to discover non-Euclidean geometric systems, which implied that the properties of space were not absolute (see Harvey, 1969, chapter 14). The working basis of physics finally changed with Einstein's general theory of relativity. This is based on a *relative* conception of space, in which the properties of space are not absolute, but dependent on the existence and distribution of matter and energy. Space is itself defined by mass and energy, and can only be studied in terms of the relations of matter and of energy through time, that is, as a space-time 'field'.

In introducing the concept of economic space and proclaiming it as 'a change in visual angle', Perroux was in effect attempting to produce a transformation in the way in which economists thought about space which was exactly analogous to that which followed Einstein's work in physics. The significance of his argument is that it highlights the fact that regional theorists have worked with a conception of space *derived from physics*. And the importance of the confusion over the meaning of the term 'economic space' is that it reflects the difficulty of applying the *physicist's* conception of relative space within the *social* sciences.

The incomplete relational concept of space

In their 'formative' period both regional science and theoretical geography drew inspiration from a small group of US social scientists who styled themselves as 'social physicists' (see Zipf, 1949; Stewart, 1950; Stewart and Warntz, 1958). The initial studies which isolated 'the effects of distance' on the location of economic activity were using an absolute conception of space *received from physics*. When the men and objects contained 'in space' are removed, there remains 'a residue of a continuous set of points', as Isard puts it (see p. 8 above), an 'empty space', whose effects on human activity are theorized through the assumption of an isotropic plain. Perroux regarded analyses based on such a conception of space as 'banal', and some regional scientists and theoretical geographers have, like him, tried to base analysis on the physicist's relative conception of space (see, for example, Berry's 'general field theory of spatial behaviour', 1968). But whether such a shift in perspective offers an adequate basis for understanding the significance of space in *social* life is highly debatable.

How, for example, is it possible to translate the law that 'if energy is transmitted from one point and takes a finite time to reach another point away from the first, the energy should be located somewhere in space between the time of transmission and the time of reception' into social scientific terms? This law of conservation of energy (quoted in Sack, 1980, pp. 56–7) implies that 'space must be characterized by energy' and is an important element in the modern physicist's view of space. But if we assume that in the social sciences space is related to human action in the same way that space is related to 'energy' in physics, how valid are the explanations of the social world that are elaborated?

In his important review of conceptions of space in social thought, Sack (1980) argues that when social scientists adopt a conception of space from physics 'they receive a view of space, the characteristics of which are beyond their purview to explain' (p. 17). Social scientists, he suggests, need to construct and work with a *relational conception of space*.

With this view it is recognized that the concepts of social science may be divided into temporal, spatial (or physical geometric) and substance. Any fact, for example my sixty-year-old house, can be described in each of these categories: in substance terms, as house; in temporal terms, as sixty years old; and in spatial terms, as a cube located at co-ordinates x and y. Some substance concepts, such as 'dome' specify physical geometric properties. But many of these which are of interest to social scientists, such as 'peasant' or 'oppression', do not. Nevertheless, all *instances* of substance concepts, that is events, have space-time properties. As Sack puts it, 'to speak of the occurrence of an event is to speak of its physical geometric properties' (Sack, 1973, p. 26). Applying the relational concept of space within social science would involve addressing 'the temporal and spatial aspects of substances' (Sack, 1980, p. 72). It would be recognized that space, substance and time are conceptually separable, but they would be linked in both description and explanation.

The problem, then, is how this link can be made. The discussions of economic space illustrate that regional theorists have attempted to treat space relationally. But unfortunately, doing this through the application of physicists' concept of relative space is bound to end in confusion. As a result, *regional development theorists have failed to conceptualize space as an integral element of social interaction.* Instead they work with an *incomplete relational concept of space,* which is essentially an absolute conception of space modified by the different interpretations of the physicist's relative conception of space.

This hybrid concept of space is basically the 'container' view against which Perroux argued so vehemently. Space is taken to be a locational matrix which contains things like cities and industries. It is an environment in which events such as the establishment of a new industry and expansion of agricultural output occur. From this perspective it is possible to write of 'the spatial *incidence* of development'. Development, however, it is defined, refers to a process of change, or a sequence of events connected by some mechanism. In talking of the spatial incidence of development, regional analysts are referring to where, 'in space', this sequence of events occurs. 'Space' is thus separated from 'process'.

The spatial environment within which events occur is not taken to be immune to influence, as in Newtonian physics. Distance relationships are socially defined; and the nature of the spatial environment is constantly being changed by human activity. But with an incomplete relational concept of space, it is assumed that it is possible to define the nature of this shaped environment at any particular instant in time.

The terms 'spatial structure' or 'spatial system' are sometimes used to refer to this abstraction. Essentially what these phrases try to describe is a momentary snapshot of the arrangement of human activity on the earth's surface. It is in this sense that Friedmann and Alonso (1964, p. 9) write that 'the spatial structure of economic development' has two aspects – 'physical and activity patterns'. The former refers to the spatial arrangement of human settlements, productive facilities, transport routes and land uses; the latter consists of the flows of capital, labour, commodities and communications which link these physical elements.

Some theorists thinking in this way have abstracted a 'slice' of human activity at a moment in time, focusing, for example, on the economic or political part of the spatial environment. This is what Boudeville does when he speaks of 'economic space' and it is in this sense that we may interpret Santos's plea that 'one should be concerned with world space as a whole and not just aristocratic space where the only flows are those of giant firms and persons of leisure' (1974). Different adjectives may be used to describe different slices of human reality and thus it is possible to multiply different types of space in this way. But they all refer to a momentary spatial cross-section of human activity.

The map is used as a device to portray the nature of the spatial environment at a given moment in time. A sequence of maps portraying physical and activity patterns at different points in time may be said to describe 'the evolution of the spatial structure' or 'the evolution of the spatial system'. And maps may be drawn which transform distance relations in a manner which reflects the way in which they are socially defined (see Figure 3, p. 16, above). The 'spatial incidence of development' at any moment is described on maps which depict the spatial distribution of particular features, such as roads and industries, which have been selected as indicators of 'development'. And a temporal sequence of such maps may be said to describe the 'development' of different locations within a country. Elements of the spatial environment can thus be seen both as the spatial context within which 'development' occurs *and* as indicators of 'development'.

Maps are an essential tool through which regional theorists *describe* the spatial distributions of human activity which are of interest to them. But in analysing these distributions with an incomplete relational concept of space, *explanations* have been constructed which suggest that the spatial environment of a city, region or rural locality *itself* exerts effects on the events which occur there, and that therefore there is an intrinsic spatial logic to the evolution of spatial distributions.

It is with this perspective that Friedmann and Alonso (1964) write:

> Regional development concerns the incidence of economic growth. It is *ultimately the result of* the location of economic activities *in response to* differential regional attractions.   (p. 20, emphasis added)

And Riddell (1970) suggests:

> Modernization is a geographic phenomenon with obvious spatial expression, its pattern of spread is not a simple contagious process, but

is strongly influenced and determined by the transport network and
urban-administrative hierarchy.   (p. 130, emphasis added)

And Stöhr (1981) argues:

Large-scale organizational linkages between areas of greatly differing
levels of development *lead* (due to factors such as unequal distribution
of power, selective factor withdrawals, unequal terms of trade, unequal distribution of scale economies) *to* increasing spatial divergence
rather than convergence of living levels.   (p. 42, emphasis added)

And Santos (1979) writes that:

The metropoli *are responsible for* macro-spatial organization.
(p. 153, emphasis added)

Each of these theorists is working with a very different conception of
how 'development' occurs. But their explanatory statements are each
based on an incomplete relational concept of space. *It is in such explanations that the spatial separatist theme is evident in regional development
theory.*

SPACE AND CONCEPTIONS OF SCIENTIFIC EXPLANATION

The purpose of this chapter is to examine the nature of the explanations
which have been constructed using an incomplete relational concept of
space. Most of the regional planning strategies outlined in the second
part of the book supposedly have some *scientific* basis and it is in these
terms that knowledge within the field will be assessed. But, at the outset,
it is worth noting that within some conceptions of what constitutes a
'scientific' explanation, it would be impossible to construct scientific
knowledge and retain the incomplete relational view of space. In fact,
and this is the first important point on the limitations imposed by that
view, *it is only possible to construct scientific explanations using an incomplete relational concept of space within a positivist and instrumentalist
conception of science.* Demonstrating this point takes us into deep philosophical waters, but it is important to grasp what is meant by positivist
and instrumentalist scientific theory and why, from certain perspectives,
such theory would not be considered to provide 'proper' scientific explanations.

The term 'positivism' has been used to embrace a variety of philosophical positions including the thesis that sensory experiences are the
exclusive source of valid information about the world, the notion that
natural and social sciences share a common methodological foundation,
and the idea that there is a categorical distinction between fact and value

(see, for example, Giddens, 1977, chapter 1). But, to simplify, the positivist view of science may be taken to be one in which, first, an 'explanation' takes the form of a *logical argument* in which the key statements are laws, that is, general statements which express the regular relationships that are found to exist in the world; and second, the truth or falsity of these laws can be assessed by systematic observation and experiment.

According to Hempel (1965), the most precise form of positivist scientific explanation is a deductive argument in which the event to be explained is the conclusion, and certain universal laws and antecedent conditions are premises. The occurrence of an event, for example, the temporary drop and then sharp rise of the mercury column in a thermometer which occurs after a mercury thermometer is rapidly immersed in hot water, can be logically deduced by applying certain general laws to the antecedent conditions. In this example, the laws would be laws of the thermic expansion of mercury and of glass, and laws about the small thermic conductivity of glass, and the antecedent conditions would be the fact that the thermometer consists of a glass tube which is partly filled with mercury and that it is immersed in water. Schematically:

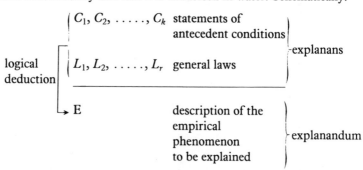

Hempel describes such a form of scientific explanation as *deductive-nomological*. Within it, the event is a logically necessary conclusion once the antecedent conditions and general laws are brought together. It represents the most precise form of positivist explanation, but not the only way that a positivist may attempt to explain an event by laws. According to Hempel, some laws, which may be arrived at through inductive reasoning, are of a statistical form expressing probabilistic trends rather than deterministic uniformities. In such so-called *inductive-statistical* explanations, the event is not a logically necessary conclusion given the antecedent conditions and laws, but rather a highly probable one.

Because positivist explanations take the form of a logical argument in which the occurrence of an event is related to certain *antecedent* conditions, such explanations can serve as the basis for making conditional predictions. Indeed, in this form of explanation, there is a 'structural identity' between explanation and prediction in the sense that explanations logically account for events which have occurred in the past while predictions logically account for events which are expected to occur in the future. In constructing an explanation, the event is known to have occurred and the scientist seeks the general laws and antecedent conditions which account for it. In making a conditional prediction, the general laws and antecedent conditions are known and an event which has not yet occurred is inferred from them.

This structural identity between explanation and prediction provides a basic test of the *adequacy* of positivist scientific explanations. Lawful relationships are established through systematic observation of the world as it is. But if an event which has not yet occurred can be successfully predicted, then the laws which inform the prediction may be held to be valid, and the explanation of the event judged to be complete.

To the positivist, scientific theories consist of laws which enable one both to explain *and* predict events, and the 'truth' or 'falsity' of these laws is established through systematic observation and experiment. The *instrumentalist* view of scientific theories is less stringent. From this perspective, the adequacy of a theory is not assessed in terms of its truth or falsity. Rather, theories are merely 'devices for the generation of successful prediction' (Keat and Urry, 1975, p. 64). Such scientific knowledge may be constructed using mathematical models, such as the gravity model. The gravity model 'explains' the volume of movement of people and goods between two places in terms of the size of those places and the distance between them, as if social interaction obeyed the laws of Newtonian physics. Social activity certainly does not respond to the forces of gravity. But from the instrumentalist perspective the fact that the model is 'unrealistic' does not matter. For when social activity is treated *as if* it obeys Newtonian laws, it is possible to derive relatively good predictions of spatial interaction. In making such predictions the main task of the scientist is not *validation*, but rather *calibration*, that is, improving 'the goodness of fit' of the mathematical model to observable data, so that it provides more accurate predictive information.

This discussion may seem abstruse to readers who are not familiar with the debates in the philosophy of science, and oversimplified to those who are. Yet it is of primary importance. For social scientists who work with an incomplete relational concept of space *necessarily* must also work within a positivist and instrumentalist conception of scientific knowledge. It is possible, within a positivist frame of reference, to identify relations of *logical* necessity and relations of *logical* probability in which spatial variables are significant. And it is possible to build mathematical models which identify spatial 'instrument' variables. But as soon as the task of understanding the social world 'scientifically' is seen as something more than gaining the ability to make conditional predictions, then no adequate scientific explanation may be constructed with an incomplete relational concept of space.

Why this is so may be most easily illustrated by introducing the *realist* view of scientific knowledge. The realist, like the positivist, assumes that there is a world 'out there', external to the scientific investigator, which exists independently of the scientist's beliefs and language of investigation, and that it is possible to construct objective, 'true' explanations. But the realist rejects the view of *causation* on which most positivist scientific knowledge is based. The laws in positivist science are founded on recurrent empirical regularities between the occurrence of events, and if one event is always (or with known probability) followed by another event, then the former is taken to be a 'cause' of the latter. This view of causation allows the construction of logical arguments through which conditional predictions may be made. But it can lead to inadequate explanations, as Hempel himself has shown.

He cites the fact that 'one of the early symptoms of measles is the appearance of small whitish spots, known as Koplik spots, on the mucous lining of the cheeks' and notes that this regular relationship might be taken to be a law which states that 'the appearance of Koplik spots is always followed by the later manifestations of the measles' (Hempel, 1965, p. 374). But though the evident relationship may be used for predictive purposes, we know that it is wrong to conclude that a patient developed fever and other symptoms of measles *because* he previously had Koplik spots. Both Koplik spots and the fever are symptoms of some underlying causal mechanism and it is this which the realist seeks. The cause of an event is thus sought in relationships which are part of the 'essence' or 'inner constitution' of the 'real' world.

These relationships lie below the surface of appearances. They may not be directly observed. Because of this, the positivist would reject any attempt to identify them as a return to non-scientific speculation. But the problems of constructing and verifying realistic scientific knowledge need not detain us here. What is significant is that once a realist view of science is adopted, it is *impossible* to construct scientific knowledge with an incomplete relational concept of space. For while the persistent positivist can, quite validly, search for recurrent empirical regularities in the location of events and on the basis of those regularities argue that the spatial environment is a significant 'cause' of what happens where, to the realist, isolating the 'effects of space' in this way would be like explaining measles by Koplik spots.

Some regional theorists have criticized Anglo-American regional development theory from this standpoint. Lee (1977, p. 26) for example, writes that:

Regional economic relations then are the spatial manifestation of material economic structures, and it follows that the spatial analysis of regional relations is subordinate to structural analysis and that spatial analysis may well distort and obfuscate fundamental structural conditions. Spatial structure is in fact a form created by the mode of production. It is *a mere reflection* of society as a whole.

And Sayer (1976), who has undertaken a comprehensive methodological critique of urban planning models, argues that:

Both gravity and utility-maximizing models abstract the *contingent* spatial and exchange relations from the very contexts and *determining relations* which give rise to them, and treat them in an isolation which excludes the possibility of proper explanation.   (p. 213)

In general, it is Marxist theorists who have criticized regional development theory from a realist viewpoint and they argue that mainstream thinking is characterized by both 'spatial fetishism' and 'reification'. To fetishize something is to invest it with powers which it does not *in itself* have, and 'spatial fetishism' is present whenever the spatial structure or spatial system is taken to be a cause of an event. 'Reification' occurs when an abstract concept is endowed with the capacity to act like a human being (see Kitching, 1978), and is found in many of the theories discussed in Part Two, such as when Friedmann suggests that 'core regions organize the dependence of their respective peripheries through systems of supply, market and administrative areas'; or when Berry argues the metropolitan centres in the USA 'organize the space economy'; or when Santos writes that the metropoli in dependent countries 'are responsible for macro-spatial organization'.

But although it has been mainly Marxist theorists who have criticized Anglo-American regional development theory from this viewpoint, it must be emphasized that a realist critique of theories based upon the incomplete relational concept of space does not require the acceptance of the Marxist theory of history. The realist's position is simply that a scientific explanation must seek the causes of events, not through finding recurrent regularities on the surface of appearances, but rather through identifying the underlying mechanisms which exist in the intrinsic structure of the real world. At present Marxist theory offers the best example of a realist explanation within the social sciences. But a scientist adopting a realistic position would argue that the theory must be tested, modified and abandoned if found to be false.

This discussion merely touches the debates in the philosophy of science over what constitutes a scientific explanation. It is important that regional development theorists are aware of the issues raised, for in the 1970s there has been a critical reappraisal of how knowledge may be constructed within the social sciences (see Bernstein, 1976), and many strong arguments have been made against positivist and instrumentalist science as a form of knowledge (see, for example, Gregory, 1978, and Olsson, 1980, for critiques related to regional theory). But in the present context, I wish to proceed with the assumption that positivism *is* an adequate type of scientific knowledge. Within mainstream Anglo-American regional development theory, the endeavour to construct scientific explanations has been made within a positivist and instrumentalist frame of reference, and the aim here is to assess it *in its own terms*.

However, even when one is this generous, it is still possible to identify fundamental logical problems which arise because of the use of an incomplete relational concept of space. For that concept of space not only requires the adoption of a particular conception of scientific explanation but is also expressed in particular *explanatory forms*. Within the literature it is possible to identify three major forms of explanation using an incomplete relational concept of space:

1 spatial analysis of polarized development;
2 functional analysis;
3 explanations based on the analysis of locational behaviour.

The rest of this chapter discusses the logic, and logical limitations, of each of these forms within a positivist and instrumentalist frame of reference.

SPATIAL ANALYSIS OF POLARIZED DEVELOPMENT

The spatial centre-periphery model

The first form of explanation stems from the coincidental publication of Myrdal's and Hirschman's work on regional disparities in the late 1950s. I separated their ideas within this text to emphasize the fact that they were addressing completely different research questions. But, as noted in chapter 3, there is a formal similarity in their approach, which has led regional theorists to equate their arguments and analyse the spatial incidence of development in terms of backwash (polarization) and spread (trickledown) effects. Friedmann and Weaver (1979, p. 115) even suggest that their work 'set the course of regional planning for the next decades', providing the 'basic paradigm' for the study of 'polarized development' in Anglo-American regional development theory.

The term 'polarized development' is used here to mean spatial disparities in development, and within the 'Hirschman-Myrdal paradigm' changes in disparities are explained by the impact which growth in the dynamic centres of a national territory has on other areas. If the positive ('spread'/'trickledown') effects are stronger than the negative ('backwash'/'polarization') effects, then it is assumed that spatial disparities will diminish; and conversely, they will increase. The exemplar of this approach is Williamson (1965), who in hypothesizing that there is a relationship between regional income inequality and national development (see chapter 3), links the terminology of Myrdal to the prognosis of Hirschman and places each of their analyses within a Rostovian view of the development process.

At the risk of adding to the tangle of jargon within the field, I shall label the general approach which explains the spatial pattern of development in terms of Hirschman's and Myrdal's famous 'effects' the *spatial centre-periphery model*. I use the adjective 'spatial' to describe this model partially because the term 'centre-periphery model' has been adopted by Friedmann to refer to a particular stage in the evolution of a country's spatial organization (see chapter 1), and because within the broader regional literature this term has also been applied in other ways (see Keeble, 1976). But, more important, I use the adjective 'spatial' to emphasize the internal logic of the analytical framework.

This logic is spatial in two senses. First, the 'centre' and 'periphery' are defined as spatial entities, that is, *locations*. This is in marked contrast to the way that sociologists sometimes use the terms. Shils (1961) for example, notes that the 'centre' or 'central zone in the structure of society', is 'a phenomenon of the realm of values and beliefs . . . a phenomenon of the realm of action'. It is 'the centre of the order of symbols, of values and beliefs, which govern society', and 'a structure of activities, of roles and persons, within the network of institutions' (p. 117). In small-group interactions it is thus sometimes said that there is an 'ingroup' and 'outgroup'. And some sections of a national society may be classified as 'marginal' or members of 'the establishment'.

And second, the spatial pattern of development is explained by the *spatial relationships* between 'centre' and 'periphery'. This is an important point to emphasize, for it is possible to describe the morphology of a national economy as some type of centre-periphery structure and analyse the economic performance of central and peripheral regions by referring to general 'centripetal' and 'centrifugal' forces. Those forces may have nothing whatsoever to do with the spatial relationships between 'centre' and 'periphery'. The invention of the blast furnace in the nineteenth century, for example, acted as a strong centripetal force on the location of the iron industry in western Europe or North America, as scattered iron works using the old charcoal-based production techniques were replaced by larger units concentrated on coalfields. The adoption of an import-substitution strategy of industrialization by developing countries may similarly act as a centripetal force as the new industries tend to be established in the national metropoli which are places with maximum access to the internal market. Such forces are excluded from consideration in the spatial centre-periphery model which, in strict terms, merely analyses how growth in the 'centre' may, through various forms of spatial interaction, have positive and negative effects on the economy of the 'periphery'.

In the terms of positivist science, the spatial centre-periphery model provides an analytical framework for the construction of what Bergmann (1958) calls 'process laws' and 'developmental laws'. A 'process law' seeks to explain the different states of a system as it changes through time by establishing 'the relevant variables interacting within the system' and 'the parameters governing interaction among the variables and the direction of the interactions' (Harvey, 1969, p. 419). 'Developmental laws' are crude process laws which show that 'if a system of a certain kind has at a certain time the character A, then it will under normal conditions at some later times successively have the characters (go through the stages) B, C, D, E, F' (Bergmann, 1958, p. 119). Within the analytical framework of the spatial centre-periphery model, the state of the system which is the object of analysis is the degree of 'development' in different *locations*, and changes in the state of the system are explained by reference to *spatial relationships* between localities which engender 'spread' and 'backwash' effects. The laws constructed within this analytical framework would be *spatial* 'process laws' and *spatial* 'development laws' in this dual sense and would suggest that there is an *intrinsic* spatial logic to the evolution of the spatial pattern of development.

As an analytical framework, the spatial centre-periphery model is very flexible. The simple two-region morphological description of the space economy which Hirschman uses (dynamic 'North' and propelled 'South') may be refined by differentiating types of region in the periphery (see, for example, Stöhr, 1975, pp. 91–101), and by superimposing a description of the 'structure of human settlements' on to the pattern of regional differences. From this perspective there may be a nested hierarchy of 'centres' within a country. Viewed at national scale, an intermediate city within a poor region may be said to be part of the 'periphery', but at the same time it can be acting as a 'centre' within its region, its surrounding hinterland being defined as its 'periphery'.

Moreover, it is possible to relate the intensity of the different effects to distance from the centre (see Richardson, 1976), and to elaborate a variety of spatial centre-periphery relations to explain the spatial pattern of development. Myrdal and Hirschman both focus upon the effects of factor movements and trade on regional disparities. But it is equally possible to inject the diffusion of technical progress and social values and spatial power relationships into the model, as Friedmann's 'General theory of polarized development' illustrates. Indeed, *any* spatial relationship between centre and periphery through which growth in the centre has 'effects' on the periphery may be legitimately included.

Such flexibility holds dangers for the unwary regional analyst, for it opens the possibility of eclectic explanations which lump together processes which properly belong to different conceptions of how economic and social change occurs. The neo-classical, Schumpeterian and Perrouxian conception of growth processes are very different, but it is easy to borrow ideas from each and suggest that together they indicate how 'spread effects' occur. But even if the traps of eclecticism are avoided, the spatial centre-periphery model offers the regional analyst a very limited framework for explaining spatial patterns of development.

The first problem with the model is that it fails to theorize the process of growth in the 'centre'. This is not a weakness if the only aim is to explain the non-local effects of growth which is occurring in a city or region, and in growth centre analysis it is assumed from the outset that, through market forces or planning intervention, growth has started in a centre. But in using the model to explain changes in spatial disparities in development it must be assumed, as Hirschman and Myrdal do, that once a momentum of growth is started in the 'centre', it is *self*-sustaining. It can be argued that certain necessary conditions must be fulfilled before this occurs. Thompson (1965), for example, hypothesizes that once a certain population level is reached in a city, its future growth is assured. But even with this refinement, the possibility that the momentum of growth may be stopped or reversed by general factors, such as the rise in oil prices, is ignored.

Within the literature, the failure to theorize growth processes in the centre is often disguised through the use of organic or mechanical analogies. The mechanical analogy is most obvious. Growth centres are described as 'suction-pumps', 'lift-pumps', 'counter-magnets' and 'generators of development impulses', and the failure of them to engender spread effects is sometimes attributed to the lack of 'transmission lines' (see Higgins, 1978). The organic analogy, in which the nation is taken to be an organism whose health depends on the strength of its 'heart' and the absence of blockages in the arteries through which 'blood' reaches is extreme-most cells, is less explicitly used, but perhaps even more pervasive. It is no coincidence that the term 'core' comes from the French word *le coeur* – the heart.

Setting aside these observations, there is a second problem which limits the utility of the spatial centre-periphery model as an explanatory framework. This is quite simply that it is *logically* impossible to use the model in the way in which it is normally applied within the literature – that is, to explain changes in the spatial disparities of development. It must first of all be assumed that the only source of economic change in the periphery comes from growth in the centre and that there are no general centrifugal and centripetal forces other than those associated with spatial relationships. But even then it can only be argued that when growth in the 'centre' is generating more negative effects in the 'periphery' than positive effects, the economic disparity between 'centre' and periphery will *increase*. It *cannot* be concluded conversely that when growth in the 'centre' is generating more positive effects in the periphery than negative effects, the disparity will *decrease*. For the disparity depends on the *difference* between how much growth has occurred in the 'centre' and how much growth is induced in the periphery. It is perfectly possible, therefore, for the spread effects of growth in the centre to be strong and backwash effects to be weak yet at the same time for economic disparities to *increase* because the induced growth in the periphery is less than the growth in the centre which is assumed to have induced it.

This logical problem may be avoided if the terms spread/backwash and trickledown/polarization effects are redefined, as they are in the following quotation:

> The cities of a country at the same time represent an interrelated system in which developmental impulses are transmitted upward and downward through the urban hierarchy. . . . Impulses transmitted from the main metropolitan centre downwards to the intermediate and small cities are principally innovation and power, while those transmitted from the small cities upwards to the main metropolitan centres are principally labour, capital and natural resources. These flows *cause* the spread and backwash effects. . . . Similar flows occur between individual cities and their respective hinterlands and also cause spread and backwash effects between them. The sum of these two sets of spread and backwash effects *determines* the geographical pattern of development over the entire country.   (Stöhr, 1975, pp. 167–8)

Backwash/polarization effects are defined here as *any* form of spatial inter-action which causes a more spatially polarized (concentrated) pattern of development; and spread/trickledown effects are those which cause a more spatially dispersed (evenly spread) pattern. Such redefinition is not an isolated example within the regional development literature (see, for example, Richardson's World Bank Report on *City Size and National Spatial Strategies in Developing Countries*, 1977). But if this change is made, the spatial centre-periphery model loses its key analytical concept, which is that growth in one place has non-local effects. There is a danger that an analysis which began as an example of circular and cumulative causation ends as an exercise in circular reasoning. Spatial disparities are said to be caused by the relative strengths of backwash and spread effects, but these effects are, at the same time, defined by their impact on spatial disparities. The mechanisms which 'cause' the spatial disparities thus lose their separateness and become coterminous with the disparities. And the only analytical task which may then be addressed is to *list* the different types of 'effects', and to specify conditions under which they are relatively strong or weak.

Strictly speaking, the only aspect of the spatial pattern of development which may be explained using the spatial centre-periphery model as an analytical framework is the way in which *peripheral* cities, regions and rural localities develop. Even then, rigorous analysis is only possible after making *a priori* assumptions about how 'development' occurs and, from this basis, showing how growth in the 'centre' has non-local effects in the 'periphery'. And the explanation is incomplete unless it is further assumed that the periphery has *no* autonomous capacity for change. If it is accepted that the periphery can develop through 'internal forces' as well as external impulses, problems of empirical testing of the model arise, for in such a situation it is very difficult to isolate that part of the economic change in the periphery which is caused by the famous 'effects'.

The spatial centre-periphery model can thus be most easily applied to explain change in the periphery *after* adopting either a dualist or a stagnationist view of conditions in developing countries. If the periphery is described as a static society, bound by tradition yet transformed through contact with a modern, dynamic 'centre', then its *development* may be totally explained by the positive effects which the dynamism of the centre has upon it. And if, conversely, the periphery is described as a malleable society, changing yet warped through contact with a rich centre, then its *underdevelopment* may be totally explained by the negative effects which the dynamism of the centre has upon it.

Spatial diffusion analysis

Some regional theorists include the diffusion of technical progress and social values as a 'spread' or 'trickledown' effect in the spatial centre-periphery model. But it is worth distinguishing the spatial diffusion analysis as a separate approach to the spatial analysis of polarized development. This may seem like splitting hairs. But the distinction is necessary for analytical clarity, as spatial diffusion analysis has some features and limitations which are not present in the model based upon the false synthesis of Myrdal's and Hirschman's work.

I use the term 'spatial diffusion analysis' to refer to a particular approach within the broader field of the theory of innovation diffusion. In that approach, the object of analysis is the *spatial form* of innovation adoption, which is described by a series of maps which depict the spatial pattern of adoptions at successive points in time. And the explanation of the evolution of the spatial pattern emphasizes the role of *spatial relationships*, particularly information flows between places, in determining the timing of adoption. The approach may be used to 'explain' the spatial pattern of development if one assumes that 'development' occurs in a city or region or rural locality after an innovation is adopted there. The spatial pattern of 'development' is then explained by the paths via which an innovation diffuses outwards from the centres in which adoption first occurs, and by the rate of diffusion. Berry's work summarized in chapter 3 is a good example of the approach. But it may also be illustrated by the following quotation from Riddell (1970), who adopts a modernization perspective on 'development':

> Modernization is a spatial-diffusion process, assuming patterns of varying intensity and rate. Its origins are localized in specific regions or zones, indexing a contact situation and the pattern of change move like waves across the map, and cascade down the urban hierarchy as they are funnelled along the transport system. (p. 45)

Such spatial analysis stems from the seminal work of Hägerstrand, *Innovation Diffusion as a Spatial Process* (1967), which was originally published in Swedish in 1953. The title of the book is significant, for it emphasizes the fact that its objective was to analyse diffusion *as a spatial process*. Hägerstrand was concerned to explain the time at which small-scale farmers within a region of central Sweden adopted innovations, such as taking advantage of government subsidies to improve pasture, or vaccinating their cattle against tuberculosis. From maps describing the spatial pattern of adoptions at different points in time over a ten to fifteen year period, Hägerstrand noted the presence of a distinct 'neighbourhood effect' − that is, a tendency for farmers who lived close to the farmers who first adopted the innovation to adopt the innovation earlier than those living further away − and he ascribed this pattern to the fact that farmers living close together tended to communicate more than those living further apart. The spatial patterns were thus explained by the distance decay in information flows within the region.

In this case, it may be legitimate to study innovation diffusion *as a spatial process*. The farmers possessed both the technical and economic means for adoption and the innovations studied were demonstrably desirable, and thus, as Blaut (1977) points out, 'information was, in essence, the only missing variable, the only element needed to set the diffusion in motion' (p. 344). But: can the same approach be used to explain innovation adoption by small-scale farmers in developing countries, where resource constraints are severe and severely skewed, and innovations may be untested outside experimental conditions? Can the approach be applied to explain innovation adoption over longer periods of time at a national scale and for different types of innovation, such as a new industry? And can the approach be applied to study 'development' *as a spatial process*?

To do so requires drastic limitations on one's perspective of how both innovation and development occur. Hägerstrand's analysis falls within what Blaikie (1978) calls the 'item-communication-adoption paradigm' of innovation diffusion, and both Blaikie (1978) and Blaut (1977) have pointed out its numerous weaknesses. In this paradigm, people adopt innovations in a similar manner to the way in which they catch diseases: through contact. The main explanatory variable is information, and once an individual knows about an innovation, it is assumed that adoption will occur sooner or later, or in the extreme instance, never, depending on the characteristics of the potential adopter. These characteristics limit the desirability and feasibility of adoption, and late adopters ('laggards') may be said to be 'resistant to change' just as some people are resistant to diseases.

In order to conceptualize innovation adoption in this manner, it is necessary to assume that discrete bits of information, which relate to a particular innovation, are flowing, somehow, across geographic space and are received by human minds within which discrete bits of knowledge are heaped, 'like apples in a basket' (Blaut, 1977). All the complexities of how individuals acquire knowledge and what makes information meaningful to them are ignored within the paradigm. Moreover, in identifying information as the major *independent* variable which explains innovation diffusion, the social structures which determine channels of communication are excluded from consideration. And in making information the *major* variable, resource constraints, such as access to the means of production, are relegated to a secondary position in the explanation of adoption and non-adoption. In the more sophisticated studies, attempts have been made to assess the relative importance of information and resource variables in innovation adoption. But such empirical exercises artificially separate variables which are interrelated.

The limitations of the 'item-communication-adoption paradigm' characterize all spatial analysis of innovation diffusion. But further weaknesses arise because of a focus upon the *spatial form* of diffusion. Once the object of explanation is a series of maps describing the evolution of the spatial pattern of innovation adoption, the analytical problem is reduced to the question of explaining why *a city* or *a region* adopts an innovation sooner or later than another one. Regional theorists have, of course, assumed that innovations are being adopted by households or entrepreneurs *in* those places. But the problem is how to introduce people into the spatial analysis.

The best 'explanations' of the spatial form of diffusion which have been devised are mathematical models, which have been either derived from epidemiology, or are based on the mechanical analogy of the gravity model. The complex equations within such models can be calibrated so that they faithfully reproduce the diffusion pattern and with an instrumentalist view of knowledge they are perfectly adequate. But they distort the social process of innovation adoption even further than the simplifications of the 'item-communication-adoption paradigm'. For example, in Berry's analysis, it is assumed that once an innovation is adopted in a town, that town will transmit information to other towns which have not yet adopted, and the innovation will be adopted in those towns, if they have a large enough population, once they receive sufficient information.

The worst 'explanations' of the spatial form of diffusion merely take a description of the spatial pattern of adoption to be an explanation. Thus, for example, when Riddell (1970) finds that 'modern' institutions 'cascade down the urban hierarchy as they are funnelled along the transport system' in Sierra Leone, he concludes that the 'geographic fabric of the country' – the transportation network and urban-administrative hierarchy – 'directs and *determines* the pattern of spatial evolution' (p. 86, emphasis added).

Spatial analysis of innovation diffusion is only possible if the social processes of innovation are grossly oversimplified. But even further assumptions are required to relate innovation adoption to 'development'. It is easiest to explain the spatial pattern of 'development' using a spatial analysis of innovation diffusion as a conceptual framework if development is equated with 'modernization', and 'modernization' is equated with the adoption of the techniques, institutions and values which are found in the industrialized west.

It certainly is possible to relate the diffusion of technical progress to economic growth and some regional theorists have constructed modified neo-classical growth models which incorporate the diffusion of innovation between regions (Fu-chen Lo, 1978). But the relationships between innovation and growth are complex and it is just too simple to assume, as Berry does in his study of the diffusion of TV stations and TV sets in the USA that 'growth occurs as a consequence of the filtering of innovations downwards through the urban hierarchy and the spread of use of the innovation among consumers residing within the urban fields of the adopting centres' (see above, p. 110). An innovation is likely to have various employment and income effects in a region. The beauty of the modernization perspective theorists who wish to analyse the spatial pattern of development within a country as the outcome of a diffusion process is that within that perspective innovation is, *by definition*, development.

Thus, just as the spatial centre-periphery model is most easily applied once a dualist or stagnationist conception of society is assumed, spatial diffusion analysis fits the view of development as modernization. Indeed, it may be said that if these approaches to the explanation of the development of cities, regions and rural localities are used rigorously, the spatial framework for analysis *pre-selects* a conception of development.

Spatial dependency analysis

In an earlier chapter, dependency was defined after dos Santos as 'a conditioning situation in which the economies of one group of countries are conditioned by the development and expansion of others' (see above, p. 135). With this definition, the analysis of dependency relationships is predicated on the application of the spatial centre-periphery model *at a world scale*. Indeed dos Santos (1973), in elaborating the nature of the 'conditioning situation', reproduces what Friedmann and Weaver call the 'Hirschman-Myrdal paradigm'. He writes that:

> A relationship of interdependence between two or more economies or between such economies and the world trading system becomes a dependent relationship when some countries can expand through self-impulsion while others, being in a dependent position, can only expand as a reflection of the expansion of the dominant countries, which may have positive or negative effects on their immediate development. (p. 76)

Such positive effects are equivalent to the 'trickledown' and 'spread' effects; while the negative effects can be equated with 'polarization' or 'backwash' effects.

Regional development theorists who undertake spatial dependency analysis argue that changes in developing countries must be understood from an historical perspective, and this raises special issues about the nature of historical explanations. But while these are important, the present discussion will focus on problems within spatial dependency analysis which arise from the logic of the spatial centre-periphery model and the assumption of the dependency theorists that the effects of the centre's expansion on the periphery is *necessarily* negative.

The logical problems are clearest in the crude applications of the dependency perspective which focus upon the spatial transfer of surplus as a cause of 'polarized development'. In such analyses the transfer of surplus is to the regional dependency theorist what the diffusion of innovation is to the regional modernization theorist. The pattern of surplus transfer is determined by the network of exchange relations between areas just as the pattern of innovation adoption is determined by the network of communications. And just as innovation brings 'development' to an area, so the transfer of surplus brings 'underdevelopment' to the source areas and 'development' to the receiving areas.

The first problem with an explanation of spatially polarized development couched in such terms is that, unlike in spatial diffusion studies, which can easily map the distribution of an artefact at different points in time, the empirical identification of 'flows of surplus' is extremely difficult. The empirical task requires some standard by which to measure the 'value' of goods and services produced in different areas. This raises very complex issues which cannot be addressed here (see Kitching, 1980, Appendix, for an introduction). But it may be noted that the simple equation of market prices with the 'value' of goods and services is misleading, as it ignores what has been invested in the production of those commodities, in terms of both physical equipment and labour-time.

Disregarding the empirical difficulties, two further limitations arise in the spatial analysis of surplus transfer. First, such analysis *requires* a conception of surplus which may be separated from the production process. Without such a conception it would be impossible to speak of 'the surplus of a region', for once the idea of 'surplus', however it is defined, is related to production, the analytical problem immediately shifts to a consideration of the 'surplus' of social groups or classes. The modes by which social groups appropriate 'surplus' from other groups may be analysed in a spatial context. But such an analysis would be very different from an account of how the surplus *of a region* is extracted *by another region*. The importance of Baran's definitions of 'surplus', summarized in chapter 4, is that they allow one to think in terms of an *area's* surplus. As soon as one adopts the classical Marxist definition of the production of surplus value under capitalism, purely spatial analysis of surplus transfer becomes impossible.

One may or may not agree with Baran's definitions of 'actual' and 'potential surplus'. But even if one does, the attempt to relate the *transfer* of surplus to patterns of development and underdevelopment is necessarily deficient, as it ignores questions about the *use* of surplus. In Baran's analysis, the size of the actual surplus sets the *upper* limits to new investment which in turn determines the rate of economic growth. A drain of surplus may be one reason why the actual surplus in a region is less than it could 'potentially' be. But this does not necessarily mean that the actual surplus is less than what it would have been *in the absence* of the interconnection of that region into the world system. And there is no reason for concluding that if the actual surplus were larger there would have been more growth within that region. Without consideration of the way the surplus is used within the region, the conclusion is merely a hypothetical assumption.

Similarly, the transfer of surplus to other regions does not necessarily mean that those regions will grow faster. Again, it depends upon the use of the surplus and, in Baran's formulation, the way in which it is capitalized in new investment. This *may* be concentrated in the regions to which surplus is transferred but, as Brewer (1980, p. 175) succinctly puts it, 'the geographical pattern of investment need not correspond at all to the geographical distribution of owners of the surplus'. The transfer of surplus, *in itself*, does not therefore provide any explanation of patterns of development and underdevelopment.

The fundamental weakness of attempts to relate the spatial transfer of surplus to patterns of polarized development is that the spatial relationship of surplus transfer is abstracted from the social processes which determine both the relationship and its development implications. The more sophisticated applications of the dependency perspective avoid this problem. Santos (1979), for example, attempts to analyse *social* and *spatial* relationships within developing countries, in terms of the way they are conditioned by spatial centre-periphery relationships at a world scale. But in such dependency analyses, logical problems immediately arise in that the world-scale relationships are assumed to be negative from the outset, and any 'development' which occurs is labelled 'misdevelopment' or 'inauthentic' development.

It cannot, of course, be denied that what is happening within the countries of Africa, Asia and Latin America is affected by the world events. But if the hypothesized process of 'authentic development' is not fully described, it becomes impossible to refute the conclusions of spatial dependency analysis empirically, as *any* change can be said to be a 'distortion' from an unspecified norm. And if the process of authentic development is associated loosely with some notion of 'self-centred' development, then everything that is occurring within dependent countries becomes 'inauthentic' *by definition*. So what appears to be an explanation is merely a tautology. And 'analysis' is reduced to a listing of facts which supposedly confirm the 'distorting' influence of multi-national corporations or verify the 'comprador' role of the state (see Bernstein, 1979).

FUNCTIONAL ANALYSIS

Functional analysis is a second form of explanation within Anglo-American regional development theory which uses an incomplete relational concept of space. It is more difficult to isolate than spatial analysis of polarized development, as it is sometimes implicit within applications of the spatial centre-periphery model and as it is often only evident in isolated statements about the 'role' of particular elements of the spatial structure, especially small and medium sized towns. But a functionalist perspective is widely applied within the field and is particularly important in that it is not only used to explain spatial distributions but also to formulate normative judgements about them. For, as we shall see, it is a form of explanation which explains what *is* in a way which suggests what *ought* to be.

The basic logic of functional explanation

The logic of functional analysis is most clearly set out by Hempel (1965). He summarizes its nature as follows:

> The kind of phenomenon that a functional analysis is invoked to explain is typically some recurrent activity of some behaviour pattern in an individual or a group, such as a physiological mechanism, a neurotic trait, a culture pattern or a social institution. And the principal objective of the analysis is to exhibit the contribution which the behaviour pattern makes to the preservation or the development of the individual or the group in which it occurs. Thus, functional analysis seeks to understand a behavior pattern or a socio-cultural institution by determining the role it plays in keeping the given system in proper working order or maintaining it as a going concern. (pp. 304–5)

A functional analysis of a spatial pattern, such as a particular city size distribution, or the presence of a network of market towns, or the existence of regional income disparities, would thus seek to determine the role which it plays in maintaining some defined social system in 'proper working order'.

The first essential condition for constructing a functional explanation is that the notion of the system being 'in proper working order' is clearly specified. This is because in functional analysis, the *effects* of a behaviour pattern or social arrangement are taken to be its *causes*, and this curious form of reasoning cannot provide an explanation unless both the system and criteria for it working 'properly' are defined.

Hempel illustrates the point with the following comparison of two functional statements:

1 The heartbeat in vertebrates has the function of circulating blood through the organism.
2 The heartbeat has the function of producing heart sounds.

(p. 305)

In both these statements, it is possible to substitute the phrase 'the heartbeat has the effect of . . .'. But one cannot argue that the latter statement somehow explains the heartbeat. It is merely descriptive. The former statement, on the other hand, can provide the basis of a functional explanation of the heartbeat, as it may be extended as follows:

3 The heartbeat has the effect of circulating the blood, and this ensures the satisfaction of certain conditions (supply of nutriment and removal of waste) which are necessary for the proper working of the organism.   (p. 305)

The presence of the heartbeat is then explained by the effects which it produces.

Within this example, both the system being analysed and the criterion of 'proper working order' may be easily identified. The circulation of blood within the living organism supplies nutrients and removes waste from its various parts, a process which is essential if it is to stay alive. But in the social sciences it is much more difficult to isolate systems and to specify the conditions in which they work properly.

Consider, for example, the following statement:

Core regions together with development corridors perform a critical role in generating impulses of economic development and transmitting them to other parts of the space economy.

(Friedmann, 1966, p. 101)

This is exactly the same as statements (1) and (2) in the paragraph above, and like the second statement it is merely descriptive if the effects produced by the core region do not somehow contribute to the 'proper functioning' of the system of which it is part. The starting-point for constructing a functional *explanation* on the basis of Friedmann's statement would thus entail defining the system in question – which in this case would probably be the nation state – and postulating that the process of generating and transmitting development impulses is essential for the survival of the social system. What 'survival' might mean in this context is debatable. But the most obvious meaning would be the reproduction of existing social relations.

The definition of the system and its conditions of proper functioning is essential for functional *explanation*. But the function-statements discussed thus far should not be confused with explanations. To formulate an explanation it is necessary to specify the conditions, both within the system and in its environment, under which the item being explained performs its function. As Hempel illustrates, 'circulation will fail if there is a rupture of the aorta; the blood can carry oxygen only if the environment affords an adequate supply of oxygen and the lungs are in proper condition; and it will remove certain kinds of waste only if the kidneys are reasonably healthy' (p. 305). We could then extend Friedmann's statement by specifying that the transmission of development impulses will only occur if there are no 'strangulation points' in core region development, as Friedmann himself puts it; if there is a well-developed urban hierarchy, and a well-knit transport network; and if the external environment of the nation state, defined by the nature of the international economic system, is founded on relations of mutual interdependence.

The conversion of statements about the 'function' or 'role' of an element within the spatial system into an explanation of that element is thus a complex task. We may exemplify what such an explanation would look like in formal terms by taking two quotations from Rondinelli and Ruddle (1978). They assert that:

1 Integration of subsistence communities into the national economy . . . is essential to national development, for commerce and trade cannot be extended without linking local and peripheral markets to major metropolitan centres. (p. 160)
2 Market towns perform functions essential to the commercialization of agriculture. (p. 175)

These statements would be converted into a functional explanation of market towns in the following way:

a At a certain time, t, the national economic system, s, functions adequately (that is, grows with equity) in a setting of kind, c (characterized by specific internal and external conditions).
b s functions adequately in a setting of kind, c, only if a certain necessary condition, n, is satisfied. In this case the necessary condition is

the commercialization of agriculture and integration of subsistence communities into the national economy.

c If trait, i, a network of market towns, is present in s, then, as an effect, condition n would be satisfied.

d Hence, at t, a network of market towns is present in s.

Functional explanation in regional development theory

Functionalism, as a working method, was first adopted in the social sciences by anthropologists. They argued that within a human group, such as an African tribe, all elements of social life should be studied as an interconnected working 'whole', and that recurrent activities, such as a funeral ceremony, may be explained by their contribution to the continued functioning of the 'whole'. Within North American sociology, the approach was propagated by the influential work of Parsons, who constructed a structural-functionalist theory of social systems which examined the *structure* of a social system in terms of the different roles which individuals and institutions play within it, and the *functioning* of that system in terms of the way the role contributes to the maintenance of the social system and the way that the system adapts to problems which threaten its continued functioning. This functionalist perspective pervades the language of Anglo-American regional development theory and terms such as 'spatial structure' and 'spatial system' represent the translation of Parsonian structural-functionalism into a spatial context.

The logic of functional analysis summarized above is one way in which 'the spatial structure of development', to use Friedmann and Alonso's phrase, has been 'explained'. But normally the necessary requirements to convert function-statements about the role of an element of spatial structure, such as a core region and market town, into a functional explanation have not been observed. And thus the statements merely provide descriptions which are similar in form to the statement that 'the heartbeat has the function of producing heart-sounds'.

Even if the stringent requirements necessary to construct a functional explanation had been followed, there are strong grounds for rejecting this form of explanation as an adequate basis for understanding the social world. The debates on this issue have been long (see Demerath and Peterson, 1967). But one central problem which social theorists have identified is the idea that a social system 'needs' certain traits in order to keep it in 'proper working order'. This idea may be appropriate for explaining the presence of organs in biological organisms, but many social theorists reject the idea that a social system has 'needs' as conceptually unsound, in that it obscures the purposive actions of individuals within society and the unintended consequences of their actions (see, for example, Giddens, 1977, chapter 2).

One may disagree on this issue for it turns upon deep questions about how society can and should be understood. But even if these objections are swept aside, functional explanations are invariably *weak* explanations. As Hempel suggests, such explanations are only strong in cases where it may be asserted that the system functions adequately in a particular setting *if and only if* a certain necessary condition is satisfied. In most cases, there are likely to be 'functional alternatives', 'functional substitutes' or 'functional equivalents' which will also satisfy the necessary condition. One could, for example, substitute 'the establishment of state and collective farms' for 'agrarian commercialization' in the example taken from Rondinelli and Ruddle. And once such substitution is possible, then the functional 'explanation' is reduced to an assertion that one *out of a set* of possible traits must exist to maintain the proper functioning of the system. This is inevitably a weak explanation, if it can be called an explanation at all, for the reasons why, in any given case, a particular trait, rather than another one in the set of functional alternatives, fulfils that need is left out of consideration.

This point is significant because regional theorists have not only used function-statements to 'explain' spatial patterns, but also to prescribe more desirable patterns. The quotation from Rondinelli and Ruddle, for example, is the basis for their prescriptive judgement that *if* the national economy is to function adequately, to grow with equity, a network of market towns must be created. And such logic also underlies Johnson's expectation that the creation of 'functional economic areas' will result in beneficial effects.

At best such judgements may be constructed through taking a weak functional explanation which recognizes the existence of functional alternatives; converting it into a conditional or *hypothetical* prediction of the form:

1 System *s* functions adequately in a setting of kind *c* only if condition *n* is satisfied;
2 *I* is the class of empirically sufficient conditions for *n* in the context determined by *s* and *c*; and *I* is not empty;
3 If *s* functions adequately in a setting of kind *c* at time *t*, then some one of the items in class *I* is present in *s* at *t*.

(Hempel, 1965, p. 316)

and finally *inverting* the hypothetical prediction to state that if a particular element is *not* present in the system at time *t*, it will *not* function adequately. I leave it to the reader to decide whether such a convolution, *which represents the best way in which a functional explanation of what IS may be converted into a prescriptive judgement of what OUGHT TO BE,* is an adequate basis for policy.

Functional explanation of spatial change

Social theorists who construct functional explanations have argued that social systems may be studied both *synchronically* and *diachronically*. In 'synchronic' analysis, the social system is abstracted at a given moment in time, and it is with this perspective that the 'spatial structure' or 'spatial system' is identified. In 'diachronic' analysis, change over time is analysed and, in a spatial context, this entails explaining how the elements and relationships of a spatial system evolve.

Within Anglo-American regional development theory, the approach to 'diachronic' functional analysis follows the logic of Parsons. His monumental work is impossible to summarize here, but we may abstract a few key points about his view of social change which can help identification of this form of analysis within the field and also provide a basis for examining some of its logical weaknesses.

The starting-point for the Parsonian account of social change is a social system which is in equilibrium with its environment in the sense that all the elements which are necessary to maintain it in 'proper working order' are present. Part of the analysis of the functioning of the social system shows the ways it 'comes to terms with the exigencies imposed by a changing environment, without essential change in its own structure' (Parsons, in Demerath and Peterson, 1967, p. 192). But in certain circumstances, the social system cannot meet all its 'functional needs' to maintain its present structure. This may arise through exogenous factors, such as the introduction of factory industry or the deterioration of the physical environment; or it may arise through endogenous 'strains', which occur when the relationships between elements in the system *themselves* set up pressures for change. In either case, the system must reorganize as it moves towards a new equilibrium.

The process of structural change has various facets, but the two most important are *structural differentiation* and *reintegration*. 'Structural differentiation' involves the creation of new roles within a social system, such as occurred with the increasing division of labour concomitant with the industrial revolution in western Europe. And 'reintegration' involves the introduction of mechanisms which regulate the social 'strains' which may be associated with 'differentiation'. For example, the creation of industrial trade unions may be seen as an institution which 'copes with' the problems of a new division of labour.

This thumb-nail sketch is all too brief. But it provides a basis for identifying the application of such logic to understanding change in *spatial
systems* within Anglo-American regional development theory. The
clearest example is found within the work of John Friedmann (again).
His account of the stages of spatial organization through which every
country passes (summarized in chapter 1), although it is based on what is
supposed to have happened in the USA, is, at the same time, the spatial
correlate of the Parsonian theory of social change. A society which
initially consists of a set of semi-autarchic regional economies in
equilibrium with their physical environment is 'disturbed' by the introduction of industry. *Spatial* differentiation follows, with industry localized in the dynamic 'centre' of the space economy. But over time, the
'spatial system' becomes more and more spatially integrated until it
finally reaches a new equilibrium in which all problems of spatial organization are resolved.

Hirschman's account of the way in which the North-South problem
within countries is resolved uses similar functionalist logic. Up to a
certain point, the 'polarization effects' of growth in the dynamic centres
of an economy exceed the 'trickledown effects', a condition which leads
to increasing regional disparities. But after a certain point, trickledown
effects strengthen *via-à-vis* polarization effects, a change which supposedly leads to decreasing disparities. The inevitability of this change is
not explained by Hirschman. But it rests upon the implicit assumptions
that the disparity constitutes a 'strain' and the social system, which
includes the state, will behave in an equilibrating manner. The strength-
ening 'trickledown effects' do not solely occur as an effect of growth in
the dynamic region, but also as an effect of the increasing regional disparities. Regional disparities will, after a certain point, have to diminish,
as the social system copes with the 'strains' which disparities set up.

Such arguments are clearly more complex than the basic logic of functional explanation introduced at the beginning of this section. And they
may be used to explain spatial changes which occur as a system evolves,
as well as the characteristics of that system at any moment in time. But
this added complexity unfortunately only brings further logical complications.

The main new problem is that just as the synchronic perspective
requires some notion of the social system being 'in proper working
order' to get beyond mere description, the diachronic perspective
requires some notion of the particular *end-state* towards which structural
change is directed. As Taylor (1979) points out, the assertion that the
system will reorganize to meet the needs of new functional imperatives
'cannot, *in itself*, establish what qualitatively new phenomena will

emerge within the structure, or which phenomena will be transformed in what direction' (p. 29). However, the extra *assumption*, that the system is directed towards a future goal, allows the prediction of the structural changes associated with given disturbances.

This implies that functional explanations of spatial change must be based on some *a priori* assumption of the goal towards which the social system is directed. Such an assumption is made within modernization theory and in that case the end-state towards which all structural changes in developing countries are supposedly directed is the condition of modernity, represented by the social structures found within western Europe and North America. But most social theorists would argue that the view that social systems are evolving towards some definable end-state is conceptually unsound.

EXPLANATIONS BASED ON ANALYSES OF LOCATIONAL BEHAVIOUR

One conspicuous feature of the explanations considered thus far is the absence of people acting as knowledgeable agents who shape the world. The metropoli, the urban hierarchies and the core regions are all said to have effects. But where are the people, acting as individuals or in groups? The last form of explanation is one which attempts to relate spatial distributions to human behaviour. But with an incomplete relational concept of space, such explanations are based on analyses of *locational* behaviour.

Analysis of locational behaviour is concerned with the location choices which individual decision-making units, such as a household or firm, make. Examples are a firm's decision about where to set up a factory, a rural migrant's decision about which city to move to, a farmer's decision about where to sell his produce and where to buy goods and services. In the analysis of such decisions, it is possible to identify 'location factors' which are characteristics of a locality which may attract or repel the individual.

Explanations based on analyses of locational behaviour may be criticized at various levels, and the reader may usefully refer to the work of Doreen Massey for a comprehensive and incisive discussion of industrial location theory (Massey, 1973; 1974). Here I shall focus upon just two problems which limit the adequacy of such explanations within a positivist and instrumentalist conception of scientific knowledge.

The first problem is that analyses of locational behaviour must be based on some 'laws of individual behaviour', and these are presently lacking in the social sciences. As a result, analysis usually proceeds from the *assumption* that people behave in a particular way. Much classical location theory, and the early work in regional science and theoretical geography, was based on the fiction of 'economic man', an individual who always sought to maximize profits or minimize costs. In Perloff's analysis of regional growth in the USA (see chapter 3), it is assumed that businessmen choose locations in order to maximize profits. And the expectation that urban-industrial growth poles in peripheral regions can act as 'counter-magnets', which divert migrants away from the metropoli, is based on the assumption, succinctly summarized by Levy and Wadycki, (1974), that 'the probability of an individual migrating from a specific origin to a specific destination is a function of characteristics which reflect the average costs and benefits of the origins and destination regions and the distance between them' (p. 201). The migrant is expected to behave as if he or she were responding to the forces of gravity, and so the greater the opportunities (mass) available within a regional centre, and the closer it is to the migration source area, the more attractive it will be.

There have been attempts to avoid such simplifications. Alonso (1975), for example, offers an interesting account of the non-economic factors influencing industrial location decisions in developing countries. But speculations of this type, however well-informed and however plausible, are not the same as scientific explanations.

In the absence of general laws of individual behaviour, it is possible to construct statistical correlation models which 'explain' locational behaviour (see, for example, Riddell, 1970, for rural-urban migration patterns in Sierra Leone). But such models are only valid in the context in which they are formulated; they invariably only offer a partial explanation of behavioural patterns; and what is unexplained, supposedly 'random' behaviour, is as much a product of the model as of the world. Moreover, if the explanatory information contained in such models is used to *predict* what 'location factors' will attract or repel individuals, it must be assumed that what pertained in the past will continue in the future.

It is questionable whether it is possible to formulate any *general* laws of individual locational behaviour if such behaviour is abstracted from the broader social and economic structure. But if progress could be made in this direction, or if one believes that economic man or mechanistic analogies offer the best working approximation in present circumstances, there is a second problem which sets strict limits to the extent to which spatial distributions may be explained through analyses of locational behaviour. The problem is how individual location decisions can be interrelated with the aggregate spatial outcome.

The most logical method of explaining aggregate regional development patterns through analysis of individual locational behaviour is that proposed by Perloff and his associates (1960). As summarized in chapter 3, their research task was to explain regional growth in the USA and they were able to relate industrial location decisions to the growth patterns they observed by distinguishing 'volume' and 'welfare' aspects of growth, and by making the object of their analysis *regional deviations* from the average national growth rate, rather than regional growth *per se*. As they recognize, the national pattern of growth is determined by such factors as technological change, capital accumulation, population growth and the discovery of natural resources. But in limiting their research question to the problem of explaining why some regions get a greater *share* of national growth than others, they could take these 'underlying determinants' to be 'external parameters', as they put it. And with the assumption that industrial growth is the basis of regional growth, volume aspects of regional growth could logically be explained in terms of the 'location factors' which attracted particular industrial sectors to particular regions (and thus the mix of fast-growing and slow-growing industries within the different regions) and in terms of particular regional characteristics which, during the period in question, made particular sectors' growth faster or slower than the national average.

Using the Perlovian method, the researcher is 'freed in the beginning from explaining the general state of the national economy' (Thompson, 1968, pp. 204–5), and may logically interrelate individual locational behaviour and regional growth patterns. It is with this logic that it is possible to make sense of Friedmann and Alonso's assertion that 'Regional development concerns the incidence of economic growth. It is ultimately the result of the location of economic activities in response to differential regional attractions' (1964, p. 20). But the Perlovian method may only explain regional deviations from the national average. And it cannot be used to predict changes unless it is assumed that the underlying determinants of growth continue to operate in exactly the same manner as they have in the immediate past.

CONCLUSION

Scientific knowledge within mainstream Anglo-American regional development theory is based on a positivist and instrumentalist conception of science and an incomplete relational concept of space. Adherence to the positivist and instrumentalist view allows the construction of scientific explanations which incompletely relate spatial distributions to the social processes of which they are an integral part. But the use of an incomplete relational concept of space sets very strict limits to what may be explained. The logic of explanation is such that unless the regional theorist is careful, what appears to be an explanation is merely a description. And if the limits to what may be explained are not observed, the 'explanations' become illogical or tautological.

The three major forms of explanation which use an incomplete relational concept of space are: (i) spatial analysis of polarized development, (ii) functional analysis, and (iii) explanations based on the analysis of locational behaviour. The first form of explanation requires so many assumptions that it cannot be said to be adequate even within a positivist and instrumentalist frame of reference. Functional analysis is rejected by many social theorists as a useful way of explaining social life, and even those who take it to be an adequate form of explanation recognize that it can only provide weak explanations. The third form of explanation rests upon either simple assumptions about human intentions, or inferences which are derived from observed behaviour patterns and which have uncertain generality.

Close examination of the logic of explanation with the field thus reveals major weaknesses. These weaknesses are apparent even though the discussion has been made in terms which offer the *least* grounds for mounting a critique. Many powerful arguments may be made against positivist and instrumentalist scientific knowledge *per se*. And if one judges the research methods used within the field against the rigorous procedures which philosophers of science suggest are required to construct scientific theories, one might conclude that it is mere flattery to describe regional development theory as 'theory'. For the hard task of *empirical* research on processes of urban and regional change in developing countries has only just begun.

It can be argued that regional development theorists have been poor scientists. But this reflects a general tendency in the social sciences and does not take us very far. The weakness of Anglo-American regional development theory as a field of knowledge cannot be attributed to human frailty. It is rooted in the structure of its theories.

7

The limits of spatial policy and territorial regional planning

In itself the logical dissertation of the last chapter serves as nothing more than an academic exercise. But it is of wider significance, for the three explanatory forms identified are the 'scientific' basis for many regional planning strategies. The purpose of the first half of this chapter is to examine the consequences which follow when knowledge constructed in this way is translated into practical action. The second half discusses the idea of 'territorial regional planning' as an alternative paradigm which rejects the idea that regional planning should be based on scientific knowledge and which supposedly rests on a different conception of space.

THE NATURE AND LOGICAL BASIS OF SPATIAL POLICY

We may begin by recalling a key feature of many of the regional planning strategies discussed in Part Two of the book. The account there emphasized the differences between the strategies, noting the various developmental perspectives upon which they are based. But the different conceptions of how 'development' occurs give a spurious appearance of diversity. For all the strategic proposals within what Friedmann and Weaver call 'functional regional planning' have a common feature. *They each attempt to achieve a more desirable spatial pattern of 'development' through changing the spatial distribution of infrastructure, economic activities and urban population or through changing the spatial pattern of interaction between areas.*

Proponents of urban-industrial growth pole policy suggest that regional growth may be accelerated *through* the implantation and expansion of large-scale industries in the major city of that region. Johnson argues that agricultural output, and the marketed surplus of a region, may be expanded *through* setting up competitive markets and agro-industries in small towns and *through* investments which increase rural–urban linkage. In the USAID strategy of integrated regional development it is believed that equitable growth may be achieved within poor, mainly rural regions *through* establishing a 'proper' urban hierarchy and fostering spatial linkages. And the advocates of selective spatial closure argue that regional development may be promoted *through* changes in the spatial distribution of power and *by* blocking certain flows of resources into and out of that region. Each of the strategies is concerned with 'locational aspects of development'. But 'location' enters strategy formulation in two ways: both in terms of ends and in terms of means. They attempt to achieve *spatially defined objectives* through *spatial means*.

The rival proposals within functional regional planning may all be defined as *spatial policies*. But they cannot be labelled 'spatial' merely because of the nature of the ends they seek to achieve. For almost all of the policies which manipulate the *aggregate economy* or plan resource allocations *within sectors* have spatially differentiated effects. As Richardson (1978) illustrates, tight monetary policies 'cut off loans to lagging regions'; protective tariffs 'raise incomes in the areas where the protective sectors are highly localized'; energy conservation and price-support measures 'depress welfare and economic activity in cold (or hot) climates'; corporate tax concessions 'benefit the wealthy high-profit regions'; and food subsidies 'raise incomes in, and reduce out-migration from, rural areas' (p. 249). The spatial implications of particular development policies – such as a shift from import-substitution industrialization to export-promotion, the devaluation of the currency and import controls, or the pursuit of land reform – may be difficult to work out. And some policies may have a uniform impact on different regions and localities within a country. But as long as there are some which do not, then it is impossible to differentiate spatial policies from 'aspatial' policies in terms of their effects. What makes a policy 'spatial' is, first, the fact that it seeks some *explicitly defined* spatial effects. But second, and most fundamentally, the fact that it tries to achieve these effects through *spatial means*.

Spatial policies attempt to achieve their objectives through the manipulation of the spatial structure and the spatial system, or through changing the spatial environment within which 'development' occurs. At the simplest level, regional planners following such policies attempt to change the spatial distribution of physical infrastructure, both in terms of the transport network and the built environment of the towns and cities within a country. Infrastructural investment may be designed to enhance the attractiveness of a city, region and rural locality to households and investors, and the simple physical planning measures can be enhanced by economic policies which are designed to change the spatial distribution of investment and living opportunities. Subsidies on capital or labour costs in particular regions are used to attract industrial investment to those regions; and the expansion of job opportunities and services in intermediate cities are used to divert rural–urban migrants away from the metropoli. Measures which ease or restrict the flow of labour and capital between localities are also adopted, along with measures designed to accelerate and channel the spatial diffusion of innovation. And finally, the regional planner pursuing a spatial policy may change the spatial distribution of power.

The means of spatial policy are thus diverse. But the expectation that it is possible to achieve spatially defined objectives *through spatial means* is logically derived from explanations which use an incomplete relational concept of space. This point may be illustrated by returning again to growth pole theory. That body of knowledge has not greatly illuminated our understanding of processes of regional development. But the confusion within it provides a key to understanding our understanding of such processes. The transformation of the growth pole concept as it was applied in regional studies (see chapter 3) is founded upon a switch from a relational to an incomplete relational concept of space, and it is through this transformation that *spatial* growth centre strategies are derived.

Consider, for example, the type of policies which may be inferred from growth pole analysis *as it was originally conceived by François Perroux*. To Perroux, the growth pole is defined as 'a propulsive unit coupled with the surrounding environment' (see above, p. 86). The propulsive unit is not a spatial unit, such as a city or a region, but an economic unit, such as a firm or an industrial sector. And the 'surrounding environment' consists of the firms and sectors with which the propulsive unit has economic relationships. These firms and sectors are not necessarily close to the propulsive unit *in geographic space*. The growth of the related units is induced by the growth of the propulsive unit, and the spatial effects which follow may be traced by projecting the 'delocalized' growth relationships into geographic space. Policies designed to change the spatial pattern of growth must take account of the projection of economic relationships in geographic space, but would not just manipulate the location of economic units. They would logically focus upon the factors which determine the growth of propulsive units and their economic relationships. And they would do so in a way which recognized, as Perroux did, that locational relationships are an integral part of the propulsive mechanism. For, as he noted, spatial agglomeration of the propulsive and propelled units can enhance the growth inducement mechanism.

The precise nature of policies which are designed to achieve spatial objectives and based on Perrouxian growth analysis is difficult to specify because of the nebulous definition of the propulsive unit and the eclectic identification of possible propulsive relationships. But one attempt to do so has been made by Lasuen (1973), who has extended the Schumpeterian basis of Perrouxian thinking in a spatial context. In his work, Lasuen identifies regularities in innovation diffusion paths between *firms*, not *places*, and explains the spatial pattern of development by projecting these economic relationships into geographic space. His analysis suffers from a number of weaknesses which stem from the failure to take account of all the complexities of Schumpeter's view of how economic change occurs, and from the simple equation of innovation and development. But what is significant here is that although the spatial pattern of innovation adoption which Lasuen finds is similar in form to the hierarchical pattern described by the spatial diffusion analysts, his logical approach to the study of diffusion patterns leads to planning measures which are very *different* from a spatial policy. To Lasuen, the spatial pattern of innovation diffusion, and thus development, may be changed through the manipulation of economic relationships and, in particular, policy should be directed towards changing the organizational structure of firms. For, according to Lasuen, innovation diffusion will be faster and more spatially dispersed in a country if firms have a multi-plant, multi-product and multi-locational structure than if they had a more simple organizational structure.

The expectation that spatial objectives may be achieved through spatial means, as it is in all growth centre strategies, is *not* based on growth pole analysis as originally conceived by Perroux, but rather on spatial analysis of polarized development. If the development of peripheral cities, regions and rural localities is seen to be determined by certain *underlying* forces which affect the national economy as a whole, but different localities in different ways, then the measures adopted to accelerate their development should logically be directed towards steering these underlying forces in the desired way. However, if the development of these places is conceptualized as it is in the spatial centre-periphery model and in the spatial diffusion analysis, then it is possible to expect that their development may be accelerated through measures which sustain and accelerate growth, and foster innovation, in a few 'central' *localities* and through measures which influence the *spatial* relationships which engender geographical trickledown effects.

The different planning strategies that may be derived from growth pole theory highlight the fact that policies designed to achieve spatial objectives through spatial means rest upon explanations which use an incomplete relational concept of space. But *all* spatial policies have this logical basis. Analyses of locational behaviour inform measures designed to change the spatial distribution of industry and urban population by making particular cities more attractive to industrialists and rural–urban migrants. Functional analysis underpins strategies which attempt to promote regional and national growth through manipulating the settlement structure and network of spatial linkages, and through fostering greater spatial integration. And the strategy of selective spatial closure is based on the notion that it is possible to promote regional growth through filtering out the negative 'backwash' effects which growth in the dynamic centres has on peripheral regions, while retaining the positive 'trickledown' effects.

THE POTENTIAL EFFECTS OF SPATIAL POLICY

The question which I wish to address here is: what effects are likely to be achieved through spatial policies? Earlier in the book it was argued that the pursuit of spatial objectives could not be considered 'desirable' in any technical sense. But if we accept these objectives as politically given, is it correct to assume that they may be achieved through spatial policies? And are such policies likely to have any predictable social side-effects? Answering these questions empirically is fraught with difficulty – as the discussion on the alleged failure of urban-industrial growth pole strategies shows. But it is possible to deduce the potential effects of spatial policies from the structure of knowledge on which such policies rest. This approach will be adopted here.

In a trivial sense, spatial policies are bound to achieve their spatial objectives. If the present state of industry or a more regular urban hierarchy are taken to be indicators of 'development', then a policy which implants industry within a poor region, or locates urban facilities in a way which defines a settlement hierarchy, can be said to have 'developed' that region. In that sense, the spatial policy is effective because it does what it does!

But spatial policies have not been advocated in this trivial sense. They are expected to achieve a set of spatial outcomes, *through the manipulation* of spatial instrument variables. Scientific explanations constructed within a positivist and instrumentalist frame of reference and using an incomplete relational concept of space provide the logical basis for this expectation. But the structure of knowledge on which the policies are based sets strict limits to the spatial effects which may be achieved through them, and influences their social side-effects.

To begin, it is worth noting that the observation that so-called 'aspatial' policies can be as spatially powerful, in terms of their effects on the spatial distribution of economic activity and population within a country, as spatial policies, has a very important corollary. It implies that *spatial policies cannot achieve their objectives unless they work in concert with sectoral and macro-economic policies*. It is perfectly possible, for example, for a government to be initiating spatial policies which are designed to *reduce* regional and rural–urban disparities in development while at the same time it is pursuing aspatial policies which have *implicit* consequences which *increase* those disparities. Under such circumstances, what the government *visibly* gives the poorer regions and rural localities with its left hand, the spatial policy, it *indirectly* takes away with its right hand, the macro-economic and sectoral policy.

It would be interesting to examine how widespread that situation is in both the richer and poorer countries of the world today. But let us proceed with the analysis of the potential effects of spatial policies with the assumption that they are not being subverted by so-called 'aspatial' policies. Even then, *the only changes in the spatial pattern of 'development' which it is possible to achieve through spatial policies are spatial redistributions*.

What this means requires some clarification. Let us suppose that we have a table, or a series of maps, such as those illustrated earlier in Figures 11 and 19, which depict the spatial distribution of various indicators of 'development' between different regions of a country. The simplest indicator which one may use is regional *per capita* income. But it is possible to add to it other economic indicators such as the distribution of industry, formal sector employment and road density; and social indicators such as infant mortality, the death rate and the education level of the population. And if one wishes to be quantitatively sophisticated, one may combine them all into some composite index which portrays, for that particular set of regions, the spatial incidence of development. The assertion that 'the only changes in the spatial pattern of "development" which it is possible to achieve through spatial policies are spatial redistributions' means that it is possible to change the *share* which a region has of the things which measure 'development'.

This is not to say that the spatial policy does not have a real spatial outcome. It *can* increase the share which a poor region has of the GNP; the share which it has of national industry or of national formal sector employment; and the share it has of national health and education facilities. It *can* thereby reduce regional disparities in 'development'. But it does so through spatial *redistributions*. In conditions of stagnation, a spatial policy which makes a poor region relatively better off *vis-à-vis* other regions does so *at the expense of* those regions. In conditions of growth, it does so by steering a greater *share* of the benefits of increasing national prosperity to the poor region. And in conditions of economic decline, it does so by steering a greater *share* of the misery of national decline away from the poor region.

Why is this so? There is one obvious and simple answer. The state development funds which are allocated to one region are the potential development funds of other regions. In any year the government has a given public expenditure budget, and a decision to increase the allocation of capital investment and recurrent expenditure within a poor region will reduce the share being spent in other regions. But this cannot be a complete answer. For most developing countries have mixed economies in which the government does not have total command of the society and economy. The government undertakes direct investment in both human and physical capital and conducts its own research to create innovations. But it also tries to steer the processes of economic and social change.

The basic reason why spatial policies can only achieve *spatial redistributions* in 'development' is that such policies do not affect the underlying determinants of social and economic *change*. And this is an inevitable consequence of the structure of the knowledge upon which they are based. It is inevitable whenever the scientific basis of policy rests upon a positivist conception of science and an incomplete relational conception of space.

The realist's critique of regional theory, outlined in the last chapter, is relevant here. For, although it is possible to construct positivist and instrumentalist explanations with an incomplete relational concept of space, and although, within a particular conception of science, these may be regarded as 'true' scientific explanation, such explanations *inevitably* leave some factors out of consideration. And what is left out has important implications for the effects which are produced when such theories are translated into practice. From a realist viewpoint, the positivist explanations based on an incomplete relational concept of space consider *contingent* relationships, on the surface of appearances, rather than *determining* relationships. If one wishes to maintain a positivist viewpoint, this critique does not undermine the explanations *as explanations*. But it implies that policies based upon such explanations will not affect the underlying determinants of events, but instead merely manipulate contingent relationships.

A spatial policy based on analysis of locational behaviour can change the spatial environment within which decisions are taken. After the identification of salient 'location factors', it is possible to undertake measures which change the spatial surface of opportunities open to entrepreneurs and migrants. But such a policy can only encourage an industrialist to go to one region *rather than* another, or a migrant from a rural area to go to a small town or intermediate city *rather than* the metropoli. Through such policies it is possible to change the spatial pattern of growth within a country, measured in terms of deviations from the national average. But it can do no more than change the *spatial incidence* of growth unless it affects the underlying determinants of growth, such as technological change and capital accumulation.

A policy based on spatial diffusion analysis can speed up the timing of innovation adoption in 'lagging' regions, by changing the spatial pattern of information flows and by creating conditions within a region which make adoption more probable. If innovation is associated with 'development', such policies can, through accelerating spatial diffusion and changing diffusion paths, reduce spatial disparities in 'development'. But it can do no more, unless it affects the underlying process through which new technology is created.

Infrastructural investment, on roads and market-places, may be made in the vicinity of a small town with the aim of improving rural–urban linkages and thereby engendering 'spread effects'. It may, for example, be expected that such a policy can improve the food distribution system so that farmers get a fairer price for their produce and the increase in demand for food in the town elicits a supply response in the surrounding rural areas. But unless this spatial policy affects the basic economic organization of the marketing system, influencing conditions of entry into trade, possibilities of forming cartels and so on, these measures will only change the pattern of *where* traders buy and sell. The *spatial* distribution of producer prices can be altered as a result, and because of this the *spatial* distribution of farm incomes may change. But the policy can do no more than change the *spatial distribution* of farm incomes, unless the policy somehow affects agricultural production and productivity.

The only way in which a spatial policy could achieve more than the spatial redistribution of 'development' would be if it affected the underlying determinants of 'development'. *Such effects may well occur. But regional development theory is not structured in a way in which they may be predicted.* 'Space' is taken to be environment in which 'development' occurs, and the main focus of theoretical enquiry has been to explain the spatial distribution of human activity. The 'feedback' of these distributions on social processes is taken into account in normative arguments about the efficiency and equity of spatial patterns, and functional analyses which serve as a basis for both normative judgements and explanatory statements. But as argued at length in Part One, the normative arguments which try to infer the growth and distributional effects of spatial patterns are weak. And as shown in the last chapter, there are many reasons to question the adequacy of functional analysis as an explanatory form. In fact, it is doubtful whether it is possible to construct any adequate knowledge about the effects of spatial policies on social processes, if the problem is conceptualized as a 'feedback' relationship between spatial distributions abstracted at a moment in time and social processes. The problem may be properly addressed once the incomplete relational concept of space is abandoned, and space is studied as an integral element of social processes. Until such knowledge is constructed, the effects which spatial policies have on the underlying determinants of development cannot be predicted.

The conclusion that 'the only changes in the spatial pattern of "development" which it is possible to achieve through spatial policies are spatial redistributions' specifies an important limitation to the efficacy of spatial policies. But it is not a trivial limitation. It implies that if the policy objective is to reduce regional and rural–urban *disparities* in development, and change the hierarchical and spatial *distribution* of the urban population, then a spatial policy can achieve this outcome. The technical arguments which suggest that such changes in spatial patterns are desirable from an economic and social viewpoint may well be weak. But if such changes are the objectives of a spatial policy, then *it can achieve its objectives.*

However, there is one important proviso. *Spatial policies can only achieve the spatial redistributions which they are designed for in conditions in which the underlying pattern of social and economic interaction remains the same.* It has been argued that an assumption of continuity is a necessary feature of all positivist and instrumentalist explanations. Lewis and Melville (1978), for example, write that if scientific explanation is equated with prediction, as it is in the positivist and instrumentalist frame of reference, 'we can *only* produce scientific explanations by assuming that existing social conditions continue to pertain' (p. 90). But the fact that spatial policies can only achieve their objectives if the underlying pattern of social and economic interactions remains the same does not *just* stem from the adoption of a particular scientific methodology. It is also rooted in the forms of explanation constructed with an incomplete relational concept of space.

For example, although it is possible, at any given moment, to identify the 'location factors' which attract a particular type of industry to a particular type of locality, changes in the production processes within that industry can lead to a complete re-evaluation of those 'location factors' by entrepreneurs. If policy is directed towards providing those location factors in chosen localities with a view to attracting that type of industry to those places, it can succeed only if such a re-evaluation has *not* taken place. Similarly, it is possible to relate the spatial pattern of innovation adoption to city size and the location of a city relative to the cities where the innovation is first adopted. Within this frame of reference, information flows are identified as a key 'explanatory' variable of the spatial pattern. And on the basis of the observed relationships, policy may be directed to improve the means of transport and thus ease communication; to increase the number of cities 'transmitting information' about innovations, by selecting a few demonstration centres in which the government acts immediately to promote adoption; or to speed up urban growth in smaller cities in remoter regions. Such policies are expected to change the spatial pattern of innovation adoption by changing the spatial pattern of information flows. But they can succeed only if there has been *no change* in the social structure which determines channels of communications.

Diachronic functional analysis is the only form of explanation from which spatial policies may be derived which does not require that the underlying pattern of social and economic interaction remains the same if the policy is to achieve its objectives. This form of explanation shows how the spatial structure and spatial system evolves as a society 'develops'. If it were an adequate explanatory form, it would provide the basis for spatial policies which were formulated in anticipation of, and in accord with, the qualitative changes in social and economic relationships which are associated with 'development'. But the teleological assumption which is a necessary element of this form of explanation – that is, that society is evolving towards some definable end-state – is of dubious validity. If it is not valid, it is uncertain exactly what will be achieved through policies based upon it. And once diachronic functional analysis is rejected as an adequate scientific basis for policy, the spatial planner must rely on explanations of contingent spatial relationships which will only hold into the future if the determining social and economic relationships remain the same.

The conclusion that 'spatial policies can only achieve their objectives in conditions in which the underlying pattern of social and economic interaction remains the same' throws considerable doubt on their utility in *developing* countries. 'Development' is normally associated with some *qualitative* change in social and economic relationships. But the argument suggests that it is impossible to predict the outcome of spatial policies under such conditions. It is only valid to expect that such policies will induce desired spatial changes *over the short run*, a time period which is defined by the limits of 'other things remaining the same'. This severely restricts the circumstances under which spatial policy can be effective, even in the sense of achieving spatial redistributions.

It contradicts the assumption which has sometimes been made that 'regional planners are in business only in the long run' (Richardson, 1976, p. 1). And it implies that in conditions of rapid change, which general development policies may try to create, a spatial policy can only achieve its objectives *by chance*.

Yet although the conclusion that spatial policies can only be effective if underlying social and economic processes remain the same is in contradiction with the developmental *rhetoric* within which spatial policies are often formulated, they may have a consistent internal *logic*. For it can be argued that *spatial policies are innately conservative*, in the sense that they serve to perpetuate the processes upon which their efficacy depends. The point has been clearly stated by Olsson (1972), who argues that this consequence is inevitable once scientific knowledge constructed from an instrumentalist and positivist viewpoint is translated into planning practice. He writes:

> By ascribing to the proposal that there is a need for planning and guided social change, we seem to imply that there is something in the projection of today's empirical world that we may wish *not to occur*. If this is correct, then I submit that the use of spatial theories and models as social engineering tools may have contradictory consequences. The reason for this warning is, of course, that practically all existing theories are positivistic and instrumentalist constructs in which theoretical statements successively have been refined to agree better and better with current observation. To argue for extensive implementation of projections derived from these spatial constructs would therefore be conservative in the true sense of the word; planning based on descriptive subject-matter models would only help to perpetuate the existing state of the world.   (p. 14, emphasis added)

Whether or not planning practice based on positivist scientific knowledge *invariably* serves 'to perpetuate the existing state of the world' is debatable. For it may be argued that such knowledge allows what Popper calls 'piecemeal social engineering', and then the truth of the proposition hinges upon whether such 'piecemeal' changes perpetuate existing processes or represent *real* changes. The argument thus becomes quite complex. But without addressing these difficult, but very important, issues, it may be asserted that *spatial policies are innately conservative, in the sense that they do not seek to affect the underlying processes of social and economic change*. And furthermore, when they are based on static functional explanations, they are specifically designed to ensure the reproduction of the existing social order.

Given the current state of knowledge it is impossible to predict the social side-effects of spatial policies. But to conclude this section, it may be noted, as a corollary of an earlier proposition, that *spatial policies can only achieve the spatial redistributions which they are designed for if existing processes of social differentiation within a country are perpetuated*. They can make particular groups of people in poorer regions better off. They can *relocate* the poor, the unemployed, the hungry and the sick and thus *spatial policies can provide the appearances of a spatial solution to social problems*. But as long as they do not tackle the fundamental processes within which these problems are rooted, the problems do not go away. They just no longer appear on the maps portraying indicators of 'development'. For, as an effect of a *spatial* policy, the poorer population may be scattered in different cities and regions rather than being concentrated in a spatial pocket of distress. It is only through *social* and *economic* policies that these problems may be tackled. And if a spatial policy is being effective in achieving the *spatial* redistributions it seeks, it is a sure sign that the processes which produce social inequalities are continuing as before.

To sum up:

1 Spatial policies cannot achieve their objectives unless they work in concert with sectoral and macro-economic policies.

2 The only changes in the spatial patterns of 'development' which it is possible to achieve through spatial policies are spatial redistributions.

3 Spatial policies can only achieve the spatial redistributions they are designed for in conditions in which the underlying pattern of social and economic interaction remains the same.

4 Spatial policies are innately conservative in the sense that they do not seek to affect the underlying processes of social and economic change.

5 Spatial policies can only achieve the spatial redistributions which they are designed for if existing processes of social differentiation within a country are perpetuated, although,

6 Spatial policies can provide the appearances of a spatial solution to social problems.

TERRITORIAL REGIONAL PLANNING AS AN ALTERNATIVE

It must be emphasized that these conclusions only refer to the *potential* effects of spatial policies. What has actually happened in practice depends on the extent to which planners pursuing spatial policies have formulated those policies on the basis of the knowledge within regional development theory. This is an important empirical question. But if it is found that planners do *not* base their interventions on this body of technical knowledge, the next question which must be asked is: what is the rationality of their actions?

The foregoing discussion outlines the effects which can be achieved through spatial policies *if* they were formulated according to the 'ideal' that planning intervention should be based on scientific knowledge. The technical basis of spatial policies is found in explanatory theories which use an incomplete relational concept of space and such theories are necessarily framed within a positivist and instrumentalist view of science. When judged as a body of scientific knowledge, these theories are found wanting. But if they are taken to be the best available – and they offer the only possible 'scientific' basis for spatial policies – then the effects of spatial policy follow logically from the forms of explanation.

These effects exist *prior to implementation* in the structure of the theories which provide the scientific basis for planning interventions. They will be produced even when a spatial policy is implemented within a cloud of developmental and egalitarian rhetoric. And they will be produced at the same time as the 'scientific' basis of policy promotes an image of unbiased, neutral intervention.

If regional planners wish to formulate policies which do not have these effects and to base their policies on scientific knowledge, they require explanations of urban, regional and rural development which are constructed in a different way from those which have been put forward in mainstream regional development theory. And if regional theorists wish to construct such explanations, they must abandon the incomplete relational concept of space and reassess the utility of the positivist and instrumentalist conception of social science.

Some regional theorists have already reached this conclusion (Lewis and Melville, 1978; Olsson, 1970, 1971, 1972, 1974a and b, and 1980; de Gonzales, 1980). And within mainstream Anglo-American regional development theory, a shift in thinking is evident with Friedmann and Weaver's proposal to abandon 'functional regional planning', with its various spatial policies, and to replace it with 'territorial regional planning'.

This so-called 'paradigm shift' has a number of dimensions. As noted in chapter 5, territorial regional planning is concerned with the integrated mobilization of human and natural resources within regions. The people of the region are engaged in the planning process, and planning measures are designed to meet local needs and to promote a general improvement in the quality of life for *all* the people in the area. The goal of 'development' efforts is no longer defined as the maximization of regional growth. It is, rather, to meet basic needs, to alleviate poverty and provide employment, to preserve equality and community, and to foster self-reliance.

The account in chapter 5 emphasized the change in developmental assumptions which is made in a shift to the new approach. But it is now possible to see its other dimensions more clearly. As well as a shift away from the growth orthodoxy of the 1960s towards a neo-populist development strategy, it involves the rejection of a rationalist type of planning, in which the planners, in isolation from the people for whom they plan, formulate and implement policies on the basis of scientific knowledge which shows the best means to achieve the ends of policies. This is replaced by a type of planning which Friedmann (1973b) calls 'transactive'. In 'transactive planning', planners work with the people and the policies are formulated and implemented through 'interpersonal dialogue marked by mutual learning' (Friedmann, 1973b, p. 389). In territorial regional planning, therefore, the knowledge upon which policy is based is constructed through social interaction between the planners and the people. This cannot be achieved using mathematical models whose inner logic is only understood by a few, privileged technical experts. And it does not necessarily require recourse to general laws, which supposedly have universal validity. The knowledge which informs territorial regional planning is rooted in the unique characteristics of a region and the particular way of thinking of the people of that region.

Moreover, territorial regional planning brings the region back to the centre of regional development policy. The placeless landscape of the regional scientist and theoretical geographer, a hierarchical system of nodes and networks on an isotropic plain, is deemed to be irrelevant. And the idea that desirable objectives may be achieved through manipulating the spatial structure or spatial system is seen as fanciful. Territorial regional planning is not concerned with space, but with *place*. A 'place' is formed through the social relationships which people have in an area over a long period of time, and its unique characteristics reflect the shared physical environment, the shared history and the shared experience of the everyday life of the people of that area. The regions in which territorial planning is conducted are supposed to be such places.

The paradigm shift from 'functional' to 'territorial' regional planning thus meets all the objections which have been raised so far. The fact that, given the current state of the art, there is a weak scientific basis for regional policy does not matter. For within territorial regional planning, the knowledge which informs policy must be constructed in a different way from that of science. And the incomplete relational concept of space – and the spatial policies which are its concomitant – is jettisoned.

THE CONCEPT OF TERRITORIAL INTERESTS

Unfortunately, however, closer examination of the logical basis of the new paradigm reveals a number of new problems. Territorial regional planning is designed to give priority to *territorial interests*. But what is meant by this term? How are these territorial units defined? And what is the relationship between 'territorial interests' at various spatial scales?

Like the terms 'territorial power' and 'territorial will' the only sensible meaning that can be given to the concept of 'territorial interests' is the interests of the people *in* a given territory. But this said, two further questions arise: (i) how are those interests defined? and (ii) is it possible to equate territorial interests with individual interests? The definition of interests is a very contentious issue within the social sciences (see Lukes, 1974). But the debates are ignored by the advocates of the alternative paradigm. Interests are merely equated with subjective preferences. If the people of a territorial unit are able to plan their development in the way they want, then the development necessarily serves their interests.

From a radical view, it is argued that an individual's expressed preferences may be manipulated by a system which works against his or her *real* interests. As soon as it is recognized that there may be a difference between a person's subjective preferences and his or her real interests – that false consciousness may exist – the alternative paradigm loses its logical force. Indeed, it could be argued that the promotion of territorial interests *reinforces* false consciousness by masking 'real' class interests through an ideology of 'community'.

Logical coherence may be maintained by asserting that there is no such thing as objective (real) interests and false consciousness. Or it may be maintained by adopting a dependency perspective which suggests that the people of peripheral regions in peripheral countries are being impoverished through backwash effects and through external control of their lives, and by limiting applications of the new paradigm to such regions. In such circumstances, giving the people of a region the power to decide the use of local resources and the allocation of the product of local labour is a necessary first condition for meeting the objective interests of those people.

To equate *individual* interests with *territorial* interests is to commit an ecological fallacy, for it is not necessarily correct to assume that developments which in an aggregate sense benefit a group of people will benefit each individual in that group equally. This is realized by the advocates of 'territorial regional planning' and thus Friedmann and Weaver (1979) in their discussion of agropolitan development, clearly state that 'where conditions of equal access to the bases of social power are established . . . a community may *rightfully* express a general or territorial interest' (p. 204, emphasis added). But what this implies is that the new approach is only logically coherent if it is embedded within a developmental philosophy which emphasizes equity. The emphasis that is put on the pursuit of greater social equity in territorial regional planning is thus not just a question of change in values, or a reassessment of what sort of 'development' is desirable. It is a *logically necessary condition* for the application of the approach.

The two questions raised thus far threaten the logical coherence of the new approach, but they do not undermine its validity given the development strategy proposed and given assumptions about the distorting and debilitating effects of the condition of dependency. However, more serious logical problems arise when we consider the ways in which territorial units are defined. The advocates of the alternative paradigm are singularly unilluminating on this important question. They write that:

> Territorially organized communities may be conceived as arising in the intersection of three abstract spaces, each with its own attributes and describing a different dimension of communal life: a common *cultural* space . . . a common *political* space . . . a common *economic* space. Although cultural, political and economic spaces intersect, they do not, as a rule, completely overlap. To the extent that they do, however, they trace the natural habit of a 'community of destiny'. Such areas of overlap may be designated as the primordial units of territorial integration (*T*) [Figure 27]. Every major area of overlap, *T*, may be

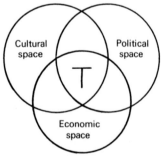

Figure 27 Primordial units of territorial integration.

Source: Friedmann and Weaver, 1979, p. 197.

further divided into component spaces, $t_1 \ldots n$, each of which will display unique characteristics within the common pattern.

(Friedmann and Weaver, 1979, p. 197)

The reader can make of this what he or she will.

The advocates of the alternative strategy point to administrative and economic considerations that have to be taken into account when drawing the political boundaries and deciding the size of territorial unit. But there are no criteria which specify the group of people which may properly enjoy territorial power. Necessarily, if the new units are to express the territorial interest, they have to be 'territorial communities'. But in some cases, well-defined communities may not exist. The possibility is not considered in detail, though Friedmann does suggest in his later work that 'Communities arise from practice. Political communities will arise from the practice of political choice' (1981). But the question then is: who structures these political choices? It appears as if it will be the task of the national government. But the idea that territorial communities are going to be created from outside contradicts the principle of self-reliance and the idea that the people will be free to decide their own development.

In some parts of some countries, regional consciousness is already manifest and expressed in political demands for autonomy. Not surprisingly, the advocates of the new paradigm refer to these regionalist movements, as they would appear to solve this problem. Demands for autonomy usually specify the areal limits to their power. However, if we accept that regional consciousness responds to changing historical and political circumstances, that they 'arise from the practice of political choice', there is a possibility that the devolution of power to 'territorial communities' will change their definition. This has, in fact, happened in federal Nigeria where regional groups, who formerly asserted that they constituted a distinct community who deserved their own state within the federal structure, split and redefined themselves into different 'territorial communities' once a new state was created.

If it is assumed that 'communities arise from practice' and if it is further assumed that the common interests which bind individuals into a 'territorial community' are their subjective preferences, then the territorial units upon which 'territorial regional planning' is based become *indeterminate*. There can be as many or as few 'territorial communities' as 'the people' want. To fix the boundaries of the territorial communities it is necessary to have some objective criteria, such as the basic needs criterion which Friedmann and Weaver use to define agropolitan districts (see above, p. 167). But the search for such criteria opens up the question of the relationships between subjective and objective interests. This hornets' nest may be avoided if territorial communities are regarded as *natural* entities – 'primordial units of territorial integration', as Friedmann and Weaver put it. But this position is inconsistent with the idea that communities must be created in some instances by political action, and is, in any case, empirically indefensible. Where a group does express a common regional identity, it is based, as Friedmann himself writes, on 'ties of *history*'.

The problem of defining the territorial units which express a territorial interest does not mean that territorial regional planning is impossible. But it does imply that the vision of the development of a region occurring by the efforts 'of its people' and 'for its people' is more complex than at first sight. And non-local intervention is not just necessary in the setting-up of the territorial units.

For territorial regional planning is based on the idea of the integral mobilization of a region's human and natural resources to benefit the people of that region. It is designed to prevent any interactions with other regions which reduce a region's potential for self-reliant development. But this goal, coupled with the pursuit of equitable development strategies within each region, raises a very odd spectre. It is of a cellular economy with perfect social inequality within each of the cells, and *inequality between them*. This outcome will not occur if there are no natural resource differences, as on the uniformly fertile, isotropic plains on which the regional scientists and theoretical geographers constructed their theories. But otherwise it can only be avoided if there is a territorial unit *above* the regions, which redistributes resources between the lower territorial units.

A nested hierarchy of territorial units is thus required to achieve spatial equality *between* territorial units. But its existence leads to an insoluble logical problem, for to sustain the notion of equitable development, equitable distribution must be achieved within the territorial units *at different spatial scales*. To achieve the equitable development of the higher order territorial units it is necessary to tax the rich lower order territorial units and subsidize the poor ones. Thus, to serve the territorial interest at one level, you have to *override* the territorial interests at the level immediately below. This problem is *not* apparent if we focus on the most disadvantaged areas and the lowest level of the nested hierarchy. But as soon as the relationship between territorial units at different spatial scales is examined, the paradigm shift to self-reliant, locally planned, equitable development appears to be based upon a number of mutually contradictory but equally necessary elements. To avoid the ecological fallacy, development efforts logically must be equitable. To ensure equity in the higher order territorial units they must be able to override the interests of people in at least some of the lower order territorial units. And yet, to achieve locally planned development, the balance of power needs to be shifted from higher to lower territorial units, and the lower territorial units should be able to override the demands of the higher ones. It is a difficult logical conundrum to escape from!

THE ORGANIC CONCEPTION OF THE REGION

Friedmann and Weaver are aware of some of these problems and in their discussion of the agropolitan development strategy they note that 'conflicts will arise among territorial units (districts and regions), each with its special interests to defend, and there will always be differences in local and/or personal viewpoints' (Friedmann and Weaver, 1979, p. 204). But they assume that those conflicts will be resolved by a national state whose role is 'at once protective, developmental, facilitative, regulatory and redistributive' (p. 203). Such a state is difficult to envisage outside Utopia and even if it existed in today's world, the practice of territorial regional planning would not match the ideal posited by Friedmann and Weaver, for it rests on a number of logical conditions which are mutually contradictory.

And if we look closely, it is possible to trace the roots of these logical problems back to the reconceptualization of space which is made in the shift from functional to territorial regional planning. The incomplete relational concept of space is abandoned. But the new paradigm still does not use an adequate concept of space for understanding and planning the *social* world. For while 'functional regional planning' is based on a conception of space derived from physics, 'territorial regional planning' is based on a conception of the region *derived from biology*.

Within a branch of biology normally called 'organismic biology' it is argued that living creatures must be studied as 'organic wholes'. The 'parts' of such a whole are said to be mutually interdependent and to function as an 'organic unity'. The standpoint of 'organismic biology' is that such 'wholes' cannot be understood through analysing the actions of their separate parts and combining the knowledge required. For the relations of interdependence between the parts mean that 'the whole is more than the sum of its parts'.

Bringing this biological perspective to bear on the analysis of society would seem to be singularly inappropriate. But there is a long history of the application of *organic analogies* to understanding social life (see Stoddart, 1967). Within geography, there is a tradition of studying the region as an 'organic unity', a 'whole', whose 'parts' are anything which is spatially included within it. This 'whole', it is said, can only be understood through examining the mutual interdependence of the complex of elements in specific areas. From this perspective, the region is sometimes treated as an organism, that is, an entity that has the capacity to act, react, adapt and create. And a region is sometimes said to have a 'personality', which reflects the mutual adaptation of its people to its environment (see Hartshorne, 1939, chapter 9). At the broader scale, the nation state has also been analysed as an organism, which is a union of people rooted in the soil of its territory – a perspective which led the German geographer, Friedrich Ratzel, to suggest that *lebensraum* – the life-area of the people – was essential for the growth of the state.

The proposal for 'territorial regional planning' falls squarely within this tradition of thought. Its project entails identifying existing or latent 'regional communities', where the people live and work in relations of mutual interdependence, sharing values which reflect the common history of that specific place; halting the erosion of these so-called 'primordial units of territorial integration' in the wake of their increasing interconnectedness with the outside world; and establishing conditions which ensure that these regions can adapt to their environment and act like living organisms. Its project is no less than *to make regions into organisms*. And from a developmental perspective, it is assumed that in the restoration of 'territorial integrity', the 'whole' will be more than the sum of its parts, and some 'vital force', previously locked up, will begin to animate community action.

It may be unnecessary to argue the inappropriatenesss of the application of the organic analogy within regional planning. But, briefly, it is worth noting three problems in territorial regional planning which arise because of the organic conception of the region.

First, within territorial regional planning the territorial units at various spatial scales – the nation, the region and the district – are *all* treated as organisms. To apply the organic analogy exactly, it is necessary to consider the nation state as a living organism and analyse how its parts, like the organs and the cells of a rat, are interrelated in a spatial hierarchy within the nation state. In proposing to make the territorial units at different spatial scales act as 'organisms', relationships which are outside the limits of the organic analogy must be introduced. Not surprisingly, the specification of these relationships represents one of the most obscure parts of the proposal.

Second, after long debates, which are summarized by Hartshorne (1954), geographers reached the conclusion that regions are not organisms which objectively exist in reality but are subjectively defined by man. If that is accepted, the 'primordial units of territorial integration' do not exist and so the 'organic wholes' must be created by someone for some purpose. This requires the introduction of concepts which are beyond the scope of the organic analogy and, as argued in the last section, the creation of territorial units poses severe problems for the logical consistency of the whole project.

Third, the belief that the restoration of territorial integrity will release some 'force' through which the people will develop themselves is based on a view of living organisms which even biologists have now rejected. This view, called 'vitalism', suggests that all living systems possess a 'life-force', which directs evolution towards the attainment of some end, or have the capacity of 'entelechy', the capacity to realize, or make actual, what is potential. 'Vitalism' was propounded by some biologists in the nineteenth century, but has been rejected as a metaphysical attempt to explain facts about living systems which were not understood at that time by reference to undemonstrable and unprovable causes. Territorial regional planners may argue that they are concerned to mobilize hidden human potentials which cannot be known by the methods of science. But even in transactive planning, in which knowledge is constructed through social learning, the assumption that the region as an organism possesses some *élan vital* must be recognized as precisely that – an assumption whose veracity must be tested through practice.

If one accepts these arguments, the organic analogy *in itself* does not provide an adequate basis either for guiding regional planning interventions or understanding their effects. This is not to say that the project of territorial regional planning to make regions into 'organic wholes' cannot be undertaken. But it requires the introduction of concepts outside the purview of 'organismic biology', and because of this both its nature and effects will be variable. Friedmann and Weaver refer to the Chinese commune system as an example of an agropolitan development strategy. But an equally good example is the creation of native authorities within the British colonies using principles of indirect rule.

The change from 'functional' to 'territorial' regional planning is said to be a paradigm shift. In some senses it is. But the philosophical assumption of functionalism is as important (if not more important) to so-called 'territorial' regional planning as it is to 'functional' regional planning. And, more importantly, both paradigms assert the significance of the spatial in determining human activity. Indeed, *territorial regional planning reflects adherence to the spatial separatist theme in a new guise.*

Just as in spatial policy, elements of the spatial structure, or spatial relationships, or 'locational factors' are taken to be causes, so, in territorial regional planning, the region is given causal efficacy. 'Organic wholes' have been defined as systems 'the behaviour of which is not determined by that of their individual elements, but where the part-processes *are themselves determined by* the intrinsic nature of the whole' (Wertheimer, quoted in Nagel, 1961, p. 391, emphasis added). Thus, when a region is treated as an 'organic whole', the behaviour of its elements is attributed to *the intrinsic nature of the region itself*. Indeed, any attempt to explain the behaviour of individual elements by reference to social and economic processes is misplaced. For 'the whole is more than the sum of its parts'.

If this position can be sustained, it provides an unassailable basis for the assumption that positive developmental effects may be achieved merely through manipulating the spatial attributes of phenomena. As the earlier sections of this chapter showed, it can be demonstrated that the outcome of spatial policy depends upon underlying social and economic processes. But territorial regional planning, which aims to arrange the phenomena of social life into 'organic wholes', *makes these processes dependent upon the nature of the whole*. It is a neat inversion. But it must be rejected, unless one believes that the organic analogy provides a useful basis for understanding and changing the world.

CONCLUSION

Spatial separatism is both a characteristic of the social organization of development studies and a working method within regional development theory. Although development theorists have been much concerned with spatial patterns of inequality at an international level, they have usually ignored the significance of space and regions in their studies of economic and social change within developing countries. Work of this type has been intensively pursued by regional theorists, who have applied the findings of development theory in a spatial context. But in doing so, they have adopted a methodology which isolates the effects of 'the spatial'.

Spatial separatism as a social fact impoverishes both development studies and regional development theory. In order to study the 'locational aspects' of development, the regional theorist must be an impossibly flexible expert. Sensitive application of theories of social, political and economic change in a spatial context is only possible if the regional theorist is a competent sociologist, political scientist *and* economist. Misinterpretation is likely to occur when the regional theorist takes ideas from their original theoretical context, and it is almost inevitable that the spatial applications will lag behind current thinking in social and economic theory. The refraction of knowledge leads to curious formulations and emphases, as we saw in the second part of the book. But in its social separation, regional development theory is not subject to the close scrutiny of the theorists who originally formulated, or who are reacting against, the ideas being applied in a spatial context. Misapplied ideas may be accepted by other regional theorists; or they may be challenged through further misapplications of social and economic theory, or simply through ideas which have been formulated as a reaction against some spatial aspect of the original misapplication. And as derived regional theories are synthesized with other derived regional theories, their assumptions about the way in which change occurs in society become obscure. It is through this process of involution that regional development theory has 'developed'.

But spatial separatism as a social fact also impoverishes development studies. Some ideas within the field, such as the thesis of urban bias, some dualist models and dependency analyses have an explicit spatial element. But they are weakened by the lack of appreciation of the problems of treating space in social theory. For the most part, space is neglected in development studies, and as a consequence explanations of social and economic change are either incomplete or distorted. As Sack (1980, p. 70) succinctly puts it, 'to explain why something occurs is to explain why it occurs where it does'. In its failure to analyse the spatiality of processes, development studies remains underdeveloped.

Spatial separatism as a working method impoverishes regional development theory and reinforces spatial separatism as a social fact. Both the normative statements and explanations formulated in regional development theory are characterized by logical weaknesses which stem from the attempt to isolate the effects of 'the spatial'. The weakness of the field encourages the belief that theorizing spatial relationships is unimportant. And the proliferating jargon, the 'in-speak' of regional theorists, discourages penetration by 'outsiders'. Moreover, the *concepts* which regional theorists use, such as 'periphery', 'backward region', 'growth centre', 'the spatial incidence of development', 'internal forces of regional change' are rooted in their *mode of conceptualizing* the relationship between space and society. In order to engage in debate, it is necessary to use this language. But to use the language, it is necessary to accept the mode of conceptualization.

Regional development theory, like much of development studies, has grown with a major policy orientation. The idea that the type of knowledge which development theorists should construct is knowledge which gives governments the ability to plan social and economic change has biased the theoretical issues treated in development studies and made the field peculiarly susceptible to the developmentalist fashions of governments and international aid agencies. But within regional development theory the policy orientation has distorted understanding. For adherence to spatial separatism as a working method is only possible if academic activity is limited to the problem of constructing a type of knowledge which provides the means for planning intervention.

Yet the weaknesses of the way in which space is conceptualized in regional development theory are most fully exposed when the field is examined as a scientific basis for regional planning. When viewed in these terms, the field is illogical. There are no strong *technical* arguments which demonstrate that the three regional policy problems most commonly identified by the governments of developing countries – regional disparities in development, the size of the metropoli and rural-urban disparities – constitute social and economic problems. It is difficult to describe the explanatory 'theories' which provide the *technical* basis for the formulation of regional planning strategies as theories, if they are examined by the criteria used to judge scientific knowledge. And the spatial prescriptions which have been advocated by regional theorists can only work if the underlying patterns of social and economic interaction within a country remain the same. If 'development' is defined as a qualitative change in social and economic relations, then the strategies advocated can only work if there is no 'development'. And although governments usually announce regional policies with a stream of egalitarian rhetoric, the prescriptions advocated can only achieve their spatial objectives if processes of social differentiation continue as before.

The analysis of the consequences which logically follow when the knowledge within regional development theory is translated into practical action exposes the deficiencies of spatial separatism as a working method. But our conclusions on the inadequacies of this working method now deepen the puzzle which arises from the context of the argument. For our *argument* suggests that, from a 'national perspective', there is no adequate technical justification for the adoption of policies to reduce regional and rural–urban disparities in development and to curb the growth of the national metropoli. And our *argument* suggests that the theories which provide a basis for deciding the means to achieve supposedly more desirable spatial distributions lead to policy prescriptions which will either be ineffective, or will only achieve their stated aims by chance. Yet it is an *observable fact* that regional planning as an activity still thrives. Spatial disparities in development and the spatial distribution of the urban population are *in practice* identified as 'problems' which need to be solved through state intervention. And despite changes in emphasis, urban-industrial growth pole strategies, rural growth centre strategies, strategies which build up a 'more complete' urban hierarchy, and strategies which 'strengthen' local and regional institutions are still being pursued *in practice* as ways of changing the spatial distribution of development and of population. The puzzle is, quite simply, to explain *why*.

The final chapter of the book offers an answer to this question. Taking up the line of discussion raised at the end of Part One, it will be argued that in the conditions which pertain in many developing countries, regional planning concepts have *political utility*. The aim of the chapter is to outline some of the more salient of those conditions and to demonstrate exactly how and why 'regional planning' has such political utility in many developing countries. In the course of the discussion, the significance of 'space' and 'regions' in 'development' will be reassessed; and the use to which 'scientific' theories can be put in practice is reappraised. In fact, the terms of our argument will be totally transformed. But in the end, with this change in perspective, the *value* of concepts which are rooted in a spatially separatist methodology should become clear.

Conclusion

The state, development and regional planning practice

> 'Regional planning has become a necessity in most countries. But nobody seems to know quite what it is, and no nation seems to know how to do it.'
>
> (Ross and Cohen, 1974)

Throughout this book no attempt has been made to define what regional planning actually is. The working definition on which the argument has been built is that regional planning is 'planning concerned with the *where* of development'. In practice there is an immense variety of planning activities which governments undertake under the name of 'regional policy and planning'. This is important to recognize, for any abstract definition which tries to pin down precisely what regional planning actually is can easily lose what is its essential characteristic – its elusiveness.

The most useful general definition of the activity that may be made is that 'regional planning is what governments define it to be'. This statement may look like an easy way out of a tricky definitional problem. But in fact it can serve as the starting-point for a difficult analytical task. For if regional planning is defined in this way, it may only be understood by examining it as an integral aspect of state policy. This means that a theory of the practice of regional planning must be located within some theorization of the state. It is a complex task. But this is what understanding regional planning in political terms entails. And only through a political analysis is it possible to understand what the activity actually is.

THE STATE, TERRITORY AND POWER

We may begin from basics. In the English language, the word 'state' is used in two distinct ways. It sometimes refers to *a set of institutions*, and it sometimes refers to *an association of people*. With the former definition, the 'state' is popularly equated with the government and the phrase 'state intervention' used interchangeably with 'government intervention'. With the latter definition, the state is presently equated with the term 'country' and thus it is possible to speak of 'Latin American states' and 'Latin American countries' interchangeably. Both these everyday ways of thinking about the state are used in sociological and political theory. On the one hand, some theorists refer to the state as 'a system of institutions' – the central and local government, the judiciary, the police and armed forces – which stand outside 'civil society', constraining and influencing relationships between individuals and groups within that society, and being, in some way and to some degree, accountable to members of that society (see, for example, Miliband, 1969). On the other hand, some theorists view the state as an association of people linked by a particular form of power relationship which is exercised through the state institutional apparatus (see, in particular, Poulantzas, 1973; 1978).

Considerable confusion may be created if this distinction is not realized. During the 1970s there was a major revival of interest in the state within social studies and there is now a complex literature in which different theorists analyse the state from a variety of liberal and Marxist perspectives. But cutting across these variations, which are rooted in different perspectives on the way society is organized, there are the different ways of thinking about what 'the state' is. If we are to elaborate a clear analysis of the state we must be clear about how we conceptualize this object of analysis. And in the present context, the state will be viewed, in the second sense, as *an association of people*.

But what is the precise nature of this association? Laski, in work published long before the recent sociological revival in state theory, succinctly summarizes its key features. He suggests that the social world is made up of all kinds of associations of people, such as churches or trade unions, which consist of individuals grouped together to achieve diverse economic, political and cultural objectives. The state is such an association. But it differs from all other associations 'in that membership is compulsory upon all who live within its territorial ambit and that it can in the last resort enforce its obligations upon its subjects' (Laski, 1934, p. 37). The characteristics which define the state as an association of people are then: the particular type of power relationship which links members of a state; the territorial demarcation of the limits of that power relationship; and the conditions for membership of the association.

The particular type of power relationship which links members of a state is a supreme coercive authority. Within any state there are many associations of people, each with their own rules. But the individuals and groups who are members of a state are all, 'in the last resort', subject to the laws of the state. As Laski (1935, p. 21) puts it, the state is 'a society which is integrated by possessing *coercive* authority which is *legally supreme* over any individual or group who is part of that society' (emphasis added). The actions of people who are subjects of a state are constrained by what is defined as legitimate behaviour in that state. And, if necessary, conformity to the laws of the association of people which is the state can be ensured through the legitimate use of physical force. This supreme coercive power is what is known as 'sovereignty'. But although it is legally supreme, it is not boundless. It has *spatial limits* which define the territorial ambit of the state. In present times, every person becomes a member of a particular state through the fate of their place of birth. And, in the end, they can only escape subordination to the laws of that state by leaving its territorial ambit.

It must be emphasized again that this is not the only way that theorists have conceptualized the state. However, strong arguments have been made to show that the most fruitful approach to theorization of the state is to define it as an association of people linked by a particular type of power relationship (see Poulantzas, 1978, Introduction). And in addition, and particularly important in the present context, the conception of the state which has been outlined is useful for it makes *territory* an integral part of state theorization. The term 'territory' connotes geographic space *and* power.

Four initial observations may be made to clarify further this view of the state. First, Laski's statement that the state is a society *integrated* by a particular form of power relationship does not imply that conflict is absent from such a society. The term 'integrated' may be understood here to be shorthand for the specific way in which the relationships between the individuals and groups in society are *mutually constrained* by a supreme coercive power, and it in no sense requires any preliminary assumptions about the nature of those relationships. The idealist view of the state assumes that 'the object of the state must be to fulfil, at the maximum possible, the desires of its citizens' (Laski, 1935, p. 34). With this view, state policy is fashioned to serve the common interest (or 'territorial interest', as Friedmann and Weaver put it), and the government expresses the *unified* will of the people. In reality, conflicts of interest riddle the association of people which is the state. And the basic theoretical problem is to explain the way in which these conflicts affect the form of the state apparatus and the nature of state policy, and how the exercise of state power affects the realization of various sectional interests. This problem may be tackled from a number of different theoretical perspectives, both Marxist and liberal.

Second, it is important to be clear about what is meant by the terms 'power' and 'state power'. Two concepts of power, which have been applied within the regional development literature, have already been introduced. In François Perroux's terms, an economic unit is 'dominant' if it can affect another economic unit while it cannot be affected by the latter (see chapter 3); and in Friedmann's 'General theory of polarized development', 'to have power is to exercise a measure of autonomy in decisions over a given environment and to have the ability to carry out these decisions' (see chapter 5). In the present context neither of these definitions, which are based on a notion of asymmetry of influence, will be used, as they do not tackle the key issue which must be addressed in any definition of power. This issue is well stated by Lukes (1974, p. 26):

> The absolutely basic common core to, or primitive notion lying behind, all talk of power is the notion that A in some way affects B. But, in applying that primitive (causal) notion to the analysis of social life, something further is needed – namely, the notion that A does so in a non-trivial or significant manner. Clearly, we all affect each other in countless ways all the time: the concept of power, and the related concepts of coercion, influence, authority, etc., pick out ranges of such affecting as being significant in specific ways. A way of conceiving power (or a way of defining the concept of power) that will be useful in the analysis of social relationships must imply an answer to the question: 'what counts as a significant manner?', 'what makes A's affecting B significant?'.

Lukes identifies various answers to this question within social theory, but underlying each is the notion that 'A exercises power over B when A affects B *in a manner contrary to B's interests*' (p. 27, emphasis added).

If power is viewed in this sense, it is possible to identify many different power relationships between the individuals and groups who form the association of people which is the state. Such relationships exist between classes, between men and women, between adults and children, between ethnic groups and so on. The ability of an individual or group to affect other individuals or groups in a manner contrary to the latters' interests is derived from various sources, such as wealth, or control of the means of production, or knowledge and organization, or the acceptance of certain forms of behaviour as 'natural'. But in all states, conflicts of interest are played out within the context of a legally supreme coercive power. This supreme coercive power is 'state power', and the uses towards which it is put not only directly support and damage the interests of individuals and groups within society, but also, in Poulantzas's words, play a 'constitutive role' in all power relations within society.

The term 'state power' is confusing for it can lead to the belief, which underlies some institutional analyses of the state, that the government and the state administration *themselves* possess power *over* 'civil society'. One may then conclude that power is a 'thing' which can be spatially redistributed by changing the form of institutional apparatus. Or that the state, a monolithic bloc of public institutions, is an instrument which can be captured by the dominant class or élite within civil society and used to promote their sectional interests against the interests of other groups. But within the present frame of reference, both these conclusions, and the belief which underlies them, are mistaken. The uses to which the supreme coercive power are put certainly allow individuals and groups to affect other individuals and groups in ways contrary to the latter's interests. But this does not mean that the institutions through which that power is exercised themselves *possess* power. They are, rather, the material expression of the ends to which state power is applied. And, as stated earlier, a key theoretical problem is to explain how the conflicts of interest and power relationships between the individuals and groups who make up the association of people which is the state affect the determination of these ends.

Third, it must be emphasized that the purposes to which state power is put and the exercise of those purposes is decided by *people* who have in some sense been deemed competent to form the government and to operate the state institutions. The state *itself* never acts. And the institutions *themselves* decide nothing. The institutions are the material framework within which decisions are made. But their internal organization certainly can affect the exercise of the state power, and the people who work in the state bureaucracies are part of the association of people which is the state. They have their own interests *vis-à-vis* other groups in society and their own divisions of interest between themselves. These interests, like those of any individual or group, may be supported or damaged by the exercise of state power.

Finally, if one takes a long historical perspective, looking, for example, at western Europe from the time of the Greek city-states, through the feudal ages to the present day, it is possible to see changes in the way in which the territoriality of the state has been socially defined (see Poulantzas, 1978, pp. 93–113). But today the territorial ambit of most states in the world is defined by frontiers which stake out a 'national territory'. Within these frontiers, the state institutions have a hierarchical-cum-territorial organization. There is a central and local government, and federal states are divided into constituent states. Administration is also organized on a regional and local basis, with different sections of the state institutional apparatus dividing up the national territory in different ways.

DEVELOPMENT AND REGIONAL PLANNING

If the state is analysed in these terms, it is possible to redefine the meaning of 'development' and to begin to make sense of regional planning activities. In the course of the argument of this book many different conceptions of 'development' have been introduced. It is evident that there is very little agreement among theorists about how 'development' occurs. But essentially the different theories of 'development' are theories of social and economic *change*, with various criteria being used to specify whether a particular type of change is 'development' or not.

The basic criteria which theorists use to specify a type of change as 'development' are: (i) whether it entails qualitative change in some sense; and (ii) whether it is 'progressive', according to some moral judgement about what constitutes progress. There is no absolute standard for deciding between these, and within each, particularly the second, a multitude of standards, which are rooted in different conceptions of the word 'good', can be applied. That there are different ways of understanding social and economic change is important. But the fact that the criteria used to specify what type of change is 'development' are arbitrary, in the sense that there is no logical basis for preferring one criterion to another, has led to sterile debates about what 'development' *really* is, and about whether a particular country is growing or developing, developing or underdeveloping, ultra-underdeveloping or misdeveloping.

But we now have a way out of this impasse. 'Development' is defined *in practice* as a PURPOSE towards which the exercise of state power is directed. That purpose involves much more than the use of state power to ensure that law and order are maintained among the individuals and groups who are members of a state. It involves much more than the use of state power to regulate the economy so that 'failures in the market mechanism' are avoided and to provide welfare support so that the 'weaker' sections of society can survive. With the adoption of 'development' as a central purpose of the exercise of state power, that power is used to organize *future* conditions of life and *future* relationships among the association of people who form a state.

By describing the purpose to which state power is put as 'development', it is implied that this power is used to create a *better future* for the people. But what 'development' means, in terms of both rhetoric and actual policy measures, varies considerably between states. In rhetoric, for example, it may mean closing the income gap with the rich countries of the world and adopting the most recent 'modern' technologies; or increasing the national growth rate and ensuring that income is more equitably distributed; or restructuring colonial institutions and re-establishing 'indigenous' ways of life; or increasing self-reliance and economic independence; or adopting 'socialist' forms of economic organization. But in all cases it is used to justify state intervention in a broad range of fields which deeply affect the lives of the subjects of the state. And what it means in specific contexts, both in rhetoric and actual policy measures, may be understood by examining how the purposes to which state power is put are determined. For that is how 'development' is defined in practice.

In developing countries today, with the adoption of 'development' (in some guise or other) as a central purpose of the exercise of state power, the strategic field of state intervention has become potentially all-embracing. New institutions are established within the state administration; public and 'para-statal' corporations and various types of state-owned banks are set up; and development plans are written. Health services, the education system, housing and personal social services are all reorganized for 'development'. And state intervention is actively directed towards increasing production, either through the establishment of state enterprises or through support to private investors, such as the provision of economic infrastructure, the organization of technical research and promotion of innovation and technology transfer, the creation of business training schemes and agricultural extension facilities, the manipulation of prices and taxes, and the negotiation of trade agreements in international markets.

Regional planning activities are part of this strategic field of intervention. In general, regional planning involves interventions which are *explicitly* directed to change the spatial distribution of physical infrastructure, population and human activities within the territory of a state. *Spatial organization*, that is, the way in which phenomena are distributed in geographic space to achieve some objective, is the central focus of regional planning. But this term should not be understood in the sense in which it has been employed by regional scientists and theoretical geographers (see Introduction). Their attempts to construct a science of the spatial organization of society are based either on the conceptually unsound assumption that a social system has 'needs' and spatial distributions are designed, by some invisible hand, to serve those 'needs', or on gross oversimplifications of human behaviour, such as the fiction of economic man. The term 'spatial organization', if it is employed in this way, will inevitably result in poor social theory. But in the context of a theorization of the state, the term is valuable. For within states, the strategic field of intervention includes measures which are intentionally designed to change the spatial distribution of population and human activities. Those measures have a purpose, that is, they are concerned with the *spatial organization* of society. And the purpose of such intentional spatial organization may be understood by examining how the purposes to which state power is put are determined.

Regional planning usually entails the *explicit* spatial allocation of resources *between sub-areas* of the territory of a state, or the co-ordination of resource allocation *within sub-areas* of the territory. These sub-areas, which are the 'regions' in regional planning, are in general larger than the territory of basic local government units of the state, though sometimes they are not (Conyers, 1983); and they are in general larger than the area covered by municipal authorities, though what a government describes as 'urban planning' may be conducted in metropolitan regions. The regions which form the basis of what governments describe as 'regional planning' activities are sometimes defined specifically for that purpose and sometimes consist of already existing administrative units of the central government. But, in either case, the initiation of regional planning will require some change in the territorial-cum-hierarchical organization of the state institutional apparatus, which may be marginal or radical. The regions, therefore, cannot be said to be arbitrarily defined. They are the material expression of the ends to which state power is applied.

The fact that regional planning involves interventions which are *explicitly* directed to change spatial distributions is of fundamental significance if we are to understand the rationale of the activity. As noted in the last chapter, both macro-economic and sectoral policies have *implicit* spatial effects. The corollary of this observation is that *the rhetoric and practice of regional planning can only be understood if we analyse it as an integral aspect of state policy.* And in developing countries, this means studying it as an integral part of state development policy.

But this presents us with a problem. For, unfortunately, theorization of the state in developing countries is still an underdeveloped part of development studies (O'Donnell, 1980; Goulbourne, 1980). And although there are some sophisticated analyses of urban planning and state policy in North America and western Europe (see, for example, Castells, 1978; and Scott and Roweis, 1977), studies of regional planning practice in developing countries from this perspective are only just beginning (see, in particular, Slater, 1983; de Oliviera, 1981).

Some general leads have been offered by Friedmann (1972) – in his 'General theory of polarized development' – in which changes in the spatial distribution of resources are related to a struggle between central and peripheral élites; and by Santos (1979), who argues that state development policies and regional policies are designed to serve the interests of multinational and monopoly capital (see chapter 5). But the argument of the former is rooted in a conception of space which will necessarily result in logical fallacies. And the argument of the latter is founded upon a mechanistic and class reductionist analysis of policy formulation whose assumptions can be easily questioned (see Jessop, 1982, chapter 2).

In this context I shall proceed with the discussion in a limited way. It must be stressed that ultimately it is necessary to ground the analysis of the formation of state development policy in some social theory which specifies the nature of sectional interests and power relationships in developing countries. Moreover, theorization must take account of the heterogeneity of the countries of Africa, Latin America and Asia. But here it will merely be assumed that conflicts of interest exist between different groups in society, and I shall hazard some generalizations by focusing upon a particular *type* of state, which will be termed a 'developmentalist state'.

POLICY FORMATION IN DEVELOPMENTALIST STATES

The idea of a 'developmentalist state' has been suggested by Cardoso and Falletto (1979). They use the term to refer to a type of state in Latin America, in which there was a weak domestic capitalist sector (as exemplified by Mexico and Chile between the 1930s and 1950s), and state policy, supported by an alliance of workers, state officials and the beginnings of a new bourgeoisie, was directed to promote industrialization. In the present discussion, the term will be used more broadly. For our purposes, a developmentalist state will be defined by two basic characteristics.

The first characteristic refers to a basic feature of the nature of state intervention. The government of a developmentalist state uses state power and state finances to increase material production, and it does so by facilitating and supporting *private capital accumulation* and by establishing *state enterprises run on profit-making principles*. The second characteristic refers to the principle of legitimacy upon which the government authorizes its rule over the association of people who form the state. The government of a developmentalist state authorizes its rule by the claim that it represents the common interest of all the people, and articulates this claim in rhetoric which says that the government is concerned with *national development*.

The reasons why state policy is directed towards increasing material production through private and state capital accumulation rather than through some communal organization of production, and why the authority of the government is legitimated through the claim that it represents the common interest of the people, rather than, say, the principle of hereditary rule or the principle that the rulers are God's representatives on earth, are very significant issues. But they cannot be addressed here. What is important is that most of the countries which have been defined earlier in the book as 'developing countries' may be conceived as 'developmentalist states'. And the formation of policy in those states may be related to a fundamental problem which the governments of those states will *inevitably* face.

That problem is simply how to obtain the consent of the people who are ruled. And it is bound to arise, for while the government *claims* to represent the common interest of all the people, and claims to be planning *national* development, the benefits of the increase in material production through private or state capital accumulation are, in the short term, necessarily distributed unequally between social groups and geographical areas. Once 'national development' is actively adopted as a major role of government, the crude and brutal effects of capitalist accumulation, cannot be taken for granted as an unfortunate side-effect of the free play of market forces. In taking on this task, the government becomes visibly identified as a prime agency which determines who prospers and who suffers in society.

There is a major contrast here between the conditions in most of the poorer countries of the world today and conditions in the now-rich countries when they first began industrializing. In the age of *laissez-faire* capitalism, there was some state intervention. But the strategic field of intervention was much more limited. In making 'national development' an end towards which state power is exercised, this field has expanded to include most aspects of the lives of the subjects of the state. And as Habermas (1973) puts it, 'the expansion of state activity has the side-effect of a disproportionate increase in the need for legitimation' (p. 377).

In these circumstances the government is likely to be trapped between the possibility of a legitimation crisis and a fiscal crisis. It will be threatened with a legitimation crisis when the people cease to believe that the government represents the common interest and express their dissent, through either legitimate or illegitimate channels (Habermas, 1973). It can avoid such a crisis by diverting state finances to provide public facilities and to subsidize essential commodities, and through promoting private and state capital accumulation in ways which lead to less inequitable outcomes. But in order to promote any type of 'development', the government must increase state revenue. And although this can in some circumstances be achieved through such means as tourism or taxing entrepôt trading activities, in general it will entail increasing *taxable* material production or making state enterprises more profitable. Legitimation expenditures tend to slow down the growth of state revenue, and then the government can find itself within a fiscal crisis, in which state expenditures outrun state revenues (O'Connor, 1973).

The room for manoeuvre of different governments varies. Those countries with oil resources are less reliant on material production increases, though the short-term fluctuations in oil prices can play havoc with state finances. Some countries have been able to raise loans through the international banking system and as aid. But the general tendency is that if the government tries to avoid a legitimation crisis through expenditures which are designed to reduce the inequalities of private capital accumulation, it will be plunged into a fiscal crisis, in which the problem of obtaining the consent of the ruled will be even more heightened. For it will be evident that the government is not only failing to serve the common interest, but also failing to fulfil what is identified as its key role – organizing a 'better future' for the subjects of the state.

Policy formation in developmentalist states entails the avoidance of both legitimation and fiscal crises, and reflects the different ways in which the government can maintain the consent of the people who are subjects of state power, while fostering the expansion of material production through private and state capital accumulation.

A first way this can be achieved is through repression. Any internal dissent, whether articulated by key individuals or social groups, can be crushed by force. The government exercises supreme *coercive* power and so opposition may be eliminated by using the police, the judiciary system and the armed forces. But although violent repressive acts are a general feature of developmentalist states (see Frank, 1981), and although repression *must* be taken into account in any adequate analysis of the formation of development policy, there are limits to the effectiveness of this means of obtaining consent. Opposition within the territory may go 'underground' or be organized outside the national frontiers. And social groups can take legal, seemingly apolitical, actions which can subvert the purposes to which state power is applied. For example, in Africa, as many governments have learnt to their cost, peasant producers can withdraw from the market economy and thereby undermine the process of private capital accumulation. The government, however repressive, is therefore not absolutely *autonomous* from social forces.

Besides repression, consent may be obtained through either *discourse* or *practical actions*. The government will necessarily claim that its policies represent the 'national interest' and serve 'the needs of the people', and the discourse of development planning documents will always tend to be couched in these terms. The introduction of a scientific, and supposedly neutral basis for making strategic planning decisions can bolster the government's claims, and has the further effect of limiting knowledge to a small group of experts. In addition, the government can shape 'public opinion' through the press and radio and, in the longer term, through the education system. Particularly important in this respect is the formation of a 'common-sense' view of what is best for the country.

The government can, for example, foster the idea that the 'modern' or any forms of organization which are 'indigenous' are somehow *good in themselves*; or that any policies which are against 'foreign interests' necessarily serve the 'national interest'; or that the benefits of 'development' will reach everybody in the end, though sacrifices have to be made now. Interestingly, such 'ruling illusions', to use Skillen's (1977) marvellous phrase, form the ground on which some of the 'theories' in development studies have been constructed.

But while discourse is an essential element in securing consent, it alone is insufficient. First, discourse can only be effective if it is related to actions which together with the discourse sustain beliefs. And second, no matter what the 'common-sense' view is, people are aware, to varying degrees, that their interests are being supported or damaged through state interventions. In the final analysis, then, the government must secure consent through its practical actions.

And here we come to a fundamental point. The government must secure consent through its interventions. But *it does not need the consent of EVERY individual or group within the association of people which is the state*. It only needs to secure the consent of those groups which are *politically powerful*, in the sense that concerted action on their part can threaten the successful achievement of the particular purposes to which state power is directed at any given moment, and the underlying objective of increasing material production through private and state capital accumulation.

Various social groups can do this. They may be trade unionists, members of professional associations, students or farmers' organizations. They may be the poorer sections of the population concentrated in the metropoli or a popular peasant movement in a peripheral area of the national territory. They may be extra-territorial, for example, a multinational corporation deciding whether to invest in a country. Or they may be the supporters of opposition political parties in representative democracies. But whatever the groups are in any particular context, the fact that there are *various* groups means that their interests are not completely mutual. *The practical actions which are the substance of development policy may thus be understood as the outcome of a negotiation of conflicting powerful interests in society mediated through the institutional apparatus of the state.*

The negotiation of the conflicting interests of various groups is mediated through the state institutional apparatus in the sense that it is state personnel and the people who form the government who take the decisions. Their choices are informed by motives which range from a desire to maximize personal gain, to a deep concern for the welfare of the people and nation. But whatever their *intentions*, their room for manoeuvre will be limited. State bureaucracies are run according to certain norms and they have an internal logic of organization. But besides this, the system of state institutions is an arena of conflict within society *as a whole*. It is an arena of conflict in which the various power relationships among the association of people which comprise the state are both played out and forged. To understand both the discourse and practical actions in any given case, one must analyse the different sectional interests in society, the ways in which these interests are mobilized into political organizations and represented within the institutions of the state, and the ways in which resistance to particular policies is organized, and repressed.

But in saying this I do not wish to imply that the rhetoric and content of policy in developmentalist states can be *mechanically* derived from an analysis of social forces. The political power of different groups varies with the purposes to which state power is put, while at the same time those purposes depend on the balance of power between those groups. State policy itself may have the outcome, intentional or not, of demobilizing social groups, and thus of reducing their power. There is a complex relationship between executive actions and discourse in the sense that the actions give meaning to the discourse, while the available language constrains possible actions. And finally, the policy-makers are not omniscient, and so whatever their purposes, the outcome may include some unintended effects. Thus, policy formation must be seen as a *process* characterized by indeterminacies which are resolved at successive moments. The outcome of this process, as Poulantzas (1978, p. 135) notes, is likely to be 'phenomenally incoherent and chaotic'. Which is precisely how national development policy actually *is* in most parts of the world.

One final qualification must be added to this picture. The coercive authority which a government possesses theoretically implies that state policy can be formulated with total disregard for the interests of any group, either within or outside the territory of the state. As argued earlier, it is impossible for the government to be absolutely autonomous of social forces over a long period. But there may be particular times when the interests of politically powerful groups are completely incompatible, and it is impossible to reach a compromise as to the purposes to which state power will be put. It is at such times that repressive, authoritarian regimes are most likely to emerge. And state policy will then be directed towards meeting the interests of particular groups in society in such a way that power relationships within society are reconstituted and a return to the 'normality' of shifting compromises effected. But exactly *how* this goal is pursued is difficult to predict.*

REGIONAL POLICY OBJECTIVES AND REGIONAL
PLANNING STRATEGIES RECONSIDERED

Once those countries which were described at the start of this book as 'capitalist developing countries' are conceived as developmentalist states, it is possible to see why so many of them are adopting some form of regional planning and to make greater sense of the rationale for the choice of particular regional policy objectives and particular regional planning strategies.

In the first part of this book, the regional policy objectives commonly adopted in 'developing countries' were identified as the reduction of regional and rural-urban disparities in 'development' and the reduction of the rate of metropolitan population growth. In Part One these objectives were taken at face value. It is possible to make more sense of them by relating them to the fact that in developmentalist states the government uses state finances to promote private capital accumulation and legitimates its authority over the people by the claim that it represents the 'national' interest. For rhetoric and planning interventions, which on the surface are designed to achieve *regional* objectives, can serve to promote capital accumulation and to legitimate government authority.

In order to sustain the belief that the government is acting in the common interest of all the people in the national territory, the government must necessarily proclaim that it intends to act in this way. The goals of development plans will thus always tend to be couched in egalitarian rhetoric, and the rhetoric is likely to include the desire to 'develop' all areas within the national territory as well as the desire to increase social justice. Moreover, if the belief of the people in the government is to be maintained, the rhetoric must be backed by *explicit* actions. The fact that most macro-economic and sectoral development policies *implicitly* have spatially differentiated effects (see above, p. 212) has the corollary

---

* See Poulantzas (1973; 1975; 1978) for one answer to this question. Poulantzas's work is *essential* reading for anyone now studying the state. His ideas have been strongly criticized in the British literature, mainly because of the Althusserian view of society on which his earlier analyses of the state are founded. But the questions which he poses are the most important ones. One may disagree with the theoretical perspective which is the foundation of his studies. But by reading Poulantzas it is possible to see the state in all its complexities, to find the critical issues which must be addressed in state theorization, and to discover some paths to understanding. His last book, *State, Power, Socialism*, is particularly important.

that attempts to reduce spatial disparities could be made through these policies. But such measures have the disadvantage that the effects are indirect and, through them, the government does not explicitly target resources to poorer areas. A regional policy, particularly if it results in visible projects in poor regions, demonstrates the validity of the government's intent. The policy may be completely subverted by macro-economic and sectoral policies which have opposite spatial effects to those which the government explicitly seeks to achieve, but it has a symbolic value.

Explicit policies to reduce spatial disparities in 'development' sustain the belief that the government is serving the 'national interest'. But at a deeper level they also enhance a sense of nationhood. One of the most important legacies of colonialism is that it created states with a 'national' territory, but no nation. Part of state policy in developmentalist states is thus directed towards *inventing* a nation. And this is particularly so in the states of Africa and Asia which gained independence after the Second World War with a set of state institutions modelled on the western democracies and with a set of frontiers which encompassed diverse ethnic and linguistic groups.

National identity is a phenomenon of the imagination. It is an attribute of oneself which one imagines one shares with some others and which those others imagine they share with oneself; and it is an attribute which the collective 'we', who have this shared perception, imagine differentiates 'us' from another such collectivity, and which that collective 'they' imagine differentiates 'them' from 'us'. That it is a phenomenon of the imagination does not imply that it is 'unreal'. It is a significant determinant of human action and it is formed through the everyday experience and shared memories of people.* Living in the same territory is an important factor in the formation of a sense of nationhood, particularly as governments can create a history and a language for a people (Poulantzas, 1978, pp. 193–220). But living in the same area is not a sufficient condition for having this sense. Regional policies may promote it through homogenizing ways of life in different parts of the national territory and by increasing social and economic interaction between areas (see Friedmann, 1967).

In addition, there are certain circumstances in which the territorial

* The definition of national identity put forward here is based on a reading of R. D. Laing's ideas on experience, identity and the behaviour of individuals in groups (see especially, Laing, 1967, chapter 4). A recent historical account of the origin and spread of nationalism illustrates the value of thinking of 'nations' as 'imagined communities' (Anderson, 1983). And Laing's broader arguments show why it is impossible to derive an understanding of nationalism following the tenets of positivist science and indicate how knowledge about national identity may be constructed.

integrity of the state is threatened. This occurs when regionally based political movements demand that a separate state be carved out of national territory or when neighbouring national states question the legitimacy of colonially defined frontiers and lay claim to part of the national territory. In such circumstances, regional policies which explicitly allocate resources to 'peripheral' regions can be particularly important in maintaining support for the central government.

The legitimacy of a government is bound to be undermined if its policies result in a fiscal crisis, in which state expenditure commitments exceed state revenue. At such times the government will be unable to meet the developmental expectations it has created. Regional policies can help a government to avoid a fiscal crisis by boosting state revenue and by containing state expenditure.

Policies which are designed to change the spatial distribution of population offer an *indirect* method of containing state expenditure. Metropolitan centres are a major drain on state finances as many expenditures, on water supply systems, transport infrastructure and sewage networks, have to be made merely to keep these agglomerations of population habitable. And this is so even when the poorest groups are clustered in shantytowns. Policies which reduce metropolitan population growth and reduce the rate of rural-urban migration offer a means of slowing down the increase in state expenditure. But in pursuing such policies, the government has to make expenditures to avoid future expenditures and whether the outcome is a reduction in the rate of growth of state expenditure depends on the precise nature of the measures adopted as well as their effectiveness in altering the spatial distribution of population.

Regional policies, particularly those which are designed to promote 'integrated' development of poor rural regions, may also provide a method of attracting foreign aid to a country. This can increase the revenue available for development planning and, if an international agency is given the task of planning change in a region, there is the additional advantage that any poor results may be attributed to the failings of the 'foreign experts' rather than the central government. Such 'sub-contracting' of regions to international agencies has become quite common in Africa and Asia in the last ten years, despite the fact that, for the central government, it entails a loss of control of many resource allocation decisions in parts of the national territory.

Foreign aid, as has been observed so often, normally has strings attached to it, and to avoid a fiscal crisis without becoming entangled in a net of external obligations a government must increase revenues derived from members of the state and from activities which take place within the national territory. For most states this can only be achieved through the expansion of material production. Regional policies may help to promote such an expansion. But their particular form in developmentalist states must be related to the fact that in such states increases in production are promoted through measures which facilitate and support private capital accumulation and through state enterprises run on a profit-making basis.

What is described as a 'regional policy' is sometimes merely a locational policy for state industries, and in the formulation of this policy complex decisions are taken because the most profitable locations for an industry are not necessarily those in which the government may demonstrate that it is serving the 'national interest'. The problem is particularly acute because the type of industries which are usually under state control, such as iron and steel or petrochemicals, are ones in which economies of scale may be derived, and the government then faces the choice between an efficient single plant, which visibly symbolizes the government's bias towards one region, and a few less efficient plants dividing production between the regions of a country. But though such trade-offs exist within the state capitalist sector, it is possible to *promote* private capital accumulation through regional policies which are *explicitly* concerned with 'developing' poorer regions and rural areas.

Let us examine this proposition in relation to some of the regional planning strategies outlined in the second part of the book. Consider first Johnson's idea to build up a network of market towns which can act as 'rural growth centres' and Rondinelli and Ruddle's strategy of 'integrated regional development'. They each aim to promote 'regional' and 'rural development', and they each attempt to achieve this objective through 'integrating agricultural producers more fully into the market economy'. If they are successful, such strategies will have the effect of increasing the accumulation of merchant capital.

To understand why this is so, let us assume an idealized society in which all agricultural producers own their means of production, each household engages in production simply to reproduce itself from year to year, and part of production is *commoditized*, in the sense that households sell some of their produce. A commodity is defined as a product which is sold and in our idealized society production is commoditized to the extent that households are not self-sufficient, and thus meet their reproduction needs by exchanging part of their production for money and by exchanging this money for other commodities.

The act of selling in order to buy logically implies a reverse process of buying in order to sell, and let us assume that there is complete division of labour between the producers and merchants who buy commodities to resell them. The merchants, in contrast to the producers, use their labour 'to make money' and they do so by turning money into commodities, reselling them as quickly as possible, buying more commodities with this money, reselling them and so on. The conversion of money into commodities and back into money describes the circuit of merchant capital in our simple society, and the accumulation of merchant capital occurs when merchants are able to make net monetary gain when reselling the commodities they bought. A net gain is achieved when the total monetary gain exceeds the expenditures which are required in buying and reselling and in purchasing commodities which ensure the subsistence of the merchant.

Regional planning strategies such as those of Johnson and Rondinelli and Ruddle will increase the accumulation of merchant capital because, if they are successful, they will promote the commoditization of agricultural production through either the geographical extension of commodity production or the intensification of commodity relations or both. This is the basis of merchant capital accumulation. But the precise content of the strategies can have further important effects.

In the absence of coercion, producers can always withdraw from commodity production if the terms of exchange are such that they derive no benefit from allocating their labour-time to producing crops or livestock for sale. This possibility arises because the farmers own their means of production and if it occurs, as it has in many African countries in recent years, it can severely reduce capital accumulation and have disastrous effects on a national economy. As long as producers control the allocation of their labour-time, the limits to 'decommoditization' are set by the extent to which the necessary consumption required to meet the subsistence of the households and the necessary items required in the production process are *purchased*. If the producer requires school clothing, kerosene or domestic utensils, for example, as elements of necessary consumption, or uses improved varieties of seed or fertilizer in the production process, he or she cannot completely withdraw from commodity production because money is needed to reproduce the household. The content of Johnson's market town strategy and the 'integrated regional development' strategy is such that, if successful, they will not only promote the commoditization of production but also establish conditions which prevent large-scale decommoditization. For the 'tempting demonstration effects' which Johnson seeks to foster raise the producers' perception of what is 'necessary subsistence' and increase the extent to which 'subsistence' consumption is money-mediated, and the agro-support facilities – distributing fertilizer, tools, seed, credit and advice – advocated by both Johnson and Rondinelli and Ruddle, all serve to monetize the production process.

As producers become more deeply embedded in the monetary economy, not only is the production of agricultural commodities *secured*, but the necessary conditions are also established for what Bernstein (1977) calls a 'simple reproduction squeeze'. Such a squeeze occurs when household producers must either reduce their levels of consumption, or intensify commodity production, or do both simultaneously in order to ensure their reproduction. A 'simple reproduction squeeze' can be created by various factors, but one way it occurs is through a reduction in the price of the commodities which the household producers sell relative to the price of the commodities they buy to support household consumption or production. This change in the terms of exchange will itself increase merchant capital accumulation, but if there are strong limits to the households reducing 'subsistence' consumption, it will have the further effect of intensifying commodity relations.

Finally, the content of the proposed 'regional development' strategies also facilitates merchant capital accumulation by directly tackling a major problem which merchants face in their search for profits − the problem that producers and consumers of commodities are separated in geographic space. In general, improvements in transportation can increase capital accumulation by reducing costs of transferring commodities and through speeding up the turnover time which it takes merchants to convert money into commodities and back into money. But the speedy completion of the circuit of capital also requires that buyers and sellers are in the right place at the right time. The emergence of marketing centres, where buyers know that they can find sellers of particular commodities and sellers know that they can find buyers, provides a co-ordinating mechanism which can fulfil this function. But the emergence of such centres is not an inevitable consequence of the logic of capital accumulation. It is the result of a myriad of human decisions, with the formation of the regular and routine buying and selling habits stabilizing the spatial pattern of centres, and the merchants' search for profits constantly disturbing it. The strategies of Johnson and Rondinelli and Ruddle, through planning infrastructural investments in marketing centres and transportation, stabilize these patterns, speed up the velocity of circulation of capital and reduce transfer costs, and thereby further facilitate capital accumulation.

Just as it is possible to increase the accumulation of merchant capital through regional policies which establish marketing centres and promote the commoditization of agricultural production, so it is possible to increase the accumulation of industrial capital through the implementation of an urban-industrial growth pole strategy. The circuit of industrial capital has three basic phases. The capitalist buys labour-power and the means of production (raw materials, machines, etc.) with money; he organizes the process of production to make commodities; and he sells these commodities for money. If the sum of money is greater than the sum advanced in the first place, the capitalist secures a profit which, if it is not spent on consumption, may be used to buy more labour-power and means of production and to expand the circuit.

Accumulation occurs through such expanded reproduction of capital, but it depends upon the production and realization of surplus value. Value may be defined as the 'socially necessary' labour-time embodied in a commodity, that is 'the labour required to produce an article under normal conditions of production and with the average degree of skill and intensity prevalent at the time' (Harvey, 1982, p. 15). And surplus value can be produced because the capitalist buys the right to determine the application of labour-power in the production process. Labour-power, as a commodity, has a value which is equivalent to the labour-time embodied in the commodities required to meet the subsistence needs of the workers. Because the capitalist controls the production process, labour-power can be put to work to produce commodities whose value is greater than itself. Surplus value is produced whenever the commodities which labour-power creates in the production process exceed the value of labour-power itself.

But the realization of surplus value does not only depend upon the control of labour-power in the production process. The capitalist must be able to find upon the market 'the right quantities and qualities of raw materials, instruments of production or labour power at a price appropriate to their individual production requirements' and 'users willing to part with an exchange value [a sum of money] equivalent to the value embodied in each commodity' (Harvey, 1982, p. 88). Moreover, the three-phase circuit of capital must be completed in a given time-period if capital is not to be devalued. The realization of surplus value is thus affected by the location of the production process; the spatial distribution of raw materials, physical infrastructures and social infrastructures, such as health and education facilities; the mobility of capital, in the form of money, commodities, or when there is a physical relocation of production, in the form of the labour process itself; the mobility of labourers if they are not employed; and the spatial distribution of effective demand for the commodities produced. Space is therefore an integral part of the accumulation process. Or, as Harvey (1982) puts it, 'the production of spatial configurations can be treated as an "active moment" within the overall temporal dynamic of accumulation and social reproduction' (p. 374).

With the exception of the transport industry, 'the production of commodities is tied to a particular location for the duration of the labour process' (Harvey, 1982, p. 381). Production requires some *fixed capital*, which in material form consists of plant and equipment, the physical infrastructures of production. Such capital has value over its working life and it can tie the capitalist to particular locations for periods which are much longer than the duration of the production process. But in its monetary form, capital is highly mobile in a geographical sense and if the capital 'embedded in the land', to use Harvey's words, is owned by someone other than the capitalist, capital may also move through the relocation of the labour process.

The capitalists' search for profits and for ways to use surplus capital lead to a geographical expansion in capitalist production. But, at the same time, the various problems which a capitalist encounters in trying to realize surplus value set up a countervailing tendency towards geographical concentration. As more capitalists and labourers cluster together, the likelihood of finding the right kind of labour-power and means of production is increased and the velocity of circulation of capital quickened.

Regional policies which have the explicit objective of increasing the 'spatial integration' of the national economy and pursue this objective through transportation and communication improvements facilitate capital accumulation. As both the costs and time of moving commodities fall, the turnover time of capital is reduced and the value of all commodities being moved falls. This can have adverse effects on some individual capitalists whose production process is tied to particular locations. But, in general, 'accumulation requires that more and more capital shifts into the production of means of transportation and communication' (Harvey, 1982, p. 379).

Transport improvements loosen the tendency towards a geographical concentration of production processes. But in countries where capitalist production is spatially concentrated in a few areas and where transport and communications are still costly, time-consuming and expensive, an urban-industrial growth pole strategy is an effective means of increasing industrial capital accumulation through the promotion and co-ordination of the geographical expansion of capitalist production. This approach, a strategy of 'concentrated decentralization', as Rodwin (1963) calls it, neatly offers capitalists the advantages of geographical concentration and of geographical expansion.

The basic physical infrastructure required for production is established through state resources, usually in advance of private investment. Social infrastructures may also be improved through public investment in housing and various social facilities. The resources for all the local infrastructural investments have, in part, been taxed from the capitalists.

But the amount of capital which they then have to 'embed in the land' before commencing production is considerably reduced. The investments in social facilities such as health and education also contribute to the reproduction of labour power. And the production of both physical and social infrastructures can create an effective demand for the commodities which the capitalists produce, a possibility which is especially well illustrated by housing projects. The selection of a few key locations as 'growth centres' has the additional effect of helping to ensure that labour-power and capital, in its various forms, is in the right place at the right time. And by judiciously fostering inter-industry linkages, some of the capitalists are given a ready market for the commodities they produce.

These remarks do little more than scratch the surface of a very complex problem. In order to analyse how regional policies can facilitate private capital accumulation, it is necessary to understand the spatiality of capital accumulation. In the account above I have taken many ideas from the work of Harvey, and the reader is advised to refer to his latest book, *The Limits to Capital* (1982) to see a tightly argued analysis which treats space as an integral element in the dynamics of capital accumulation and social reproduction. But to grasp these dynamics in developing countries, it must be recognized that capitalist relations of production are not fully developed. Thus work such as that of Lipietz (1980), which examines the articulation between household commodity production and capitalist production, may offer a more complete approach to understanding.

But although the observations which I have made on the accumulation logic of regional planning strategies are over-simplified, they nevertheless suggest an important hypothesis. It is that:

> Given the conditions which prevail in the countries of Latin America, Africa and Asia, it is possible to use regional policies to promote private capital accumulation *and* to legitimate the authority of the government.

This is *possible* because the government can support its claim that its policies are in the 'national interest' by announcing that state intervention is designed to reduce spatial disparities in 'development', while the specific measures introduced in the name of developing poor areas can facilitate private capital accumulation. And it is *likely* because the commoditization of agricultural production is spatially uneven and capitalist production is geographically concentrated in a few urban centres in many of the countries of those three continents.

This hypothesis will have to be refined to take account of the heterogeneity of conditions in Africa, Asia and Latin America. But at a general level it is useful for it points to some intrinsic features of regional policy which help us to 'decode' what that activity means in particular countries.

The first and most important feature is the *metonymical* nature of policies to develop areas. A metonym is a word which is used when the name of an attribute or adjunct of something is substituted for the thing meant. For example, it is possible, *in the name of developing an area*, to promote private capital accumulation. The area may be a region, a city or a group of rural localities, and policy measures can have the effect of 'developing' that area, if 'development' is measured with certain indicators. But whatever 'development' does occur there is an *adjunct* of private capital accumulation.

The metonymical nature of regional policies means that it is possible to achieve hidden policy objectives through measures which have as their adjunct 'area development'. But the second important feature of regional policies is that the achievement of these concealed objectives depends on *how* the area is 'developed'. *The nature of the regional planning strategy adopted to achieve overt spatial objectives must be a central focus of analysis if we are to understand how regional policies can achieve covert social objectives.* What seems to be exactly the same policy may serve different purposes in different countries, and a change in strategy in one country may be designed to ensure that the same purposes are served. To 'decode' regional policies we must recognize, with Pickvance (1981), that such policies are chameleons.

REGIONAL THEORY AND REGIONAL PLANNING PRACTICE
IN DEVELOPMENTALIST STATES

If it is possible to use regional policies to promote private capital accumulation and to legitimate the authority of the government in developmentalist states, then the adoption of some type of regional policy will be a particularly attractive option in the formulation of state development policy. As the debates on redistribution with growth suggest, there is often a trade-off between the goal of maximizing national growth and the goal of fostering a more equitable income distribution. Policies which change the spatial distribution of economic activities, population and infrastructure are unlikely to promote redistribution with growth. But they offer the opportunity of achieving legitimation with accumulation.

This opportunity can provide a basic starting-point for analysing the proliferation of regional planning activities in developmentalist states.

But it would be wrong to conclude that regional policies are adopted 'because they serve legitimation and accumulation functions'. To suggest such an explanation would be to fall into the traps of functional analysis. Within the general framework of policy formation outlined earlier in this chapter, the adoption of regional policies and their specific nature can only be understood by analysing how the conflicting interests of various social groups within a country are mediated through the institutional apparatus of state. And it is at this point that analysis becomes most interesting – and most difficult.

The problem is that we must be able to theorize social relationships within developmentalist states in a way which does not conceive society as a spaceless aggregate. All the people in the national territory are subject to state power. But we cannot understand the formation of state development policy, and the position of regional planning within it, unless we theorize the *space-time constitution* of the sectional interests, power relationships and political struggles which influence policy. In order to grasp the nature of regional planning activities, it is necessary to analyse the formation and social composition of regionally based political groups, which may or may not be demanding more resources for 'their' area, and which may or may not be using regional identity as a means of political mobilization. One must consider how the interests of such groups and the interests of groups which are not localized within a particular area of the territory of the state are realized by changes in the spatial distribution of infrastructure, population and activity. One must furthermore understand how the interests of localized and non-localized social groups are jointly mediated within a state apparatus which itself has a territorial organization. One must study how changes in the territorial-cum-hierarchical organization of the state institutions can change power relationships within society. And one must analyse the ways in which policies with explicit regional development objectives are complementary with, competitive to or substitutions for, macro-economic and sectoral policies which have spatial implications.

Our knowledge of what Giddens calls 'the space–time constitution of social systems' is so slight that it is difficult to make any general argument at the moment. I shall not attempt the task. The whole purpose of putting 'Regions in Question' has been to lead the reader to this point. I have tried to get at the significance of 'space' in 'development' by negating a body of theory and clearing the ground for analyses based on a relational concept of space. The earlier parts of this chapter, in which territory is included as an integral part of state theorization and the spatiality of capital accumulation is discussed, illustrate what such a change in the conceptualization of space entails. And through this switch in perspective, and by examining regional planning activities as political choices, we have derived some general propositions which can help to 'decode' what regional planning is in practice. But a full understanding of the practice must be rooted in some theorization of social relationships in which space is an integral element.

The construction of such knowledge is a future task. It is a task which forces the theorist on to an uneasy ground where the insights of neither class analysis nor cultural studies are in themselves sufficient. And the implication of the argument of this book is that it is a task for *social theorists* in general, not regional theorists.

A full understanding of regional planning practice in developing countries may await such knowledge. But some final remarks on the general nature of regional planning practice, and its relationships to regional development theory *as it is presently constructed*, are in order.

One important feature of regional policies is that they can be used *intentionally* to mobilize political support and demobilize political opposition. At a superficial level this may be observed in parliamentary democracies where popular representation is organized on a territorial basis and votes are bought through the explicit spatial allocation of resources. Examples of such 'pork-barrel' politics are a good indicator of how a regional policy may be used, but within our framework of analysis the tactics of mobilization and demobilization must be analysed at a deeper level. Bates (1981), for example, has shown how the opposition of the peasantry to governments in Africa has been fragmented by a two-sided strategy in which policy measures which depress prices for *all* producers in rural areas are pursued in conjunction with policy measures which return a portion of these revenues to *some* producers in the form of *divisible* benefits. The location of projects is a major element in such a strategy, and through locational decisions benefits are conferred upon supporters and withheld from political opposition. Similarly, decentralization and the reorganization of political and administrative regions may be used as part of a strategy designed to reconstitute a balance of power among dominant groups within a state and has been adopted by various military regimes, such as that which ruled Nigeria in 1976.

But although the potential of regional policy as a means of political mobilization and demobilization can add to the attractiveness of a regional policy from the government's point of view, the adoption of measures which *explicitly* direct state resources to particular localities and regions, and the establishment of institutions which can co-ordinate resource allocation within sub-areas of the territory of the state can, at the same time, create problems. *For it is logically impossible to have a neutral allocation of resources in geographic space.*

As soon as industries, public facilities or projects are located, some people will be nearer to them than others and will thus derive more benefits. Inequalities in physical access may be blurred if resources are allocated to regions and each region is treated on an equal basis. But this will not reduce the inequalities *within* regions. And if resource allocations are currently unequal, the attempt to equalize them will entail the worse-off regions gaining more resources at the expense of those which are better-off. When state resources are growing quickly this can be achieved through decreasing the rate of growth of resource allocations to the better-off regions. But in conditions of stagnation, what the poor regions gain quite literally must be taken away from the rich regions.

Moreover, as soon as co-ordinating mechanisms are established to plan resource allocations at the regional level, conflicts will become apparent between the achievement of national objectives and the achievement of regional objectives. The government may claim that its policies are designed to serve the 'common good' of all the people in the national territory. But however that idea is defined, the pursuit of the 'common good' at the national level will be in contradiction with its pursuit at the regional level, and vice versa. A policy which hypothetically serves the 'common good' of the people in the national territory will not serve the 'common good' of the people in some of the regions within that territory; a policy which hypothetically serves the 'common good' of the people in a region will not serve the 'common good' of the people in some of the districts within that region; and a policy which hypothetically serves the 'common good' of the people in a district will not serve the 'common good' of the people in some of the localities within that district. The only conditions in which these relationships would not hold would be where there are no natural resource differentials, and such conditions are only found in the textbooks of regional scientists.

For legitimation purposes, regional policies will be shrouded with a rhetoric which suggests that they are concerned to reduce spatial disparities. But intrinsic to their nature is the fact that they are explicitly biased *against* some spatially defined groups. And because of this, the adoption of some form of regional planning by a government can have the *unintentional* effect of mobilizing political groups which demand more resources and rights for 'their' region.

These regionalist political movements have a peculiar nature. The articulation of local and regional identity can be a potent force for political mobilization. But the spatial attributes with which one identifies oneself and with which one is identified are only one out of a set of attributes one has – I am a man, a university lecturer, white, *and I live in Wales*. One's spatial attributes also are defined at various spatial scales – I am a resident of Swansea, of Wales, of Britain *and* of western Europe. Local and regional identity may therefore become politically salient in particular circumstances, but as those circumstances change, other attributes, such as class or race or sex, can become more significant. Moreover, one right of the subjects of most states is their freedom to move almost anywhere within the national territory, and so anyone who lives in an area which they perceive to be 'neglected' or 'disadvantaged' can migrate to seek their fortune elsewhere. This option means that regionalist movements are only likely to be well organized in two sets of circumstances. The first occurs when people have much to lose by moving. The second occurs when people have no immediate prospect of realizing their interests *anywhere* within the territorial ambit of the state, and see the creation of a new sovereign state in 'their' territory, or the modification of the territorial-cum-historical organization of the existing state institutional apparatus, as the best means to promote their interests. Strong regionalist movements thus tend to have a class basis, for example when a faction of capital is committed to immobile investment (see Harvey, 1982, chapter 13); or an ethnic basis, when place of birth is an integral part of ethnic identity and spatial concentration a necessary condition for maintaining the group's way of life; or a broader cultural basis, when a linguistic or religious minority within the state is subject to laws which apply throughout the state's territory but which are contrary to their way of life; or some combination of these (see Hechter and Levi, 1979).

The peculiarities of regionalist political movements make them as difficult to 'decode' as regional policy itself. But whatever their bases, regional 'neglect' can be a powerful political rallying-cry which a government may unwittingly provoke through adopting a regional policy. And then, depending on the balance of power of the various social groups influencing state policy, the precise form of the regional policy may change to meet the regionalist demands.

To understand regional policies, one must take account of the fact that they are EXPLICITLY *biased against spatially defined groups and* IMPLICITLY *biased in favour of socially defined groups.* The latter intrinsic feature gives them their chameleon-like quality. The former means that, for the government, a regional policy can be a chameleon that stings.

And once this is recognized, the logic of regional development theory *as it is presently constructed* begins to make sense. Looking back over the concepts discussed in the main body of this book it is clear that the field is characterized by 'persuasive definitions'. Such definitions imply that the phenomenon being defined is inherently good (see Machlup, 1958). 'Regional balance' and 'growth poles' are both of this type. Specifying what they mean precisely is an almost impossible task. But they make useful political rhetoric. The notion of 'spread effects' is of a similar type. Regional theorists have devoted great efforts to finding them, and they have remained elusive. But from a political point of view, the idea that if resources are spatially concentrated in particular localities and regions, the 'benefits of development' will eventually trickledown into other areas is an essential way of maintaining support in the neglected areas.

Regional development theory is structured in a way in which it can be used to justify regional policies which are biased in favour of social groups and against spatially defined groups. The fact that it is constructed as a body of 'scientific' knowledge gives the spurious appearance that it is neutral, that it offers a technically rational way of choosing the best means to achieve given ends. But, in reality, the propositions contained within the field are *ideological*.

To say this does not imply that regional development theory has been deliberately constructed to serve particular social interests. The intentions of regional theorists cannot be inferred from the uses to which their theories are put. And it does not imply that it is possible to have some form of knowledge of society which is 'scientific', which may be set against another form which is 'ideological'. An ideology is taken here to mean a set of beliefs which supports or damages the interests of a group in society. And in this sense most of social theory is ideological. But the realization that regional development theory *is* ideology demands that it be studied *as* ideology.

This can only be done by examining how the theory is used *in practice*. No abstract generalizations may be made about whose particular interests the theory supports and damages. But the *characteristic* which gives the *theory* its ideological flexibility and potency is clear.

It is that characteristic which, throughout this book, I have termed 'spatial separatism' – that is, the structuring of the theory in a way which separates space from social processes. The working method at present used in the field gives rise to insoluble logical problems. But the logical problems of the theory are at the same time ideological opportunities. The conflation of social problems located *in* cities and regions with problems *of* those cities and regions, the commitment of ecological fallacies and confusion of 'place prosperity' with 'people prosperity', and the displacement of analysis from an examination of social relationships to an examination of spatial relationships, have all stymied adequate theorization, and all stem from the conceptualization of space. Yet, with this conceptualization, it is possible to formulate metonymical regional policies which serve diverse social interests in the name of developing an area, and appear to be technically rational. Thus, the conceptualization of space on which regional development theory rests is not only the source of its logical weaknesses. It is also the source of its ideological power.

A guide to further reading

The main body of this book focused upon mainstream thinking within regional development theory. But the argument has drawn upon the work of various theorists who reject the method of analysis which permeates the mainstream, and attempt to make space an integral part of social theory. One of my aims in negating the validity and utility of spatial separatism has been to promote closer study of the ideas within this literature. This personal, and therefore highly selective, guide is intended for readers who wish to undertake this task.

The best place to start is Harvey (1973). That book consists of a set of essays divided into two parts: 'liberal formulations' and 'socialist formulations'. The transition reflects Harvey's own evolution in thinking, and follows the realization that the former approach leads to an analytical 'impasse' of 'formless relativism'. The method of historical materialism is seen as the only way to escape this impasse. The results of this mental leap are elaborated in a preliminary way in the 'socialist formulations' in Harvey (1975), and are most fully set out in Harvey (1982).

Harvey's empirical work in the 1970s focused on urban issues, and the debates in urban studies at that time were much concerned with the problem of conceptualizing the relationship between space and society. Two edited volumes, Pickvance (1976) and Harloe (1977), provide good introductions to the new perspectives which were put forward, and Saunders (1980) offers a synoptic and critical review of both old and new approaches within urban studies. Castells (1977), originally published in 1972, is important to examine, as this work strongly influenced the debates within the field. But a livelier introduction to his ideas is found in Castells (1978), and his most recent thinking is set out in Castells (1983). Mingione (1981) puts forward an alternative approach to those of both Harvey and Castells. His arguments interrelate urban and regional issues, and deserve the closest attention.

The changes which occurred in urban studies in the 1970s are beginning to occur now in regional studies. Massey (1978) gives an excellent concise statement of general issues, and her empirical work, mainly undertaken with Meegan, demonstrates the deeper understanding which may be gained through application of a new approach to regional problems. See, in particular, Massey and Meegan (1979); Massey and Meegan (1982); and Massey (1984). New perspectives in European regional theory are set out in Carney et al. (1980) and, for those who read French, both Lipietz (1980) and Dulong (1978) are well worth studying.

All the references thus far are to analyses which adopt some or other Marxian perspective on society. It may be, as Harvey concluded in 1973, that Marxist political economy offers the only way out of the illogicalities of spatial separation. But, as I suggested in the conclusion, this exit may merely lead to another trap. For to understand regionalism the insights of neither cultural analysis nor class analysis are in themselves sufficient. The problem, then, is one of method. Gregory (1978) offers an introduction to different approaches to understanding which have been applied in geography; and Olsson (1980), although it is a difficult book to read, raises many important questions about understanding understanding.

On conceptions of space, Sack (1980) is essential reading. Giddens (1981) attempts to show how the 'space-time constitution of social systems' may be theorized, though unfortunately the deep insights on this issue contained in Poulantzas (1978) are ignored in the account. And Blaikie et al. (1979) provide an empirical study of a developing country which adopts a socio-spatial perspective.

Finally, two journals worth perusing are the *International Journal of Urban and Regional Research* and *Society and Space*.

Bibliography

Some of the important articles within the literature are reprinted in two readers – Friedmann and Alonso (1964) and Friedmann and Alonso (1975). All page numbers in the text for articles reproduced therein refer to these volumes.

Abler, R., Adams, J. S. and Gould, P. R. (1971) *Spatial Organization: A Geographer's View of the World*, Englewood Cliffs, Prentice-Hall.

Alonso, W. (1964) 'Location theory'. In Friedmann, J. and Alonso, W. (1964).

Alonso, W. (1968) 'Urban and regional imbalances in economic development', *Economic Development and Cultural Change*, 17 (1), 1–14. In Friedmann, J. and Alonso, W. (1975).

Alonso, W. (1971), 'The economics of urban size', *Papers and Proceedings of the Regional Science Association*, 26, 67–83. Reprinted in Friedmann, J. and Alonso, W. (1975).

Alonso, W. (1975) 'Industrial location and regional policy in economic development'. In Friedmann, J. and Alonso, W. (1975).

Anderson, B. (1983) *Imagined Communities: Reflections on the Origin and Spread of Nationalism*, London, Verso.

Appalraju, J. and Safier, M. (1976) 'Growth centre strategies in less-developed countries'. In Gilbert, A. (ed.) *Development Planning and Spatial Structure*, London, John Wiley.

van Arkadie, B. (1978) 'Review article: town versus country', *Development and Change*, 8 (3), 409–15.

Armstrong, H. and Taylor, J. (1978) *Regional Economic Policy and its Analysis*, Oxford, Philip Allan.

Baran, P. (1957) *The Political Economy of Growth*, New York, Monthly Review Press.

Barkin, D. (1972) 'A case study of the beneficiaries of regional development', *International Social Development Review*, 4, 84–94.

Bates, R. H. (1981) *Markets and States in Tropical Africa: The Political Basis of Agricultural Policy*, Berkeley, University of California Press.

Beckmann, M. J. (1972) 'Equilibrium versus optimum: spacing of firms and patterns of market areas'. In Funck, R. (ed.) *Recent Developments in Regional Science*, London, Pion.

Bergmann, G. (1958) *Philosophy of Science*, Madison, University of Wisconsin.

Bernstein, H. (1977) 'Notes on capital and peasantry', *Review of African Political Economy*, 10, 60–73.

Bernstein, H. (1979) 'Sociology of underdevelopment versus Sociology of development?'. In Lehmann, D. (ed.) *Development Theory: Four Critical Studies*, London, Frank Cass.

Bernstein, R. J. (1976) *The Restructuring of Social and Political Theory*, London, Methuen.

Berry, B. J. L. (1961) 'City size distribution and development', *Economic Development and Cultural Change*, 9, 673–87.

Berry, B. J. L. (1968) 'Interdependency of spatial structure and spatial behaviour: a general field theory formulation', *Papers and Proceedings of the Regional Science Association*, 21, 205–27.

Berry, B. J. L. (1969a) 'Policy implications of an urban location model for the Kanpur region'. In Desai, P. B., Grossack, I. M. and Sharma, K. N. (eds) *Regional Perspective of Industrial and Urban Growth*, Bombay, Macmillan.

Berry, B. J. L. (1969b) 'Relationships between regional economic development and the urban system', *Tijdschrift voor Econ. en Soc. Geografie*, 60, 283–307.

Berry, B. J. L. (1971a) 'City size and economic development: conceptual synthesis and policy problems, with special reference to South and Southeast Asia'. In Jakobson, L. and Prakash, V. (eds) Volume 1, *South and Southeast Asia Urban Affairs Annual Urbanization and National Development*.

Berry, B. J. L. (1971b) 'Hierarchical diffusion: the basis of developmental filtering and spread in a system of growth centres'. In Hansen, N. M. (ed.) (1971) *Growth Centres in Regional Economic Development*, New York, The Free Press.

Blaikie, P. (1978) 'The theory of the spatial diffusion of innovations: a spacious cul-de-sac', *Progress in Human Geography*, 2, 268–95.

Blaikie, P. (1980) 'Regional planning: a sheep in sheep's clothing? A political economic appraisal of regional planning as an agent of social change', mimeo.

Blaut, J. M. (1961) 'Space and process', *Professional Geographer*, 13 (4), 1–7.

Blaut, J. M. (1977) 'Two views of innovation diffusion', *Annals of the Association of American Geographers*, 67, 343–9.

Boudeville, J.-R. (1966) *Problems of Regional Economic Planning*, Edinburgh, Edinburgh University Press.

Bramhall, D. F. (1969) 'An introduction to general spatial equilibrium'. In Karaska, G. J. and Bramhall, D. F. (eds) *Locational Analysis for Manufacturing: A Selection of Readings*, Cambridge, Mass., MIT Press.

Brewer, A. (1980) *Marxist Theories of Imperialism*, London, Routledge & Kegan Paul.

Bromley, R. J. and Gerry, C. (1979) *Casual Work and Poverty in Third World Cities*, New York, John Wiley.

Brookfield, H. C. (1971) *Melanesia: A Geographical Interpretation of an Island World*, London, Methuen.

Brookfield, H. C. (1973) 'On one geography and a Third World', *Transactions, Institute of British Geographers*, 58, 1–20.

Bunge, W. (1966) *Theoretical Geography*, Lund Studies in Geography, Series C1, Lund, Gleerup.

Button, K. J. (1976) *Urban Economics*, London, Macmillan.

Byres, T. J. (1979) 'Of neo-populist pipedreams: Daedalus in the Third World and the myth of urban bias', *Journal of Peasant Studies*, 6 (2), 210–44.

Cardoso, F. H. and Falletto, E. (1979) *Dependency and Development in Latin America*, Berkeley, University of California Press (originally published in Spanish, 1971).

Carney, J., Hudson, R. and Lewis, J. (1980) *Regions in Crisis*, London, Croom Helm.

Castells, M. (1977) *The Urban Question*, London, Edward Arnold (French edition first published 1972).

Castells, M. (1978) *City, Class and Power*, London, Macmillan (French edition first published 1972).

Castells, M. (1983) *The City and the Grassroots: A Cross-Cultural Theory of Urban Social Movements*, London, Edward Arnold.

CEPAL (1980) *Regional Development Planning in Latin America*, E/CEPAL/ILPES/R.17.

Cheema, G. S. and Rondinelli, D. A. (1983) *Decentralization and Development: Policy Implementation in Developing Countries*, Beverly Hills, Sage Publications.

Chenery, H. *et al.* (1974) *Redistribution with Growth*, Oxford, Oxford University Press, published for the World Bank.

Chisholm, M. (1962) *Rural Settlement and Land-use*, London, Hutchinson.

Conroy, M. E. (1974) 'Rejection of growth centre strategy in Latin

American regional development planning', *Land Economics*, 44 (4), 371–80.

Conyers, D. (1983) 'Bridging the gap between North and South: towards a common approach to intra-regional planning', paper presented at the Annual Conference of the Development Studies Association, Brighton, September 1983.

Coraggio, J. L. (1974) 'Towards a revision of the growth pole theory', *Viertel Jahres Berichte*, 53, 283–308.

Currie, L. (1979) 'Is there an urban bias? Critique of Michael Lipton's *Why Poor People Stay Poor*', *Journal of Economic Studies*, 6 (1), 86–105.

Dahrendorf, R. (1959) *Class and Class Conflict in Industrial Society*, London, Routledge & Kegan Paul.

Darwent, D. F. (1969) 'Growth poles and growth centres in regional planning: a review', *Environment and Planning*, 1 (1), 5–31, Reprinted in Friedmann, J. and Alonso, W. (1975).

Demerath, N. J. and Peterson, R. (1967) *System, Change and Conflict*, New York, The Free Press.

Dos Santos, T. (1969) 'The crisis of development theory and the problem of dependence in Latin America'. In Bernstein, H. (ed.) (1973) *Development and Underdevelopment*, Harmondsworth, Penguin.

Douglass, M. (1979) 'Agropolitan development: an alternative for regional development in Asia', University of East Anglia, Development Studies Occasional Paper No. 59.

Dulong, R. (1978) *Les Régions, l'État et la Société Locale*, Paris, PUF.

Dunham, D. (1982) 'Some views on research in the field of regional development and regional planning', mimeo, Institute of Social Studies, The Hague.

El-Shakhs, S. (1972) 'Development, primacy and the system of cities', *Journal of Developing Areas*, 7, 11–36.

El-Shakhs, S. and Obudho, R. (eds) (1974) *Urbanization, National Development and Regional Planning in Africa*, New York, Praeger.

Fay, B. (1975) *Social Theory and Political Practice*, London, George Allen & Unwin.

Fei, J. C. H. and Ranis, G. (1964) *Development of the Labour Surplus Economy*, Homewood, Illinois, Irwin.

Foucault, M. (1980) 'Questions on geography'. In Gordon, C. (ed.) *Power/Knowledge: Selected Interviews and Other Writings 1972–77*, New York, Pantheon.

Frank, A. G. (1967) *Capitalism and Underdevelopment in Latin America*, New York, Monthly Review Press (expanded edition, 1969).

Frank, A. G. (1981) *Crisis: in the Third World*, London, Heinemann.

Friedmann, J. (1959) 'Regional planning: a problem in spatial integration', *Papers and Proceedings of the Regional Science Association*, 5, 167–78.

Friedmann, J. (1963) 'Regional planning as a field of study', *Journal of the American Institute of Planners*, 29 (3), 168–75. Reprinted in Friedmann, J. and Alonso, W. (1964).

Friedmann, J. (1966) *Regional Development Policy: a Case Study of Venezuela*, Cambridge, Mass., MIT Press.

Friedmann, J. (1967) 'Regional planning and nation-building: an agenda for international research', *Economic Development and Cultural Change*, 16 (1), 119–30.

Friedmann, J. (1972) 'A general theory of polarized development'. In Hansen, N. (ed.) (1972) *Growth Centres in Regional Economic Development*, New York, The Free Press (page numbers from reprint in Friedmann, J. (1973a)).

Friedmann, J. (1973a) *Urbanization, Planning and National Development*, London, Sage Publications.

Friedmann, J. (1973b) *Retracking America: A Theory of Transactive Planning*, New York, Doubleday, Anchor.

Friedmann, J. (1979) 'On the contradictions between city and countryside'. In Folmer, H. and Oosterhaven, J. (eds) (1979) *Spatial Inequalities and Regional Development*, Leiden, Nijhoff.

Friedmann, J. (1981) 'The active-community: towards a political-territorial framework for rural development in Asia', *Economic Development and Cultural Change*, 29, 226–61.

Friedmann, J. and Alonso, W. (1964) *Regional Development and Planning: a Reader*, Cambridge, Mass., MIT Press.

Friedmann, J. and Alonso, W. (1975) *Regional Policy: Readings in Theory and Applications*, Cambridge, Mass., MIT Press.

Friedmann, J. and Douglass, M. (1978) 'Agropolitan development: towards a new strategy for regional planning in Asia'. In Lo, Fu-chen and Salih, K. (eds), *Growth Pole Strategy and Regional Development Policy*, Oxford, Pergamon.

Friedmann, J. and Miller, J. (1965) 'The urban field', *Journal of the American Institute of Planners*, 31 (4), 312–20.

Friedmann, J. and Weaver, C. (1979) *Territory and Function: the Evolution of Regional Planning*, London, Edward Arnold.

Giddens, A. (1977) *Studies in Social and Political Theory*, London, Hutchinson.

Giddens, A. (1981) *A Contemporary Critique of Historical Materialism, Vol. 1. Power, Property and the State*, London, Macmillan.

Gilbert, A. G. (1974) *Latin American Development: A Geographical Perspective*, Harmondsworth, Penguin.

Gilbert, A. G. (1975) 'A note on the incidence of development in the vicinity of a growth centre', *Regional Studies*, 9, 325–33.

Gilbert, A. G. (ed.) (1976) *Development Planning and Spatial Structure*, London, John Wiley.

Gilbert, A. G. and Goodman, D. E. (1976) 'Regional income disparities and economic development: a critique'. In Gilbert, A. G. (ed.) *Development Planning and Spatial Structure*, London, John Wiley.

de Gonzales, G. M. (1980) 'Regional planning under the transition to socialism', Monograph Series, No. 11, Swansea, Centre for Development Studies.

Goulbourne, H. (ed.) (1980) *Politics and the State in the Third World*, London, Macmillan.

Gould, P. R. (1970) 'Tanzania 1920–63: the spatial impress of the modernization process', *World Politics*, 22 (2), 149–70. Reprinted in Friedmann, J. and Alonso, W. (1975).

Gould, P. R. (1979) 'Geography 1957–77: the Augean period', *Annals of the Association of American Geographers*, 69 (1), 139–50.

Gregory, D. (1978) *Ideology, Science and Human Geography*, London, Hutchinson.

Griffin, K. (1977) 'Review of Lipton's *Why Poor People Stay Poor*', *Journal of Development Studies*, 14, 108–10.

Grigg, D. (1967) 'Regions, models and classes'. In Chorley, R. J. and Haggett, P. (eds) (1967) *Models in Geography*, London, Methuen.

Habermas, J. (1973) 'Problems of legitimation in late capitalism'. In Connerton, P. (ed.) (1976) *Critical Sociology: Selected Readings*, Harmondsworth, Penguin.

Hägerstrand, T. (1967) *Innovation Diffusion as a Spatial Process*. Translated from Swedish by A. Pred and G. Haag, Chicago and London, University of Chicago Press.

Haggett, P. (1965) *Locational Analysis in Human Geography*, London, Edward Arnold (second edition, with A. D. Cliff and A. Frey, 1977).

Hansen, N. M. (1967) 'Development poles in regional context', *Kyklos*, 20, 709–25.

Harloe, M. (ed.) (1977) *Captive Cities*, London, Edward Arnold.

Hartshorne, R. (1939) *The Nature of Geography*, Lancaster, Pennsylvania, Association of American Geographers.

Hartshorne, R. (1954) *Perspective on the Nature of Geography*, Chicago, Rand McNally.

Harvey, D. (1969) *Explanation in Geography*, London, Edward Arnold.

Harvey, D. (1973) *Social Justice and the City*, London, Edward Arnold.

Harvey, D. (1975) 'The geography of capitalist accumulation: a reconstruction of the Marxian theory', *Antipode*, 7 (2), 9–21. Reprinted in Peet, R. (1977) *Radical Geography*, Chicago, Maaronfu Press.

Harvey, D. (1982) *The Limits to Capital*, Oxford, Basil Blackwell.

Hechter, M. and Levi, M. (1979) 'The comparative analysis of ethno-regional movements', *Ethnic and Racial Studies*, 2 (3), 260–73.

Hempel, C. G. (1965) *Aspects of Scientific Explanation*, New York, The Free Press.

Hermansen, T. (1972) 'Development poles and related theories: a synoptic approach'. In Hansen, N. M. (ed.) (1972) *Growth Centres in Regional Economic Development*, New York, The Free Press.

Higgins, B. H. (1959) *Economic Development: Principles, Problems and Policies*, London, Constable.

Higgins, B. (1978) 'Development poles: do they exist?'. In Lo, Fu-chen and Salih, K. (eds) *Growth Pole Strategy and Regional Development Policy: Asian Experience and Alternative Approaches*, Oxford, Pergamon.

Hilhorst, J. G. M. (1971) *Regional Planning: A Systems Approach*, Rotterdam University Press.

Hilhorst, J. G. M. (1980) 'On some unresolved issues in regional development thinking', *Institute of Social Studies, Occasional Paper*, No. 51, The Hague.

Hilhorst, J. G. M. (1981) 'Peru: regional planning 1968–77; frustrated bottom-up aspirations in a technocratic military setting'. In Stöhr, W. and Taylor, D. R. F. (eds) *Development from Above or Below?*', Chichester, John Wiley.

Hirschman, A. O. (1958) *The Strategy of Economic Development*, New Haven, Yale University Press.

Hoch, I. (1972) 'Income and urban size', *Urban Studies*, 9, 299–328.

Holland, S. (1976a) *Capital versus the Regions*, London, Macmillan.

Holland, S. (1976b) *The Regional Problem*, London, Macmillan.

Hoover, E. M. (1975) *An Introduction to Regional Economics*, New York, Alfred A. Knopf (second edition).

Hoselitz, B. F. (1953) 'The role of cities in the economic growth of underdeveloped countries', *The Journal of Political Economy*, 61, 195–208.

Hoselitz, B. F. (1955) 'Generative and parasitic cities' *Economic Development and Cultural Change*, 3, 278–94.

Hotelling, H. (1929) 'Stability in competition', *Economic Journal*, 39, 41–57.

Isard, W. (1956a) *Location and Space Economy*, New York, John Wiley.

Isard, W. (1956b) 'Regional science, the concept of the region and the regional structure', *Papers and Proceedings of the Regional Science Association*, 2, 13–29.

Isard, W. (1960) *Methods of Regional Analysis: An Introduction to Regional Science*, New York, John Wiley.

Isard, W. (1975) *An Introduction to Regional Science*, Englewood Cliffs, Prentice-Hall.

Isard, W. *et al.* (1969) *General Theory: Social, Political, Economic and Regional*, Cambridge, Mass., MIT Press.

Isard, W. and Vietorisz, T. (1955) 'Industrial complex analysis and regional development', *Papers and Proceedings of the Regional Science Association*, 1, 227–47.

Jessop, B. (1982) *The Capitalist State: Marxist Theories and Methods*, Oxford, Martin Robertson.

Johnson, E. A. J. (1970) *The Organization of Space in Developing Countries*, Cambridge, Mass., Harvard University Press.

Johnston, R. J. (1979) *Geography and Geographers: Anglo-American Human Geography since 1945*, London, Edward Arnold.

Jorgenson, D. W. (1969) 'The role of agriculture in economic development: classical versus neo-classical models of growth'. In Wharton, C. (ed.) *Subsistence Agriculture and Economic Development*, Chicago, Aldine.

Kaldor, N. (1972) 'The irrelevance of equilibrium economics', *Economic Journal*, 82, 1237–55.

Keat, R. and Urry, J. (1975) *Social Theory as Science*, London, Routledge & Kegan Paul.

Keeble, D. E. (1967) 'Models of economic development'. In Chorley, R. J. and Haggett, P. (eds) *Models in Geography*, London, Methuen.

Keeble, D. E. (1976) *Industrial Location and Planning in the United Kingdom*, London, Methuen.

Kitching, G. N. (1978) 'Reification, explanation and regional planning', *Occasional Paper No. 9*, Swansea, Centre for Development Studies.

Kitching, G. N. (1980) *Class and Economic Change in Kenya: The Making of an African Petite-Bourgeoisie*, New Haven, Yale University Press.

Kitching, G. N. (1982) *Development and Underdevelopment in Historical Perspective: Populism, Nationalism and Industrialization*, London, Methuen.

Koopmans, T. C. and Beckmann, M. J. (1957) 'Assignment problems and the location of economic activity', *Econometrica*, 25, 53–76.

Kuklinski, A. (ed.) (1975) *Regional Development and Planning: International Perspectives*, Leiden, Sifthoff.

Laing, R. D. (1967) *The Politics of Experience and the Bird of Paradise*, Harmondsworth, Penguin.

Laski, H. J. (1934) *A Grammar of Politics*, London, George Allen & Unwin.

Laski, H. J. (1935) *The State: in Theory and Practice*, London, George, Allen & Unwin.

Lasuen, J. R. (1969) 'On growth poles', *Urban Studies*, 6 (2), 137–61.

Lasuen, J. R. (1971) 'Multi-regional economic development: an open-system approach'. In Hägerstrand, T. and Kuklinski, A. (eds) *Information Systems for Regional Development: A Seminar*, Lund Studies in Geography, Series B, Human Geography, No. 37, Gleerup.

Lasuen, J. R. (1973) 'Urbanization and development – the temporal interaction between geographical and sectoral clusters', *Urban Studies*, 10, 163–88.

Lasuen, J. R. (1974) 'A generalization of the growth pole notion'. In Thoman, R. S. (ed.) *Proceedings of the Commission on Regional Aspects of Development of the International Geographical Union, Volume I, Methodology and Case Studies*, Canada.

Lee, R. (1977) 'Regional relations and the economic structure of the EEC', pp. 19–35. In Massey, D. B. and Batey, P. W. J. (eds) *Alternative Frameworks for Analysis*, London Papers in Regional Science, 7, London, Pion.

Leinbach, T. R. (1972) 'The geography of modernization in Malaya', *Tijdschrift voor Econ. en Soc. Geografie*, 63, 262–77.

Levy, M. B. and Wadycki, W. J. (1974) 'What is the opportunity cost of moving? Reconsideration of the effects of distance on migration', *Economic Development and Cultural Change*, 22 (2), 198–214.

Lewis, J. and Melville, B. (1978) 'The politics of epistemology in regional science'. In Batey, P. W. J. (ed.) *Theory and Method in Regional Analysis*, London, Pion.

Lewis, W. A. (1954) 'Economic development with unlimited supplies of labour', *Manchester School of Economics and Social Sciences*, 22, 139–91.

Linsky, A. S. (1965) 'Some generalizations concerning primate cities', *Annals of the Association of American Geographers*, 55, 506–13.

Lipietz, A. (1980) 'The structuration of space, the problem of land, and spatial policy'. In Carney, J., Hudson, R. and Lewis, J. (eds) *Regions in Crisis: New Perspectives in European Regional Theory*, London, Croom Helm.

Lipton, M. (1977) *Why Poor People Stay Poor: A Study of Urban Bias in World Development*, London, Maurice Temple Smith.

Lo, Fu-chen (1978) 'The growth pole approach to regional development: a case study of the Mizushima industrial complex, Japan'. In Lo, Fu-chen and Salih, K. (eds) *Growth Pole Strategy and Regional Develop-ment Policy: Asian Experience and Alternative Approaches*, Oxford, Pergamon.

Lo, Fu-chen and Salih, K. (1978) *Growth Pole Strategy and Regional Development Policy: Asian Experiences and Alternative Approaches*, Oxford, Pergamon.

Lo, Fu-chen and Salih, K. (1981) 'Growth poles, agropolitan develop-ment, and polarization reversal: the debate and search for alterna-tives'. In Stöhr, W. B. and Taylor, D. R. F. (eds) *Development from Above or Below?*, Chichester, John Wiley.

Logan, M. L. (1972) 'The spatial system and planning strategies in developing countries', *Geographical Review*, 62, 229–44.

Lösch, A. (1938) 'The nature of economic regions', *Southern Economic Journal*, 5, 71–8.

Lösch, A. (1954) *The Economics of Location*, New Haven, Yale Univer-sity Press.

Lukes, S. (1974) *Power: A Radical View*, London, Macmillan.

Mabogunje, A. O. (1980) *The Development Process: A Spatial Perspec-tive*, London, Hutchinson.

Mabogunje, A. O. and Faniran, A. (eds) (1977) *Regional Planning and National Development in Tropical Africa*, Ibadan, Ibadan University Press.

McCrone, G. (1969) *Regional Policy in Britain*, London, George Allen & Unwin.

Machlup, F. (1958) 'Equilibrium and disequilibrium: misplaced con-creteness and disguised politics', *Economic Journal*, 68, 1–24.

Massey, D. (1973) 'Towards a critique of industrial location theory'. In Peet, R. (ed.) (1977) *Radical Geography*, London, Methuen.

Massey, D. (1974) 'Is a "behavioural theory" really an alternative?'. In Massey, D. and Morrison, W. I. (eds) *Industrial Location: Alternative Frameworks*, Centre for Environmental Studies, Conference Paper 15.

Massey, D. (1978) 'Regionalism: some current issues', *Capital and Classes*, 6, 106–25.

Massey, D. (1984) *Spatial Divisions of Labour: Social Structures and the Geography of Production*, London, Macmillan.

Massey, D. and Meegan, R. (1979) 'The geography of industrial reorganization: the spatial effects of restructuring the electronical engineering sector under the Industrial Reorganization Corporation', *Progress in Planning*, 10 (3), 155–237.

Massey, D. and Meegan, R. (1982) *The Anatomy of Job Loss: The How, Why and Where of Employment Decline*, London, Methuen.

Mera, K. (1973) 'On urban agglomeration and economic efficiency', *Economic Development and Cultural Change*, 21 (2), 309–24.

Mera, K. (1975) *Income Distribution and Regional Development*, Tokyo, University of Tokyo Press.

Meyer, J. R. (1963) 'Regional economics: a survey', *American Economic Review*, 53, 19–54.

Miliband, R. (1969) *The State in Capitalist Society*, London, Weidenfeld & Nicolson.

Mills, E. S. and Lav, M. R. (1964) 'A model of market areas with free entry', *Journal of Political Economy*, 72, 278–88.

Mingione, E. (1981) *Social Conflict and the City*, Oxford, Basil Blackwell.

Misra, R. P., Sundaram, V. K. and Prakasa Rao, V. L. S. (1974) *Regional Development Planning in India: a New Strategy*, Delhi, Viking.

Misra, R. P. and Sundaram, K. V. (1978) 'Growth foci as instruments of modernization in India'. In Kuklinski, A. (ed.) *Regional Policies in Nigeria, India and Brazil*, The Hague, Mouton.

Morrill, R. L. (1970) *The Spatial Organization of Society*, Belmont, Calif., Wadsworth.

Moseley, M. J. (1974) *Growth Centres in Spatial Planning*, Oxford, Pergamon.

Myrdal, G. (1957) *Economic Theory and Underdeveloped Regions*, London, Duckworth.

Nagel, E. (1961) *The Structure of Science: Problems in the Logic of Scientific Explanation*, London, Routledge & Kegan Paul.

Nicholls, W. H. (1961) 'Industrialization, factor markets and agricultural development', *Journal of Political Economy*, 69 (4), 319–40. In Friedmann, J. and Alonso, W. (1975).

Nichols, V. (1969) 'Growth poles: an evaluation of the propulsive effects', *Environment and Planning*, 1, 193–208.

North, D. C. (1955) 'Location theory and regional economic growth', *Journal of Political Economy*, 63 (3), 243–58. In Friedmann, J. and Alonso, W. (1975).

O'Connor, J. (1973) *The Fiscal Crisis of the State*, New York, St Martin's Press.

O'Donnell, G. (1980) 'Comparative historical formations of the state apparatus and socio-economic change in the Third World', *International Journal of Social Science*, 32 (4), 717–29.

Odum, H. W. (1934) 'The case for regional-national social planning', *Social Forces*, 13, 6–23.

Odum, H. W. and Moore, H. E. (1938) *American Regionalism: a Cultural Historical Approach to National Integration*, New York, Henry Holt.

278 BIBLIOGRAPHY

Ohlin, B. (1933) *Interregional and International Trade*, Cambridge, Mass., Harvard University Press.

de Oliviera, F. (1981) 'State and society in north-east Brazil: SUDENE and the role of regional planning', pp. 170–89. In Mitchell, S. (ed.) *The Logic of Poverty: The Case of the Brazilian North-East*, London, Routledge & Kegan Paul.

Olsson, G. (1970) 'Logics and social engineering', *Geographical Analysis*, 2, 361–75.

Olsson, G. (1971) 'Correspondence rules and social engineering', *Economic Geography*, 47, 545–54.

Olsson, G. (1972) 'Some notes on geography and social engineering', *Antipode*, 4, 1–22.

Olsson, G. (1974a) 'Servitude and inequality in spatial planning: ideology and methodology in conflict', *Antipode*, 6, 16–21.

Olsson, G. (1974b) 'The dialectics of spatial analysis', *Antipode*, 6, 50–62.

Olsson, G. (1980) *Birds in Egg/Eggs in Bird*, London, Pion.

Parr, J. B. (1973) 'Growth poles, regional development and central place theory', *Papers and Proceedings of the Regional Science Association*, 31, 172–212.

Perloff, H. S. *et al.* (1960) *Regions, Resources and Economic Growth*, Baltimore, Johns Hopkins Press for Resources for the Future Inc.

Perloff, H. and Wingo, L. (1961) 'Natural resource endowment and economic growth'. In Spengler, J. J. (ed.) (1971) *Natural Resources and Economic Growth*, Washington DC, Resources for the Future Inc. In Friedmann, J. and Alonso, W. (1975).

Perroux, F. (1950a) 'Economic space: theory and applications'. In Friedmann, J. and Alonso, W. (1964).

Perroux, F. (1950b) 'The domination effect and modern economic theory'. In Rothschild, K. W. (ed.) *Power in Economics*, Harmondsworth, Penguin.

Perroux, F. (1955) 'Note sur la notion de pôle de croissance', translated by I. Livingstone. In Livingstone, I. (ed.) (1979) *Development Economics and Policy: Selected Readings*, London, George Allen & Unwin.

Perroux, F. (1961a) *L'Economie du XXe Siècle*, Paris, Presses Universitaires de France.

Perroux, F. (1961b) 'La firme motrice dans la région et la région motrice', *Théorie et Politique de L'Expansion Régionale*, Actes du colloque international de l'Institut de Science Economique de l'Université de Liège, Préface de M. Paul Harsin.

Perroux, F. (1968) 'Les investissements multinationaux et l'analyse des pôles de développement et des pôles d'intégration', *Revue Tiers Monde*, 19, 239–65.

Pickvance, C. G. (ed.) (1976) *Urban Sociology: Critical Essays*, London, Tavistock.

Pickvance, C. G. (1981) 'Policies as chameleons: an interpretation of regional policy and office policy in Britain'. In Dear, M. and Scott, A. J. (eds) *Urbanization and Urban Planning in Capitalist Society*, London, Methuen.

Popper, K. R. (1957) *The Poverty of Historicism*, London, Routledge & Kegan Paul.

Popper, K. (1963) *Conjectures and Refutations*, London, Routledge & Kegan Paul.

Poulantzas, N. (1973) *Political Power and Social Classes*, London, New Left Books and Sheed & Ward (first published in French, Paris, 1968).

Poulantzas, N. (1975) *Classes in Contemporary Capitalism*, London, New Left Books (French edition originally published 1974).

Poulantzas, N. (1978) *State, Power, Socialism*, London, Verso.

Pred, A. R. (1976) 'The inter-urban transmission of growth in advanced economies: empirical findings versus regional-planning assumptions', *Regional Studies*, 10, 151–71.

Redfield, R. and Singer, M. B. (1954) 'The cultural role of cities', *Economic Development and Cultural Change*, 3, 53–73. In Friedmann, J. and Alonso, W. (1975).

Reiner, T. A. (1964) 'Subnational and national planning: decision criteria', *Papers and Proceedings of the Regional Science Association*, 14, 107–36.

Richardson, H. W. (1969) *Regional Economics: Location Theory, Urban Structure and Regional Change*, New York, Praeger.

Richardson, H. W. (1972) 'Optimality in city size, systems of cities, and urban policy: a sceptic's view', *Urban Studies*, 9, 29–48.

Richardson, H. W. (1973a) *Regional Growth Theory*, London, Macmillan.

Richardson, H. W. (1973b) *The Economics of Urban Size*, Farnborough, Saxon House.

Richardson, H. W. (1976) 'Growth poles pillovers: the dynamics of backwash and spread', *Regional Studies*, 10, 1–9.

Richardson, H. W. (1977) *City Size and National Spatial Strategies in Developing Countries*, Washington DC, World Bank Staff Working Paper, No. 252.

Richardson, H. W. (1978) *Regional and Urban Economics*, Harmondsworth, Penguin.

Richardson, H. W. (1979) 'Aggregate efficiency and interregional equity'. In Folmer, H. and Oosterhaven, J. (eds) *Spatial Inequalities and Regional Development*, Leiden, Nijhoff.

Richardson, H. W. and Richardson, M. (1974) 'The relevance of growth centre strategies to Latin America', *Economic Geography*, 51, 163–78.

Riddell, J. B. (1970) *The Spatial Dynamics of Modernization in Sierra Leone: Structure, Diffusion and Response*, Evanston, Northwestern University Press.

Robinson, G. and Salih, K. B. (1971) 'The spread of development around Kuala Lumpur: a methodology for an exploratory test of some assumptions of the growth pole model', *Regional Studies*, 5, 303–14.

Rodwin, L. (1963) 'Choosing regions for development'. In Friedmann, J. and Alonso, W. (1964).

Rondinelli, D. A. (1980) 'Spatial analysis for regional resource development: a case study of the Philippines', *Resource Systems Theory and Methodology Technical Papers, no. 1*, Natural Resources Programme, United Nations University, Tokyo.

Rondinelli, D. A. and Ruddle, K. (1978) *Urbanization and Rural Development: A Spatial Policy for Equitable Growth*, New York, Praeger.

Rosenstein-Rodan, P. N. (1943) 'Problems of industrialization of eastern and south-eastern Europe', *Economic Journal*, 53, 202–11. In Argarwala, A. N. and Singh, S. P. (eds) (1963) *The Economics of Underdevelopment*, New York, Oxford University Press.

Rosenstein-Rodan, P. N. (1961) 'Notes on the theory of the big push'. In Ellis, H. and Wallich, H. C. (eds) *Economic Development for Latin America*, London, International Economic Association.

Ross, G. W. and Cohen, S. S. (1974) 'The politics of French regional planning'. In Friedmann, J. and Alonso, W. (1975).

Rostow, W. (1971) *The Stages of Economic Growth: A Non-Communist Manifesto*, Cambridge, Cambridge University Press (second edition; first published 1960).

Sack, R. D. (1972) 'Geography, geometry and explanation', *Annals of the Association of American Geographers*, 62, 61–78.

Sack, R. D. (1973) 'A concept of physical space in geography', *Geographical Analysis*, 5, 16–34.

Sack, R. D. (1974a) 'Chorology and spatial analysis', *Annals of the Association of American Geographers*, 64, 439–52.

Sack, R. D. (1974b) 'The spatial separatist theme in geography', *Economic Geography*, 50, 1–19.

Sack, R. D. (1980) *Conceptions of Space in Social Thought: A Geographical Perspective*, London, Macmillan.

Salih, K. *et al.* (1978) 'Decentralization policy, growth pole approach and resource frontier development: a synthesis of the response in four south-east Asian countries'. In Lo, Fu-chen and Salih, K. (eds)

Growth Pole Strategy and Regional Development Policy, Oxford, Pergamon.

Santos, M. (1974) 'Geography, Marxism and underdevelopment', *Antipode*, 6, 1–9.

Santos, M. (1979) *The Shared Space*, London, Methuen (originally published as *L'Espace Partagé*, 1973).

Saunders, P. (1980) *Social Theory and the Urban Question*, London, Hutchinson.

Sayer, R. A. (1976) 'A critique of urban modelling: from regional science to regional political economy', *Progress in Planning*, 6 (3), 187–254.

Schaefer, F. K. (1953) 'Exceptionalism in geography: a methodological examination', *Annals of the Association of American Geographers*, 43, 226–49.

Schultz, T. W. (1950) 'Reflections on poverty within agriculture', *Journal of Political Economy*, 53, 1–16.

Schultz, T. W. (1951) 'A framework for land economics – the long view', *Journal of Farm Economics*, 33, 204–15.

Schumpeter, J. A. (1939) *Business Cycles: A Theoretical, Historical and Statistical Analysis of the Capitalist Process*, abridged, with an introduction by Rendig Fels (1964), New York, McGraw-Hill.

Scitovsky, T. (1954) 'Two concepts of external economies', *Journal of Political Economy*, 62, 143–51.

Scott, A. and Roweis, S. T. (1977) 'Urban planning in theory and practice: a reappraisal', *Environment and Planning*, 9, 1097–111.

Shils, E. (1961) 'Centre and periphery'. In *The Logic of Personal Knowledge: Essays Presented to Michael Polanyi*, London, Routledge & Kegan Paul.

Siebert, H. (1969) *Regional Economic Growth: Theory and Policy*, Scranton, International Textbook Co.

Skillen, A. (1977) *Ruling Illusions: Philosophy and the Social Order*, Hassocks, Sussex, Harvester.

Slater, D. (1974) 'Contribution to a critique of development geography', *Canadian Journal of African Studies* 8 (2), 325–54.

Slater, D. (1975) 'Underdevelopment and spatial inequality: approaches to the problem of regional planning in the Third World', *Progress in Planning*, 4 (2).

Slater, D. (1983) 'The state and territorial centralization: Peru 1968–78', *International Journal of Urban and Regional Research*, 4.

Smith, C. A. (ed.) (1976) *Regional Analysis. Volume 1 Economic Systems*, New York, Academic Press.

Soja, E. W. (1968) *The Geography of Modernization in Kenya: A Spatial*

Analysis of Social, Economic and Political Change, New York, Syracuse University Press.

Soja, E. W. and Tobin, R. J. (1972) 'The geography of modernization: paths, patterns, and processes of spatial change in developing countries'. In Brunner, R. and Brewer, G. (eds) *Ordered Complexity: Empirical Theories of Political Development*, Illinois, Glencoe.

Sovani, N. (1964) 'The analysis of overurbanization', *Economic Development and Cultural Change*, 12 (2), 113–22. Reprinted in Friedmann, J. and Alonso, W. (1975).

Stewart, J. Q. (1950) 'The development of social physics', *American Journal of Physics*, 18, 239–53.

Stewart, J. Q. and Warntz, W. (1958) 'Macrogeography and social science', *Geographical Review*, 48, 167–84.

Stoddart, D. R. (1967) 'Organism and ecosystem as geographical models'. In Chorley, R. J. and Haggett, P. (eds) *Models in Geography*, London, Methuen.

Stöhr, W. (1975) *Regional Development: Experiences and Prospects in Latin America*, The Hague, Mouton.

Stöhr, W. B. (1981) 'Development from below: the bottom-up and periphery-inward development paradigm'. In Stöhr, W. B. and Taylor, D. R. F. (eds) *Development from Above or Below? The Dialectics of Regional Planning in Developing Countries*, Chichester, John Wiley.

Stöhr, W. B. and Taylor, D. R. F. (1981) *Development from Above or Below? The Dialectics of Regional Planning in Developing Countries*, Chichester, John Wiley.

Stöhr, W. and Tödtling, F. (1977) 'An evaluation of regional policies – experiences in market and mixed economies'. In Hansen, N. M. (ed.) (1978) *Human Settlement Systems: International Perspectives on Structure, Change and Public Policy*, Cambridge, Mass., Ballinger.

Stöhr, W. and Tödtling, F. (1977) 'Spatial equity – some antitheses to current regional development doctrine', *Papers and Proceedings of the Regional Science Association*, 38, 33–53.

Stöhr, W. and Tödtling, F. (1979) 'Spatial equality – some antitheses to current regional development doctrine'. In Folmer, H. and Oosterhoven, J. (eds) *Spatial Inequalities and Regional Development*, Leiden, Nijhoff.

Tarrow, S., Katzenstein, P. J. and Graziano, L. (eds) (1978) *Territorial Politics in Industrial Nations*, New York, Praeger.

Taylor, J. G. (1979) *From Modernization to Modes of Production: a Critique of Sociologies of Development and Underdevelopment*, London, Macmillan.

Ternent, J. A. (1976) 'Urban concentration and dispersal: urban policies in Latin America'. In Gilbert, A. (ed.) *Development Planning and Spatial Structure*, New York, John Wiley.

Thomas, M. D. (1972) 'Growth pole theory: an examination of some of its basic concepts'. In Hansen, N. M. (ed.) (1972) *Growth Centres in Regional Economic Development*, New York, The Free Press.

Thompson, W. R. (1965) *A Preface to Urban Economics*, Baltimore, Johns Hopkins University Press for Resources for the Future Inc.

Thompson, W. R. (1968) 'Internal and external factors in the development of urban economies'. In Friedmann, J. and Alonso, W. (1975).

Townroe, P. M. (1979) 'Employment decentralization: policy instruments for large cities in less developed countries'. *Progress in Planning*, 10 (2), 85–154.

Utria, R. D. (1972) 'Regional structure and Latin American development', *Latin American Urban Research*, 2, 61–84.

Vapnarsky, C. A. (1969) 'On rank-size distribution of cities: an ecological approach', *Economic Development and Cultural Change*, 17 (4), 584–95.

Wanmali, S. and Khan, W. (1970) 'Role of location in regional planning with particular reference to the provision of social facilities', *Behavioural Sciences and Community Development*, 4 (2), 65–87.

Weaver, C. (1981) 'Development theory and the regional question: a critique of spatial planning and its detractors'. In Stöhr, W. B. and Taylor, D. R. F. (eds) *Development from Above or Below?*, New York, John Wiley.

Webber, M. (1964) 'Culture, territoriality and the elastic mile', *Papers and Proceedings of the Regional Science Association*, 11, 59–69.

Williamson, J. G. (1965) 'Regional inequality and the process of national development: a description of the patterns', *Economic Development and Cultural Change*, 13 (2), 3–45. In Friedmann, J. and Alonso, W. (1975).

Wingo, L. (1972) 'Issues in a national urbanization policy for the United States', *Urban Studies*, 9, 3–28.

Winnick, L. (1966) 'Place prosperity v. people prosperity: welfare considerations in geographic redistributions of economic activity'. In Real Estate Research Program, *Essays in Urban Land Economics in Honour of Leo Grebler*, Los Angeles, University of California Press.

Zipf, G. K. (1949) *Human Behaviour and the Principle of Least Effort*, Cambridge, Mass., Addison-Wesley.

Author index

Subject index